THE AFFECTIVE LIFE OF LAW

THE CULTURAL LIVES OF LAW

Edited by Austin Sarat

RAVIT REICHMAN

The Affective Life of Law

Legal Modernism and the Literary Imagination

STANFORD LAW BOOKS

An imprint of Stanford University Press
Stanford, California

Stanford University Press
Stanford, California

Printed in the United States of America on acid-free, archival-quality
paper

Library of Congress Cataloging-in-Publication Data
Reichman, Ravit Pe'er-Lamo.
 The affective life of law : legal modernism and the literary
imagination / Ravit Reichman.
    p. cm. — (The cultural lives of law)
 Includes bibliographical references and index.
 ISBN 978-0-8047-6166-6 (cloth : alk. paper)
 1. Law and literature—History—20th century. 2. Law in literature.
3. Trials in literature. I. Title. II. Series: Cultural lives of law.
 PN56.L33R45 2009
 809'.93355—dc22
                                                        2008042355

Typeset by Thompson Type in 10/14.5 Minion

For my parents,
Erella and Benny Reichman

Contents

Acknowledgments

Every book contains untold stories of intellectual debts, friendships, and commitments, and it is with immense pleasure that I give voice to some of the many who have helped shape my own. At Yale, Shoshana Felman and Peter Brooks opened possibilities for my work through their commitment to ethical questions that cross disciplinary boundaries. Their discerning sense of the place of literature within such questions fostered my convictions of what I wanted to do and why. I received much encouragement and feedback early on and since from Evelyne Ender, Pericles Lewis, and William Deresiewicz.

Many colleagues at Brown helped to press this book into existence through their comments, criticism, and enthusiasm: Nancy Armstrong, Timothy Bewes, Jean Feerick, Arlene Keizer, Kevin McLaughlin, and Leonard Tennenhouse. I would especially like to acknowledge Tamar Katz, who read the full manuscript and offered invaluable suggestions. Other colleagues—Paul Armstrong, Mutlu Blasing, Jim Egan, Olakunle George, Philip Gould, Jacques Khalip, Rolland Murray, Deak Nabers, Thangam Ravindranathan, Ralph Rodriguez, Vanessa Ryan, Mark Swislocki, and Esther Whitfield—helped to create an ideal environment in which to hone my ideas. I could always count on Stuart Burrows for his critical lucidity and subtlety, to say nothing of his unrivaled sense of humor. Deborah Cohen, whose own scholarship sets an outstanding example for modernists, pointed me toward archival materials that proved illuminating and crucial. It is hard to conceive of having written this book without the watchful eye of Daniel Kim, the only humane form of surveillance I can imagine. He has been in the thick and thicket of this project from the very beginning, has known it in its many guises, and has brought his brilliance to countless discussions of its contents. His friendship, as much as his generous collegiality, has made all the difference in these pages.

Brown University provided generous support for this project over the years. I am grateful for funding which enabled me to conduct research in England, and for a Wriston Fellowship in the spring of 2008. My writing benefited richly from a fellowship at the Cogut Humanities Center, and I thank Michael Steinberg and my companion fellows for a stimulating and productive semester. My graduate and undergraduate students were a constant source of creativity and conviction. It was consistently gratifying to be part of vibrant, thought-provoking classroom conversations, many of which helped me to rethink the material in this book. Jane Donnelly, Lorraine Mazza, Suzie Nacar, Marilyn Netter, and Ellen Viola have made Brown a wonderful (and blessedly functional) place in which to teach and work.

Austin Sarat encouraged this project from its earliest stages, giving me my first opportunities to develop it in workshops and during a semester-long stay at Amherst College as a Copeland Fellow. Tireless in his efforts to make interdisciplinary approaches to law and humanities a rich intellectual landscape, he has cultivated—and continues to nurture—the intellectual and professional ground that has been so crucial to my work. A summer visiting fellowship at Birkbeck School of Law presented a rare opportunity to think and write in a more explicitly legal context. My psychoanalysis reading group compatriots Anne Dailey, Susan Schmeiser, Sylvia Schafer, Adam Sitze, and Martha Umphrey have been wonderful sources of new ideas, and have helped me to strengthen and refine old ones. I thank also Nan Goodman, Piyel Haldar, Susan Sage Heinzelman, Naomi Mezey, Hilary Schor, and Nomi Stolzenberg for sharing their expertise and sustaining me with their enthusiasm.

Many dear friends have made writing this book a matter of means rather than ends, and have accompanied me along the way in more ways than I expected or deserved. Chaya Halberstam and Lisa Silverman, kindred spirits both, have been priceless interlocutors from the very beginning, and their discerning insights across time and place—from New Haven to London, Chicago to Maine—were indispensable at every turn. Patricio Boyer's thoughtfulness and overall wisdom were never in short supply. Emily Balić brought her usual sharpness to more of these pages than she bargained for, and helped to clarify what it was I wanted to say. Pat Chu weighed in at a crucial moment, and I am indebted to her acumen and her uncanny ability to read between, through, and in spite of the lines. Augusta Rohrbach got things on track in so many ways with her unique merging of clarity, subtlety, and insight. Anya Vajpeyi, whose penetrating questions always cut to the heart of the matter, knew exactly what to do and when. I could not have done without the contributions of Barry Wimpfheimer and Rhoda Pagano Dermer. Pep Vicente, Alison Falby, Michelle Frazier, Jordanna Fraiberg LeVine, Kara Murphy, Sharon Musher, Marcus Pyka, and Macarena Saez were irreplaceable. Liz Cohen and Jason Perlmutter made sure I had a roof over my head at all times, as did Daniel Kim and Jennifer Walrad. Inge Schneier Hoffmann was instrumental and always insightful.

At Stanford University Press, Kate Wahl gave her support to this book with enthusiasm and graciousness, and made its publication a reality. Joa Suorez saw that everything came together smoothly, and did so with much-appreciated cheerfulness. I also wish to thank Margaret Pinette for making the production process worry free, and Randy Stevens for her sharp editorial eye. Sincerest thanks to my anonymous readers for their liberal and detailed comments, which helped to make this a better book.

In the course of finishing this book, I had the singular pleasure of coming into an extended family. I am grateful to Ted Weesner Sr.; Janet Schofield; Anna Weesner; John, Lucas, and Joseph Schlesinger; Steven Weesner; Abbey Box; Mary Louise Long; and the indomitable Dwight Long for giving me so many places to call home. The memory of Sharon Weesner, whom I never had the honor of meeting, has been on my mind as I completed this project, focusing my attention time and again on what counts in both work and life.

My sister, Hila Reichman, never fails to inspire me with her unparalleled eye for detail, her astounding wit, and her ability to find the right turn of phrase for just about everything. I am grateful to her and to my brother-in-law, Josh Podietz, for their unflagging support, to say nothing of their bottomless patience with unreturned phone calls and e-mails. Oren Asher Podietz, clearly refusing to be a postscript, arrived just in time. My aunts, uncles, and cousins from near and far were unfailingly supportive, and the gatherings and celebrations that took place in tandem with writing this book are impossible, happily, for me to tease out of its pages.

Ted Weesner has given me just cause to feel amazed at my luck, illogically taking on this and a few other commitments as this book was nearing completion. My companion and collaborator, he made finishing it seem less like an ending than a beginning.

My parents, Erella and Benny Reichman, gave me that generous and precious gift of a love of language and, casting common sense aside, never asked me to go to law school. For that freedom of heart and mind, among so many other intangibles, I am grateful beyond measure. This book is dedicated to them, with love.

In Chapter Two, I have drawn freely on my 2002 essay "'I am quite a stranger to the ways of the place': The Strange Character of Law," published in *Studies in Law, Politics and Society* 25 (2002), Emerald Publishing Group Ltd. An earlier version of Chapter One was published as "'New forms for our new sensations': Woolf and the Lesson of Torts" in *Novel: A Forum on Fiction* 36.3 (2003): 398–422. Copyright NOVEL Corp. © 2003. Reprinted with permission. A version of Chapter Four appeared in the volume *Law and Catastrophe,* eds. Austin Sarat, Lawrence Douglas, and Martha Merrill Umphrey (Stanford, CA: Stanford University Press, 2007). I gratefully acknowledge permission to republish these pieces here.

THE AFFECTIVE LIFE OF LAW

Introduction

Legal Modernism

For war is the hardest place . . . [I]f comprehensive and consistent moral judgments are possible there, they are possible everywhere.

—Michael Walzer[1]

This book is about legal justice, social justice, and the narrative spaces between them. It is about how our sense of justice and responsibility changes in the wake of war, that "hardest place" where our firmest convictions falter and our sense of what we ought to do—indeed of what we *can* do—erodes. And it is about how we come to restructure our world in the aftermath of catastrophe through fiction, in narratives that begin in literature but leave their mark on our culture's experience of law. Indeed, this exploration attempts to understand the very relationship between law, literature, and the modern social world, elaborating a method of cultural analysis that sheds light on how a shared sense of commitment develops among the subjects of a juridical order. It offers, moreover, a meditation on what modernity means, legally and aesthetically, bringing into focus a complex ethical framework that I call "legal modernism."

For literary critics, it has become commonplace to link modernist experimentation with subjectivity to the trauma of World War I. Building on this connection between the trauma of war and cultural innovation,[2] I work from the intersection of law and literature to reach a different conclusion. Rather than understanding modernist novelists as simply *responding* by producing accounts of the failure of viable literary subjectivity in the face of modern warfare, I read them as using the genre's capacity for narrating subjectivity (and the subject's relation to history) to create a *responsible* vision of how the modern citizen could and should rebuild a just social world. Taking Virginia Woolf's trilogy of postwar novels—*Jacob's Room, Mrs. Dalloway,* and *To The Lighthouse*—as paradigmatic,

I see them as directly engaging challenges to the law raised by the modernization that culminated in World War I. Moreover, though I make no claim that modernist novels had a direct effect on the law of their time, I argue that the legacy of these modernist forays into subjective understandings of the juridical laid the experimental groundwork for the legal modernism of the post–World War II era—that is, the radical transformations in law brought about by that war. Our understanding of concepts such as Crimes Against Humanity or Crimes Against the Jewish People is a legacy of modernism's relationship to narrative and subjectivity. My work here is to examine the inheritance of this legacy.

The Affective Life of Law, then, addresses the legal modernism of the novel between the wars, the legal modernism produced by the International Criminal Tribunal and Israeli criminal law in response to revelations of Nazi atrocities, and the connections between them. It moves from fictional explorations of the juridical nature of culture in the interwar period to nonfictional struggles to narrate the trials that came into being after the Holocaust. I emphasize the way narrative strategies developed by modernist writers Virginia Woolf and Rebecca West contribute to Hannah Arendt's post–World War II accounts of the birth of legal modernism at the Eichmann trial. While Woolf, West, and Arendt form the centerpieces of my analysis, I also draw from a range of literary and cultural figures to show how a generation of writers and thinkers engaged the most difficult crises of their times.

The relation between legal and literary modernism that I envision runs deeper than analogy or equivalence. Far from being mirror images or replicas of each other, they exist in a *contingent* relationship, in which the parameters and stakes of ethical life are set out in literature and reified—ever imperfectly—in law. These imperfections, in turn, reenter literature, bodying forth narratives that console, lament, and imagine possibilities that remain inexpressible in legal terms. Their connection is thus one of mutual implication and necessary complementarity.[3] The narratives of responsibility I examine appear as symptoms or manifestations of a complex emotional thicket: our innermost hopes, our most inconsolable anguish, and our deepest bewilderment.

It should be stressed that *The Affective Life of Law* does not seek to provide a comprehensive historical account of either legal or literary modernity. The movement it traces, however, must be understood within the framework of certain important historical shifts, sea changes characterizing the beginning of the twentieth century, which saw subsequent transformations in the common law. Signs of technological progress could not be teased apart from symptoms of social and ethical upheaval: the expansion of railways and the growth of cities; the spread of the motor car and with it, automobile accidents; the rise of factories and consequently, of industrial accidents. Legal doctrine was not far behind in responding to the emergence of this increasingly impersonal, mechanically inflected world. The early part of the twentieth century was marked in law by efforts to develop a legal account of traumatic injury; by the shift from old notions of noncriminal harm (which traditionally fell under the legal category of trespass) to the doctrine of negligence as a means of assigning blame. These modifications responded not just to a world altered by mechanization, urbanization, population growth, and bureaucracy. They also served as markers of people's sense of how the world they had known was becoming less and less recognizable and habitable: the burgeoning anxieties about who was responsible when no one appeared blameworthy; the confusion of diagnosing and treating injury that was psychological rather than physical; the anguish of realizing that long-held ideas of inheritance no longer made sense in an era when so many young men died before they had a chance to make wills—or, for that matter, to accumulate enough wealth worthy of a will. These subjective conditions demanded expression not only in the pages of literature and history but also in the annals of law. In keeping with the trajectory of modernist studies, then, I connect historical and cultural upheaval with aesthetic innovation and subjectivity. But the history I attend to is legal, and the aesthetic innovation at the heart of this book's concerns is not only that of modernist fiction but also of new legal forms and juridical language.

Among the transformations in the first half of the twentieth century, and to a great extent at work in all of them, is the modern condition of anonymity, which emerges as one of the central aesthetic, ethical, and historical problems of modernity.[4] If Emmanuel Levinas saw ethics as rooted in the face-to-face encounter, the opportunities for such moments were becoming increasingly rare in the twentieth century—which certainly goes a long way in explaining why Levinas saw them as so very fertile to begin with. In both legal and literary modernism, making sense, and making do, with this anonymity required nothing less than a new ethical subject—or in some cases, a traditional ethical subject recast in modern terms.

By thinking about responsibility after war through both tort law—the body of law associated with private harms and individual compensation—and the private world of modernist "fictions of interiority," I am well aware of the incongruence that comes of setting private justice and public trauma alongside each other. But I invite such inconsistency because I believe that responsibility begins precisely in questions that seem far too personal to accommodate the public nature of war. It is no coincidence that these supposedly private questions are the very issues being worked out in the interwar period in both novels and courtrooms, which looked to individuals to determine the shape of social and legal responsibility. One of the main achievements of recent modernist studies has been to complicate this binary relationship between public and private, finding more in Woolf, Joyce, or Proust than their so-called inward turn and refocusing our attention on how such subjectivity participated in our most public endeavors: the formation of nationalism, the creation (or reclaiming) of culture, the establishment of political order, or the critique of bureaucracy, to name a few.[5]

In this book's understanding of modernity, the public and private intersect—or more aptly, collide—at the site, state, or body of injury, which I suggest can only be recognized in individual terms. It is here, faced with the mass trauma of World War I, that Walter Benjamin would conceptualize an injured Europe through the individual, vulnerable body in "The Storyteller" (1936):

> For never has experience been contradicted more thoroughly than strategic experience by tactical warfare, economic experience by inflation, bodily experience by mechanical warfare, moral experience by those in power. A generation that had gone to school on a horse-drawn streetcar now stood under the open sky in a countryside in which nothing remained unchanged but the clouds, and beneath those clouds, in a field of force of destructive torrents and explosions, was the tiny, fragile human body.[6]

What began as this "tiny, fragile human body," however, would eventually set the terms of political identity, creating nations and communities from injured bodies and, in Wendy Brown's diagnosis, laying the groundwork "for infelicitous formulations of identity rooted in injury" and "litigiousness as a way of political life."[7] The personal becomes political under modernism in new, jurisprudential ways, and my intention in these pages is to read the narrative sources—literary and legal—of this jurisprudence of injury.

Given that my analysis of law is primarily cultural and rhetorical, I have chosen to emphasize the shared heritage of common law, a shareability implied by its very name. As such, I move fluidly between British and American texts so as to gain a wider cultural perspective, rather than one confined exclusively to a specific nation's legal or literary history. The argument I develop pertains to a broader legal consciousness, one that emerged on both sides of the Atlantic around the same period, a time when both Great Britain and the United States faced similar historical pressures of modernization and industrialization, when decisions served (as they had historically done) as precedents in both countries, and when modernism was making its cultural presence felt in London as in New York. Thus, some chapters—most notably, Chapter 2 on *Mrs. Dalloway*—take their legal material from one nation (here, Judge Benjamin Cardozo's opinion for the New York Court of Appeals in *Palsgraf v. Long Island Railroad*) and their literature from another (Woolf's resolutely English novel). The transit from the Long Island Railroad to the streets of London implies neither causality nor pure coincidence. *Palsgraf* may not have influenced *Mrs. Dalloway*, but the two texts share a mutual historical basis in their attempt to engage the pervasive question of what strangers owe to each other in the modern city. Their narratives, in other words, represent the shaping of an ethical landscape in which expectations of responsibility needed to be redrawn—narrowed, in *Palsgraf*'s case, and widened, in Woolf's.

It is no doubt obvious that my arguments in this book can only have emerged from the body of work that is law and literature theory. But let me explain in more detail how modernist studies and law and literature studies seem to me to dovetail, and also about how I hope this book suggests new avenues for both. The field of law and literature today is as varied as the range of approaches and methodologies in both of its subfields. No clear consensus exists as to what law and literature is or does. There are thematic approaches that examine trials, imprisonment, or capital punishment; philosophical or rhetorical work on the speech acts of legal discourse; and psychoanalytic treatments of law's place in our experiences of trauma or desire, to name just a few modes of inquiry.[8] What binds this diverse interdisciplinary field together—indeed, what makes it a "field" to begin with—is an underlying belief that the texts of law and literature jointly contribute to what legal scholar Robert Cover called a *nomos* or normative universe. A nomos, it should be stated, is not synonymous with ideology or dogma. Less articulable and more supple, a normative universe emerges from the integration of our acts, ideologies, beliefs, and associations—and more generally, from the assimilation and psychic calibration of the countless narratives that enter our diverse frames of reference.

Placing law and literature on equal footing, Cover insists in "Nomos and Narrative"[9] that in the formation of a nomos, the law participates as but one normative possibility among many. One may find a particular nomos expressed in a legal opinion, and another at times conflicting normative framework articulated in literary, religious, or political discourses. The range of *nomoi,* like the expanse of texts, is limitless, and the practical business of daily life depends on how (or whether) these normative worlds coexist. Though the term might seem somewhat technical or abstract, it is useful for my purposes because it helps us envision as related the various forms of a community or collectivity shaped around a shared, normative set of values. The nomoi my study examines include the commitment to compensating everyone for their injuries, the belief that we can pass along our possessions to future generations, and the conviction that even the dullest instances of justice ought to be remembered.

I should emphasize here some subtleties of a point crucial to the trajectories of my argument: the idea that the modernist novel contributes to this nomos differently from its predecessors in that it is "normative." Drawing as I do from the field of law and literature studies, normative means something quite different than it does in literary or cultural studies. In a legal framework, the term refers to a belief in what *ought* to be as opposed to what *is.* It involves the conviction that the law can help to move society toward this goal of "ought" by initiating changes consonant with shifting perceptions, innovations, and progress. In literary studies, the term *normative* generally means, following Foucault, the imposition of culturally and arbitrarily shaped norms—sexual, racial, national—upon a social reality. Normative, in this context, has pejorative connotations associated with punishing difference and rewarding conventionality. And while it can certainly take on such negative registers in legal discourse, I use it to refer to the commitment of moving from is to ought, a move that is particularly helpful in recognizing a crucial difference between modernist writers and their predecessors. Victorian writers like Charles Dickens or George Eliot mounted their criticism through social realism's ethical critique; their novels contain strong ideas of what is wrong with the world, but little about how to address these wrongs. Writers in the twentieth century, however—at least those with whom this book is concerned—would press these ethical claims into normative ones, suggesting not only what was wrong with the world, but also how the affective experiences produced by these wrongs could be harnessed to do something right. Thus, central to my understanding of Woolf's fiction is the claim that she pursues an ethical vision of how a world tragically altered by World War I can be inhabited along normative lines, emphasizing *how* to live rather than *what* is wrong. From this vantage, I argue that Woolf's preoccupations with responsibility and memory after the war posit her as a profoundly normative novelist rather than just a sensitive observer of modern life.

My discussion of how a nomos is rebuilt in the aftermath of war approaches the legal modernism of both law and literature through a range of emotional responses to justice or injustice, affective experiences that I see as central to the ethical and normative imagination.[10] Drawing upon the interrelationship of affect and justice, I attend not to discrete emotions like love or grief but to intuitions and sensibilities that need to be narrated because they cannot be summed up by any one term. These feelings about "the way things ought to be" are arrived at only through sentences or entire narratives—discourses that I locate in both literature and law. I look to the messy contours of emotional life in order to understand how justice, as an official and unofficial ethic of responsibility, builds itself upon a substructure of sensibility.

If subjectivity figures prominently within modernist studies, it is not an altogether foreign presence in legal studies. Oliver Wendell Holmes Jr., the proverbial father of modern American law, declared in his famous opening to *The Common Law,* "The life of law has not been logic: it has been experience."[11] In turning away from the prospect of justice as a science, denying it mechanical predictability, Holmes embraced the supple, elusive realm of feeling and intuition: "The felt necessities of the time, the prevalent moral and political theories, intuitions of public policy, avowed or unconscious, even the prejudices which judges share with their fellow-men, have had a good deal more to do than the syllogism in determining the rules by which men should be governed."[12]

Expanding upon Holmes's claim, we might say that responsibility has a *sensibility,* an underlying rhetorical, psychological, and normative structure that stimulates (and stipulates) modern law as it does modernist fiction. This sensibility forms the infrastructure upon which the syllogistic propositions and reasoned decisions of law, like the forms of fiction, are built. Perhaps it should not surprise us, then, when radical innovation in literature happens at a time of radical innovation in law, or at least that literary invention is followed by the realization that the law will have to be drastically changed because it is no longer adequate to the exigencies of modern life.

My convictions here should be clear: law is not limited to what happens in the courtroom. Its reaches run far deeper: we live in a legal world, inhabit a legal culture, even if we never come before a jury or witness a trial.[13] Just as a legal opinion can be literary without discussing a novel, so can a work of literature be juridical (and, I believe, is more likely to be so) without depicting a trial. In this richer vein, Woolf's ideas about accidents and character, the treatment of strangers, and the negotiation of the material world of possessions, incorporate or recast some of the basic principles in torts and property.

In liberating Woolf from a tradition of scholarship that identifies her with domestic or largely private concerns, this book shares a sensibility with others who have discovered in her work a rigorous engagement with public life, but sets her texts within the specific contours of a legal imagination.[14] The book's first section thus posits Woolf as a normative writer who draws on the power of a juridical imaginary to shape her response to the war. I examine Woolf's novels alongside concepts from torts and property law, reading her as an intellectual deeply engaged with issues of ethics and judgment, the urgency of which was particularly felt in the wake of World War I. To think about the legal imaginary through a writer unconcerned with law in practice—with trials, attorneys, or judges—ultimately allows us to appreciate more fully the complex relation between law and culture. And it brings into view a figure quite different from the politically detached author Woolf is generally taken to be. Engaging her works in this uncharacteristically juridical way both suggests how the literary imagination contains deep legal structures—and in turn, how the legal imagination partakes of the literary.

With this in mind, Chapter 1 considers how injury—and specifically the accidental, traumatic injuries of World War I—challenges conventional notions of character, responsibility, and community. Through tort law's concepts of negligence and duty of care, I examine how law accounts for accidents and how this legal treatment of accidents informs a modern literary sensibility in Woolf's first experimental novel, *Jacob's Room*. This postwar novel both appeals to and extends legal notions of duty of care and negligence, questioning the viability of relying on past precedent—in law, the doctrine of *stare decisis*—to respond to unprecedented historical tragedy.

Chapter 2 extends the analysis of tort law and interwar responsibility to Woolf's next novel, *Mrs. Dalloway,* examining the importance of "stranger cases" in tort law, as well as the estranging language of legal decisions like the landmark opinion *Palsgraf v. Long Island Railroad*. By comparing the law's treatment of strangers to *Mrs. Dalloway,* I show how Woolf challenges the postwar generation to pursue the very encounters that tort law aims to regulate. If law works to set limits on potential plaintiffs by asking who might foreseeably be affected by an act, Woolf—unconstrained by legal procedure—insists that unforeseeable encounters with strangers create the most potent opportunities for responsibility.

Chapter 3 considers Woolf's *To the Lighthouse* as a work that refigures the law's relationship to inheritance in the context of war. World War I inaugurated a new kind of memorial culture, one that invoked traditional techniques of memory but infused them with a normative—and distinctly legal—sensibility. This discourse unfolded in a context that challenged traditional notions of inheritance, marked by the painful and widespread occurrence of the return of dead soldiers' personal effects to their families at a time when the war dead were not repatriated. The arrival of these unwilled belongings was often met with confusion: it was unclear what one was to do with them or whether to keep them at all. This chapter examines the business of inheriting such painful and impractical effects, a process I call traumatic inheritance. In detailing how traumatic inheritance lies at the heart of postwar mourning and commemoration, I demonstrate how *To the Lighthouse*'s conception of memorial architecture balances the public display of war memorials (such as London's Cenotaph) with the private sense of grief and memory, and thus offers the possibility of inheriting without a will.

The first half of *The Affective Life of Law*, then, examines fictional legal modernism through these three novels by Virginia Woolf. The second section of the book examines how the relationship between law and literature characteristic of modernism is radically reworked after World War II. The Nuremberg and Eichmann trials signaled a dramatic shift in how the collective trauma of war came to be represented in both legal and literary terms. For if World War I placed new pressures on novelists, the unimaginable scale of atrocity inflicted by the Third Reich thrust the burden of representation onto jurists, carving justice out of the remnants of society. Chapter 4 traces how an ethical responsibility for trauma on a mass scale shifted from the literary to the legal sphere by taking up Rebecca West's three-part series for *The Daily Telegraph*, "Greenhouse with Cyclamens." West lived through the two world wars and wrote extensively on both. Her aesthetics, like her politics, follow the trajectory of modernism; indeed, her biography could be seen as emblematic of modernism itself. Her work appeared in the inaugural issue of *Blast*, the avant-garde journal founded by Wyndham Lewis, and she was an early suffragette and a lifelong, self-proclaimed feminist. After World War II, she wrote about treason, Nuremburg, and many other trials, and her writing in the public press added a new civic dimension to her role as a woman of letters. And like many of her female contemporaries, including Virginia Woolf, West dealt with the far-reaching ethical questions of her times through attention to the ordinary world, privileging everyday experience as a means of grasping the ethical possibilities of a world shattered by war.

As a modernist novelist who then turned to a nonfiction narration of Nuremburg, West, in the shape of her career and in her literary preoccupation with the quotidian, instantiates my claim that our Arendtian notions of contemporary justice have roots in modernist understandings of narrative subjectivity. My reading of West's coverage of the Nuremburg trial examines her depiction of the legal event as a powerful instance of modernist self-consciousness. The trial may have been newsworthy, but it was also, to quote Walter Benjamin's criticism of journalism, "poor in noteworthy stories."[15] In seeking out these stories for herself, West discovers legal drama outside the courtroom and thus creates possibilities, through her modernist sensibility in fiction, to commit an event as unprecedented and extraordinary as Nuremberg to memory and to convey what it felt like to bear witness to historical justice. Rather than approaching the trial as a monumental turning point in jurisprudence, West describes it as a staggering instance of boredom "on a huge, historic scale." Her insistence on dullness inaugurates a strategic and psychological process through which postwar legal experience and ultimately, modern legal memory, are born. In shaping the trial's afterlife through narratives that seem to have little to do with the Tribunal's proceedings, West suggests that "legal drama" is no less than an oxymoron—and in the process, posits a uniquely historical connection between literature and law, one decidedly normative in its claims.

If West's contribution to a wider understanding of law's impact on the historical and narrative imagination remains largely overlooked, her attention to legal banality is given new life in Hannah Arendt's notion, seventeen years later, of the banality of evil. Yet the resonance between West and Arendt goes beyond their respective appreciation of banality, whether of law (West) or the bureaucratic criminal (Arendt). Indeed, these writers represent necessary companion pieces to a deeper appreciation of the relationship between law and narrative in the twentieth century. Witnessing the two most famous post-Holocaust trials as reporters, West and Arendt provide us not with erudite explanations of international law but with narratives that trace a modern, cultural, and literary encounter with justice. Chapter 5 is devoted to Arendt's famous account of the

Eichmann trial, *Eichmann in Jerusalem: A Report on the Banality of Evil.* My reading of Arendt as a modernist writer maintains that her narrative's most significant contribution was not, as is commonly noted, her insistence on the defendant's ordinariness as an inherent feature of his relationship to radical evil. In contrast to this view, I claim that the value of Arendt's work lies in its enunciation of a sense of responsibility with counterintuitive roots in Anglo-American tort law rather than international criminal law.

My treatment of Arendt illuminates how her evaluation of the trial draws upon a basic tenet of torts, the neighbor principle, which sought to define negligent behavior by setting limits on people to whom one owes a duty of care. In a manner resembling Woolf's earlier treatment of social obligation in *Mrs. Dalloway, Eichmann in Jerusalem* widens the legal scope of due care by imagining the trial as identifying not simply a nation of victims, litigants, or witnesses, but a society comprised of neighbors obligated to listen to each other. The book's final movement thus completes my outline of a genealogy that runs from a modernist literary sensibility that is fundamentally concerned with ethics to Arendt's development of the concept of social responsibility in the notion of "care for the world," by which she meant the investment in institutions such as a legal system or a political process. I read this "care" and this "world" as a set of emotional and ethical responses undergirding these public institutions and which, in turn, these institutions—law and trials, novels and culture—are meant to safeguard.

In elucidating how modernist fiction and law together arrive at new ways to address the various forms of postwar injury, the chapters that follow bring us time and again to an incontrovertible fact: that all of the central figures in *The Affective Life of Law* are women. While feminist ethics lie beyond the scope of this book, one would be hard-pressed not to adumbrate the potent connections between the iterations of care that provide its explicit and implicit framework: the legal formulation of "duty of care" in torts, Arendt's "care for the world," and the ethic of care associated with the feminist interventions of Carol Gilligan in psychology and Robin West in law.[16] In literature, we find a related sense of care in the careful attention to the everyday, an investment in the allegedly trivial long associated with women's writing.[17] At the very least, these connections between legal and feminist thought suggest that there is something resolutely ordinary about even the most revolutionary moments of justice, and that the question of whether these moments have a life beyond the law—a cultural and social future—has to do with whether they can be absorbed into everyday experience and its attendant emotions. Whether we choose to *give* it that future is itself a normative question: a matter not of what justice is, but of what it *ought* to be—and of how we get to this "ought."

Modernist writers like Woolf, West, and Arendt put forth a notion of commitment built upon the experience of *feeling* responsible. How, to return to Holmes, might we trace and elucidate the felt necessities and intuitions that enter not only the life of law, but the broader sense of justice upon which we construct this law and against which we test it? What does responsibility look and feel like in the aftermath of historical catastrophe? It is my hope that the narrative maps through which these inarticulate sensibilities are expressed—or often suppressed, put up with, or transformed—demonstrate how a normative world is built over a scaffolding of affect. To talk about a nomos in the wake of the two world wars is to address an emotional, intuitive world, and to step into the daunting task of making practical differences from intangible but all-too-real experiences.

PART I

Modernism's Legal Forms

CHAPTER ONE

Woolf and the Lesson of Torts

It must not be forgotten that "duty" got into our law for the very purpose of
combating what was then feared to be a dangerous delusion . . . that the law
might countenance legal redress for all foreseeable harm.

—John G. Fleming, *An Introduction to the Law* of Torts[1]

In Chapter Five of *Northanger Abbey,* Jane Austen presents her readers with an
introspective scene of reading. Anticipating the critical disapproval of novels
common in her day, Austen depicts her heroine, Catherine Morland—whose
main quandary seems to be that she reads too much—reading novels. Catherine's
act of reading prompts an aside from Austen, who defends her craft against those
who would attack it as an irresponsible way to squander one's time. Stepping out
of her plot momentarily, Austen declares:

> Yes, novels; for I will not adopt that ungenerous and impolitic custom so common
> with novel writers, of degrading by their contemptuous censure the very perfor-
> mances, to the number of which they are themselves adding . . . Alas! if the heroine
> of one novel be not patronized by the heroine of another, *from whom can she expect
> protection and regard*? I cannot approve of it. Let us leave it to the Reviewers to abuse
> such effusions of fancy at their leisure, and over every new novel to talk in threadbare
> strains of the trash with which the press now groans. *Let us not desert one another; we
> are an injured body.*[2]

Austen's ironic remark is a call for defense, for novelists to take responsibility for
their craft by standing up for each other. In its appeal to the fact of injury, however, her language suggests something more. Austen's rhetorical flourish implies
that there is an aspect of the injured body—seen here in its corporate, communal
sense—that brings us out of our self-absorption and complacency, demanding
that we act responsibly, ethically, in the presence of others. By offering injury as
a symbol for the ethical imperative to respond to each other and to come to one

another's defense, Austen offers us a vantage point from which to examine what it might mean to take responsibility within literature. Her aside, this chapter will argue, would take on new literary exigencies a century later with the first mechanized war and the birth of modernism.

Moving between the individual and the collective—from the denigrated heroine of the novel to the authors who bring her to life—Austen inflects her wry vindication with an imaginative potency born of addressing the general through the force of the particular. It is through this relationship between the particularized and the corporate that I propose to consider the connection between injury, responsibility, and the novel. For although a number of Austen's predecessors such as Samuel Johnson often viewed novels with contempt, many novelists of the time nonetheless insisted that literature, through force of character and sentiment, was precisely where individual and social responsibility for others could begin.

In pursuing the notion of responsibility, I intend to set it against its more official expression in the common law, and specifically within the narratives of accidents, injuries, and ensuing responsibilities that comprise the body of tort law. Responsibility, we might say, is the underpinning of torts, and torts of responsibility. What can tort law's narratives tell us about the best—most careful, least negligent—way to act? How does law talk about unprecedented situations in order to determine who is responsible? More specifically, how does it make sense of accidental injury—which also becomes, in many instances, the experience of unspeakable trauma? By exploring these questions first in law and then in literature, I do not claim merely that the two offer different approaches to the same sets of circumstances—though in part, this is often the case. Rather, I intend to explore their different responses to injuries in order to identify the sensibility involved in the experiences of pain and catastrophe that accompany them—in other words, to look at the forms of their respective responses so as to tell the story of the underlying emotional content of literature and law. In doing so, I explore the way in which Austen's defense of the novel gathers new, literal momentum after World War I. In a sense that she could not have anticipated, her playful tone is stripped of all irony, sounding instead a note of urgency in the face of war's distinctively modern brutality.

Tort law will stand at the center of my analysis both because of the field's attention to injury and because of the importance of its role in an industrializing society. The historical context that shapes tort law's grammar of responsibility finds its literary counterpart in the devastation of World War I, the staggering casualties of which were unseen by those on the home front in England, not only because the war was fought abroad but also because so many of the injuries that it produced were of an emotional, traumatic nature. This war placed pressure on literary forms, demanding a shift of idiom and representation. This same pressure would also ultimately require the law to come to terms with the demands of a world shattered by industrial warfare. In an increasingly mechanized social sphere, law sought to offer a particular kind of clarity—an intelligibility born of its burden to both represent injury and to make sense of it through judgment. But its attempts at clarity were often undone by the unrepresentable nature of the cases before it, which confounded law's language of visibility and causality. The bewildering, disorienting experience of trauma in both literature and law gives rise to similar intuitions and feelings, culminating in a new ethics of responsibility—what Virginia Woolf called "new forms for our new sensations."[3]

Literature's practical capacity to act in the world and, by extension, to do justice in it, was called into question with renewed pressure by World War I, which became a unique challenge not only to novelists but also to the idea of responsibility at its broadest level. Samuel Johnson's eighteenth-century admonitions found their twentieth-century echo in the cultural critic Walter Benjamin, whose concern with the ills of novel reading had a more specific political and historical problem in mind: the crisis of war. He writes in "The Storyteller" (1936):

> The novelist *has isolated himself.* The birthplace of the novel is the solitary individual, who is no longer able to express himself by giving examples of his most important concerns, *is himself uncounseled, and cannot counsel others.* To write a novel means to carry the incommensurable to extremes in the representation of human life. In the midst of life's fullness, and through the representation of this fullness, *the novel gives evidence of the profound perplexity of the living.*[4]

Benjamin's grim pronouncement issues not from the crisis of war alone, but from the breakdown in communication that followed it—a symptom of language grown brittle and meaningless. "With the [First] World War," Benjamin reflects, "a process began to become apparent which has not halted since then. Was it not noticeable at the end of the war that men returned from the battlefield grown silent—not richer, but poorer in communicable experience?"[5] Traditional representations of war, with their notions of strength, bravery, and heroism, could offer little consolation to a generation for whom individual agency had been overwhelmed by mechanized warfare and staggering numbers of the dead, wounded, and missing.

If legal certainty is often viewed as a counterpoint to literary indecision, it also offers itself as a social antithesis to the isolation of novel reading. For law cannot afford the luxuries of silence, even—or perhaps especially—when it issues from incomprehensible historical events. Faced with unthinkable situations and charged with the double burden of both representing and judging them, law seems to offer clarity and action in moments of chaos. By its own account, law concerns itself with responsibility and aims, to return to Benjamin's formulation, to offer counsel and clarity, and to bring the solitary individual into a relationship with others.

Law offers an important way to think through the representational challenges of historical crisis because its presence is felt most powerfully not in the smooth course of life, but in its rupture. "Let us not desert one another; we are an injured body," urges Austen, her manner reminiscent not only of a literary admonition but also of a legal command. Law is set in motion at the moment of injury and responds by balancing individual circumstances against the broader interests of a community. I approach law, then, in its own moment of crisis: during the rise of industrialization, when accidents became the rule rather than the exception and the march of progress demanded that judges and lawyers address its collateral harm. I then turn to the particular and peculiar form of injury initiated by this industrial heritage, which posed a new problem for the medical, military, and legal communities: the widespread occurrence of traumatic injury in World War I. Developing a legal language for accidents is one thing; creating a language for the psychological harm these accidents produce is another, drastically different challenge. Ultimately, the innovations of literature in the wake of these new injuries illuminate the extent to which jurists—and more broadly, the official registers of the British government and military—were unable to find a means of addressing trauma on its own terms. These terms, I hope to show, can only be discovered through radical transformation of the sort that the modernist novel allows. But it can only be recognized as necessary to begin with through the trials and errors of law.

Torts and Accidents

Torts emerged as an independent area of law only in the mid-nineteenth century in response to new circumstances that were often the product of technological innovation and industrialization.[6] Unprecedented situations—automobile collisions, injuries in factories or on construction sights—produced so many cases of damage and injury that a unified system was needed to define the bounds of responsible behavior. "In all human activities the law keeps up with improvement and progress brought about by discovery and invention,"[7] wrote one American judge in 1905 in an opinion involving an automobile accident. The pressure to keep law current, to absorb the latest innovations, meant that judges had to formulate new doctrines and reshape legal remedies to absorb the by-products of the Industrial Revolution.[8]

The legal principle of negligence developed during this period, enabling judges to assign fault only in situations involving the absence of ordinary care. Those who caused harm would now be liable only if their action created an *unreasonable* risk of harm. This meant, naturally, that law had to specify the meaning of "reasonable" as it defined the level of care individuals owed to each other. Under this new form of liability, blame was assigned only if the injuring party had not behaved with due care to prevent an accident, replacing the law's earlier reliance on formal categories of culpability, such as strict liability. Of course, the shift to a standard of due care did not imply that accidents could be eliminated. The law, Guido Calabresi insists in *The Costs of Accidents,* is built upon the tacit acceptance of these accidents that, while tragic, are countenanced to accommodate larger social interests:

> Our society is not committed to preserving life at any cost. In its broadest sense, the rather unpleasant notion that we are willing to destroy lives should be obvious. Wars are fought. The University of Mississippi is integrated at the risk of losing lives. But what is more pertinent to the study of accident law, though perhaps equally obvious, is that lives are spent not only when the *quid pro quo* is some great moral principle, but also when it is a matter of convenience. Ventures are undertaken that, statistically at least, are certain to cost lives.[9]

Calabresi's understanding underscores his conviction that accidents are calculated risks, their inevitability woven into the very fabric of law. The negligence principle itself implies that not all injuries can be redressed, that some will be unavoidable even when due care is taken, and that this inevitability is a cost that society must be willing to bear.

Holmes v. Mather, an 1875 decision of the Court of Exchequer in England, illustrates this point in a manner both commonsensical and tragic. The facts in the case are straightforward and, on a crowded street, not terribly surprising: a woman standing on the sidewalk is knocked down by a team of horses and severely injured. She sues the owner of the horses, confident that since they hit her, the court will rule in her favor. Countering this, however, the defense in *Holmes v. Mather* argued that the accident was unavoidable: the groom, despite his best efforts, lost control of his horses after they were startled by a barking dog. Although he attempted to steer them back on course, he could not prevent them from running into the plaintiff. Since the driver had done everything in his power to avoid the accident, he could not be held negligent. Yet this reasoning did little to address the ethical dilemma posed by the plaintiff's counsel: "If somebody must suffer, why should it be the innocent plaintiff, instead of the defendant, who chose to exercise his horses in the public streets?"[10] The injured woman did nothing to provoke the accident; why should she have to bear its burden when the horses should have been under the plaintiff's control?

Justice Bramwell, ruling for the defense, answers this question quite pragmatically. His reasoning offers a sketch of ordinary life shaped in equal measure by experience, unpredictability, and chance: "For the convenience of mankind in carrying on the affairs of life," he argues, "people as they go along roads must expect, or put up with, such mischief as reasonable care on the part of others cannot avoid." The logical result of doing otherwise, Bramwell insists, is that "you might as well argue that if the driver had not started on that morning, or had not turned down that particular street, this mischief would not have happened."[11]

Holmes v. Mather presents us with a glaring and matter-of-fact reminder of legal resignation, or what we might call law's sense of commonplace tragedy. This resignation dictates that in any accident, someone must suffer, no matter how unfortunate or unfair that suffering may seem.[12] Those who bear the costs of accidents are not always the people who caused them. To live in the modern world, this logic suggests, is to take risks—risks worth taking not on some high moral ground but simply "for the convenience of mankind." Several years later in the United States, Oliver Wendell Holmes, Jr. went a step further than *Holmes v. Mather,* removing the burden of injuries from inevitable accidents outside the law's purview altogether:

> The general principle of our law is that loss from accident must lie where it falls, and this principle is not affected by the fact that a human being is the instrument of misfortune . . . In the language of the late Chief Justice Nelson of New York: ". . . All the cases concede that an injury arising from inevitable accident, or, which in law or reason is the same thing, from an act that ordinary human care and foresight are unable

to guard against, is but the misfortune of the sufferer, and lays no foundation for legal responsibility" . . . A man need not, it is true, do this or that act,—the term *act* implies a choice,—but he must act somehow.[13]

The reasoning enunciated by Bramwell and Holmes runs counter to our loftiest expectations about jurisprudence. They remind us that law often surrenders to life—a life that can leave individuals who had no hand in their injuries with no answers, no compensation, and empty consolations. This pragmatic resignation, Bramwell and others imply, is the consequence of fashioning a legal system that works, one that does not buckle under the strain of its times.

But even as legal practitioners reinforced and fine-tuned the doctrine of negligence throughout the end of the nineteenth and the beginning of the twentieth centuries, the law remained ill-equipped to handle a fundamental change in the nature of a particular subset of the accidental injuries for which it was developed. Traditionally, torts cases addressed physical injury; if it was visible, it was actionable. But with the rise of accidents and accident litigation, courts found themselves confronted with a new kind of harm: psychological trauma. And the task of attending to these more intangible costs of accidents at the turn of the twentieth century presented jurists and policymakers alike with a thoroughly new challenge.

A Jurisprudence of Psychological Injury

In 1861, the renowned English judge Lord Wensleydale famously declared in the English case of *Lynch v. Knight*, "Mental pain or anxiety the law cannot value, and does not pretend to redress, when the unlawful act complained of causes that alone."[14] How, then, did the law come to value emotional trauma on its own terms, and what can this process tell us about the legal grasp of psychological injury? Is there, in fact, a jurisprudence of trauma? In what follows, I want to suggest that the law is still far from a proper language for trauma, and that the path it has taken in developing what language exists has been characterized by its own traumatic symptoms: denial, latency, and a resistance to fully recognizing the difference between one form of trauma and another. This is not to suggest that there is no particular legal language through which to refer to trauma: one can think of two powerful examples of such language in legal categories such as the Nuremberg trial's Crimes Against Humanity and the Eichmann trial's Crimes

Against the Jewish People, which I take up in the second part of this book. The difficulty with such categories, however, is that the harm they address is collective, whereas trauma in its strict sense denotes an individual phenomenon; indeed, the earliest legal opinions on what jurists once called "nervous shock" focused on individual rather than group injury. The tension between the discourse of war trauma and the foundational rhetoric of trauma within law thus offers a productive place to examine what trauma means to law, how its multiple meanings create a more complex canvas than any one term can suggest, and finally how literature—and Woolf's fiction in particular—offers a starting point for refiguring the relationship between narrative and invisible injury.

In illustrating this claim, I propose to look at two examples, the first from tort law and the second from military justice during World War I, which together clarify the disjunction between disparate legal remedies for psychological harm. The first example marks a turning point in the common law, a moment when we see the early signs of judges shaping a jurisprudence of psychological injury. In the 1901 opinion *Dulieu v. White & Sons,* the British High Court ruled that a plaintiff could recover damages for nervous shock even though no actual impact was involved in the accident. The plaintiff, Mrs. Dulieu, was working behind the bar at her husband's tavern when a driver lost control of his team of horses and drove them into the building. Although Mrs. Dulieu was not physically injured, her fear at seeing the horses crash into the tavern precipitated a state of nervous shock. She was several months pregnant and shortly afterwards gave birth to a premature, mentally impaired child. Subsequently, she sued the horses' owners and won, becoming the first plaintiff to be awarded damages without sustaining physical injury.

The reasoning behind Mrs. Dulieu's victory, however, is not what one might expect. Rather than attempting to understand the nature of nervous shock, the court relied on the established principle of negligence, citing an individual's right to personal safety in the confines of her home. The most important question for Justice Phillimore in the case was not the nature of the injury but the duty of care that the defendants owed Mrs. Dulieu. Once a breach of duty is established, "the fact of one link in the chain of causation being mental only makes no difference. The learned counsel for the plaintiff has put it that every link is physical in the narrow sense. That may or may not be. For myself, it is unimportant."[15] The nature of her trauma, in other words, has no substantive bearing on the case; as far as Phillimore is concerned, Mrs. Dulieu might just as well have sued for damages to the pub, since what mattered to the court was the defendant's negligence.

In ruling for the plaintiff, the *Dulieu* court set two conditions that would be upheld by judges on both sides of the Atlantic. First, the plaintiff's mental distress had to be accompanied by a physical manifestation—in Mrs. Dulieu's case, her miscarriage. Second, the plaintiff needed to establish that her shock resulted from fear for her own safety. "There is, I am inclined to think, at least one limitation," reasoned Justice Kennedy in the case. "The shock, where it operates through the mind, must be a shock which arises from a reasonable fear of immediate personal injury to oneself. A. has, I conceive, no legal duty not to shock B.'s nerves by the exhibition of negligence towards C., or towards the property of B. or C."[16] The holding in *Dulieu* created a chain of associations from psychological injury—whatever shape it may take—to physical harm, allowing the judges to invoke the more familiar principle of negligence.[17]

In reaching its decision, the *Dulieu* court distinguished the plaintiffs' positions from those of an earlier, unreported case, *Smith v. Johnson,* which ruled that unrelated third parties were not entitled to compensation. Although both courts entertained the possibility of remote injury, they nonetheless maintained that the law, bound by the doctrine of *stare decisis*—the practice of anchoring decisions in past precedents—need not take such injuries into account. At the heart of jurisprudence, then, is not a commitment to the new but a clear sense of the old: an insistence that every situation be represented in terms of the elements it shares with the judgments that came before it.[18] By constantly interpreting and adhering to its own past, the law ensures that its decisions are anything but revolutionary: they settle without unsettling.

Still, law is constantly troubled by the very matters it sets aside. The judge in *Dulieu* is himself uneasy about the possibility of the remote injury described in *Smith v. Johnson,* in spite of the fact he places such injury outside law's purview.[19] *Smith v. Johnson*—whose anonymous names underscore the case's invisible status—involved a plaintiff who witnessed the accidental death of a stranger and demanded compensation for nervous shock. His claim was rejected on the grounds that the relationship between the dead man and the plaintiff was too remote to cause emotional distress. Reconstructing the case in subsequent opinions, courts continually invoked it as a precedent dictating that unrelated bystanders could not recover damages. But in spite of this, *Smith v. Johnson* continued to haunt judges by reminding them that such injuries were possible, if not action-able. As an unreported case, it enters law as a ghostly, sourceless illustration of circumstances that law will not recognize.

Negligent Soldiers

In spite of the fact that courts rarely addressed the nature of mental distress in its own right, cases such as *Dulieu* and its followers nonetheless laid the ground-work for dealing with a phenomenon that, less than two decades later, would swell to epidemic proportions during World War I. In the overwhelming number of cases of shell shocked soldiers—and the fear that some of them were malinger-ing, faking symptoms to avoid the trenches—it became all the more urgent to come up with a decisive stance on traumatic injury. Tragically for many soldiers and their families, this official insight often came too late. I want to consider briefly one exemplary instance of this belated assessment: the case of a British soldier, Private Harry MacDonald, who was court martialed and shot for deser-tion in 1916. His case came before the Ministry of Pensions after the war, when his wife asked for a widow's pension rather than a compassionate allowance[20] —an award that the War Office, unsurprisingly, did not support. As Lord Derby, Secretary of State for War, wrote in a letter to the Ministry of Pensions, "The Army Council feel very strongly that to give pensions in such cases is really to put the coward on the same footing as the hero."[21] The Ministry of Pensions con-sequently reopened the case to determine whether Private MacDonald had been wrongly executed. A memo to Sir Matthew Nathan, Secretary of the Ministry of Pensions, describes the situation in the following terms:

> I am seriously concerned over the case. (. . .) I don't think the Army authorities would from the lay point of view come very well out of it.
> The record shows (1) The man went through Hell in the Dardanelles (2) Wounded in the Field (3) Suffered from Shell Shock (4) Is given M.D. a usual thing when the Dr. hasn't time either for proper examination or thinks the man is seeking to evade duty, being a shell shock patient is it surprising he wandered back to Etaples? I don't think so. (5) if the man had the Counsel even if the sentence had been the death penalty it would under the circumstances have been committed. (6) My general conclusion is that this is not a usual case of cowardice or desertion the man was a volunteer and it does not appear as if the man had rec'd at the hands of the C.M. [Court Martial] that generous consideration which we are continuously assured is given and that the desire is to find extenuating circumstances on the man's behalf.[22]

At stake in this account of the episode are questions of duty and negligence in their multiple iterations: the duty that the state owes its war widows and the responsibility it owes its soldiers to give them the best care and medical evaluations possible; the duty that soldiers, in turn, owe their country—and their manhood.[23]

When Parliament formed its Committee on Shell Shock in 1920 (which published its report in 1922), it acknowledged the relationship between war neuroses and more ordinary forms of nervous shock. A case like *Dulieu* may thus differ in degree from that of Private MacDonald, but it did not necessarily differ in kind. Yet the discrepancies in how negligence figures in these cases point to a fundamental problem that arises in the transformation of the theory of nervous shock from an individual to a more collective account. Framed within the political pressures of war and nationalism, the burden of duty and negligence has nowhere to go; we do not speak of war injuries as anyone's "fault" when injury is the goal of war to begin with. Under such circumstances, negligence is displaced onto the traumatized individual, rather than directed at the source of the shock. There is no place for negligence in this equation because, put simply, there is no negligence in war. There are, of course, war crimes, and more recently, Crimes Against Humanity. But these fall under a different rubric, one of criminal rather than tort law. *In times of war, law is silent,* as Cicero famously put it—at least when it comes to negligence. And, one might add, justice is belated.

The passage from individual shock to collective trauma adds a layer of complexity to the development of a jurisprudence of trauma. No individual case such as *Dulieu* or others like it can fully account for the overwhelming occurrence of war neuroses among soldiers. Trauma, in its strictest sense, is an individual phenomenon; indeed, we are still trying to find a satisfactory way to talk about collective trauma, or put differently, to rescue the individual from the terms assigned by collective trauma—broad categories such as victims or survivors that leave blank the particulars of victimization or survival. This particularity is perhaps the hardest task of all in the creation, or rather the tenuous existence, of a jurisprudence of trauma.[24]

As law struggled with the question of how to establish and judge psychological harm,[25] judges, lawyers, military and government personnel, and the medical community had to confront these injuries on a larger scale than ever before during World War I. The countless cases of shell shock that were often met with suspicions of malingering;[26] the assault on traditional notions of heroism; the grief felt by individuals in both public and private: all of these heralded a new era in which injury manifested itself most prominently in emotional distress. The classic mode of representing such trauma through its physical manifestations—law's mode—was rendered obsolete under these changed historical circumstances. Law's effort to respond adequately to emotional distress allows us to understand the larger crisis of representation triggered by the war. For the limitations of legal discourse speak to the wider, human limits of mourning—and to the representational problems posed by immeasurable grief. Law's efforts shed light on a wider, nonlegal sensibility through which people identify injury by adhering to physical symptoms, to familiar relationships, and to the remoteness or proximity of harm.

Invisible Injury and World War I

When injured bodies are invisible, when the dead lie in unmarked graves abroad, the problem of testifying to their injuries through tort law's precedents and principles becomes insurmountable. Even those who did not hear Benjamin's postwar silence found a like-minded, deafening repetitiveness in efforts to address the ongoing war—a recycling of old tropes now worn threadbare. "The war has used up words," Henry James reflected; "They have been weakened, they have deteriorated like motorcar tyres."[27] James's up-to-date metaphor brings the war's mechanization to bear upon a rapidly industrializing world, suggesting that even its most prominent symbols of progress could not keep up with the hyper-industrialized warfare in the trenches. Metaphors sounded worn-out, phrases hackneyed, and shibboleths tired, as language and literature collapsed under the unique pressures of the war.

In an effort to make sense of the conflict, many turned to traditional ideals of heroism, finding some solace in the belief that it was honorable to die for one's country and that their sons, husbands, brothers, or friends had not been killed in vain.[28] For many others, however, there would be no such sense of purpose, and no knowledge of how those who did not return met their deaths. As Samuel Hynes perceptively argues:

> The new soldiers came to the war believing that individual wills would have a role there, that what a man did—his decisions, his actions—would affect whether he lived or died. The new weapons of war challenged that conviction: *they made death accidental*. It wasn't the violence or the power or the cruelty of those weapons that made the war different; it was the vast randomness and anonymity of their ways of killing.[29]

War was no longer a series of causes and effects or a dramatic narrative that ended in a jubilant homecoming; it was a colossal series of errors, an inexplicable tangle of chaotic events—a tragedy that eroded the knowledge of why and how men died. Soldiers came home not because they were brave, but because they were lucky.[30]

The difficulty of narrating World War I in England stemmed in part from the fact that it was fought abroad; with press coverage heavily censored, civilians at home had little sense of what was happening on the battlefields. Geoff Dyer, in his account of postwar remembrance, *The Missing of the Somme,* perceives this situation as one that manifested itself in the most literal of ways—in England's undamaged physical landscape:

> Soldiers returned from this zone of obliteration to an England virtually untouched by war. The Second World War left London and other major cities cratered and ravaged by the Blitz. After the Great War the architecture and landscape of England were unchanged except, here and there, for relatively slight damage from air raids. Apart from the injured, there was no sign of a war having taken place.[31]

The fact that the war dead were not repatriated meant that the work of mourning, ordinarily accompanied by burial, needed new forms of expression—new acts, new sites and new language.[32] The absence of traditional rituals was experienced, as Dyer describes it, like an intangible illness. "It was as if a terrible plague had swept invisibly through the male population of the country—except there were no bodies, no signs of burial, no cemeteries even. Ten percent of the males under forty-five had simply disappeared."[33]

Life after 1918 bore the weight of an experience without representation, and a need to face the war's incommensurability: to reconcile the feeling that everything felt different with the fact that it looked the same. Dyer thus asks, "How to make visible this invisible loss? How to do the work of ruins? How to inscribe the story of what had happened on a death-haunted landscape which was, apparently, unmarked by the greatest tragedy to have affected the nation?"[34] Language would have to stand in for these absent ruins through risks of expression, form, and style. Literature would have to reflect "the profound perplexity of the living," offering little by way of consolation, but as I hope to show through Virginia Woolf's example, something by way of counsel.

We might thus look to Austen's exhortation—"Let us not desert one another; we are an injured body"—as an appeal to focus not on injury in its isolated, contained form, but on the collective experience of harm. This experience exceeds the physically damaged body, whose injuries are transmitted and absorbed by an entire community. The response to this collective injury means that Austen's words would resound differently for a novelist like Virginia Woolf, who must recast Austen's humor in addressing an invisible yet profoundly traumatic harm. In thus reformulating the novel, Woolf directs us toward normative possibilities beyond law's scope. For the imagined possibility that law takes pains to contain— that even those remote from another's physical injury can attest to emotional harm—is something that threatens a legal framework, but galvanizes a normative world. In thus expanding the pervasiveness of injury, we might ask: How can accidental, psychological, and collective injuries be represented and addressed in the aftermath of the war?

The Distinction of *Jacob's Room*

Law portrays injury from the outside; it focuses not on the individual experience of injury but on how one injury fits into a pattern of recognizable (and primarily visible) harm. By relating harms to one another and placing them side by side for the purposes of comparison, law is able to move from describing to judging. But this position only partly articulates or redresses psychological injury. Legal reasoning addresses emotional injury by yoking it to physical harm; as such, it contains a glaring incompleteness, a blindness to the unseen symptoms of trauma around which legal discourse circles but which it never fully grasps.

Literature, by contrast, does not need to work around this incompleteness. Unburdened by the demand to invoke the language of the past, literature can enlist language in the task of representing a shattered world—and in doing so, give voice to invisible injuries. Literature's power to speak to these injuries is made manifest in Virginia Woolf's *Jacob's Room,* which forces its readers to face the slaughter of World War I through a decidedly unremarkable individual. The necessity of accounting for so many "unremarkable" deaths confronts the living in spite of the fact that on the surface, life appeared unchanged, but underneath this surface it was profoundly altered. Woolf insists that there is a duty of care one owes to the dead in these conditions, as well as to the living who are injured by the shock and sorrow of bereavement. This duty exists in mutated, unofficial form, resisting Holmes's claim that injury "is but the misfortune of the sufferer." When these injuries cannot be seen—and so cannot be recorded officially—Woolf suggests that it is nonetheless possible to account for them in unofficial ways. In articulating this accountability, *Jacob's Room* does not impose an answer so much as pose a question, one grounded in both experience and intuition. Law, as Holmes understood it, is built not upon a set of unyielding propositions but instead on a host of "felt necessities," intuitions that drive Woolf's work as well. As Edward Bishop notes in his introduction to the novel's holograph edition, "Led by intuition rather than theory, she was not trying out a new method but moving toward one."[35] The question of how to articulate and respond to changes we cannot see is of pressing importance to Woolf. Already in 1916, she felt convinced that it was imperative to find "new forms for our new sensations,"[36] and that writers who did not develop such forms were, in effect, irresponsible. In an essay from 1918, she expressed her feeling that after the war, realistic literary descriptions of the prewar family presented a world which "the war had done nothing to change."[37]

Woolf begins to address this new state of affairs in her first experimental novel, *Jacob's Room*, published in 1922—the same year that the War Office published its *Report of the Committee of Enquiry into "Shell-Shock."*[38] The story of Jacob Flanders, who is killed in World War I, is also the articulation of an invisible injury: Jacob's fatal wound which is left undescribed, alluded to only obliquely at the novel's conclusion. *Jacob's Room*, then, tells the story of someone who does not return, whose injured body is left behind on the battlefields of World War I. But it is also the story of the altered state of affairs experienced by the living— itself a kind of injury that must be recorded. "Today people live in rooms that have never been touched by death,"[39] writes Walter Benjamin, noting how we confine the dying to sanatoria and hospitals. *Jacob's Room* suggests a different understanding of this idea, presenting its readers with an empty room indelibly "touched by death." The story of this room adumbrates, more broadly, the story of countless rooms that would remain empty after the war. John Mepham thus understands the novel as reflecting "a general cultural malaise. Many people no longer felt at ease with traditional forms and ceremonies of mourning. Many people felt bereft of a traditional public language for the expression of grief."[40] *Jacob's Room* constitutes Woolf's effort at a new language for grief in general and postwar grief in particular.

Woolf's project takes shape before her narrative begins, with the title *Jacob's Room*, evocative both for what it states and omits. For it withholds Jacob's full name, which we ultimately learn is Jacob Flanders, a thinly veiled reference to Flanders Fields—if not the site of his death, then at least suggestive of it.[41] But his name also reflects Woolf's own literary inheritance, harking back to the heroine of Daniel Defoe's *Moll Flanders,* published 200 years earlier in 1722. Woolf positions her narrative, then, against another kind of story—the eighteenth-century narrative of character, a clutch of novels bearing such eponymous titles as *Pamela, Joseph Andrews, Tristram Shandy,* and *Robinson Crusoe.* The sense of character elaborated in these novels—in which the details of an individual life are drawn out in order to bring the individual into sharp focus, and to distinguish this individual as exemplary—is no longer viable in Woolf's historical moment. As novelistic precedents, these life stories prove inadequate to record the unremarkable, obscure life.

In her subtle reference to *Moll Flanders,* Woolf takes issue with the anachronistic assumption that knowing an individual's name is the first step to knowing her fully. The old sense of character is no longer workable, no longer acceptable under the violently altered conditions of postwar life. Jacob's university essay at Cambridge, of which we learn only the title—"Does History consist of the Biographies of Great Men?"[42]—thus becomes a kind of alternate title for *Jacob's Room.* It also becomes a central question of the novel, one that Woolf answers with an unequivocal "no." The characters of noteworthy individuals—the Moll Flanderses of the world—have been replaced with the empty spaces of the dead: not Jacob Flanders but Jacob's room, Flanders Fields.

Jacob's Room thus turns away from an exhaustively represented individual, offering instead a partially developed image, painted with broad and swift brush strokes, of an unremarkable anti-hero. A "deconstructed bildungsroman," as Christine Froula has called it, the novel "does not tell Jacob's story but unwrites it to expose the social forces that initiate him into masculinity and leave him dead on the battlefield."[43] We glean details of Jacob's life—his childhood experiences near the ocean, his student days at Cambridge, his life in London, and his travels to Italy and Greece—in brief and loosely structured vignettes. For the most part, however, Jacob escapes us: even his uniqueness turns out to be borrowed from the novel's reflections on eighteenth-century architecture. "The eighteenth century has its distinction. Even the panels, painted in raspberry-coloured paint, have their distinction" (70). At this point, the narrative is interrupted by a free-indirect reportage that shifts the focus from the panels to Jacob's appearance: "'Distinction'—Mrs. Durrant said that Jacob Flanders was 'distinguished looking.' 'Extremely awkward,' she said, 'but so distinguished looking'" (70).

Mrs. Durrant's fleeting, unfinished thoughts suggest that, in fact, Jacob is anything but an eighteenth-century man of distinction. Our understanding of him is built around a series of incomplete episodes and blurred images. We share the inchoate reflections of Mrs. Norman, who sits across from Jacob in the same train compartment and lets her mind wander from the figure in front of her to her own son: "[E]ven at her age, she noted his indifference, presumably he was in some way or other—to her at least—nice, handsome, interesting, distinguished, well built, like her own boy?" (31). A rather frustrated, or at any rate resigned, narrator interjects at this point: "One must do the best one can with her report. Anyhow, this was Jacob Flanders, aged nineteen. It is no use trying to sum people up. One must follow hints, not exactly what is said, nor yet entirely what is done." (31). The narrative's question mark—"presumably," Mrs. Norman wonders, "he was distinguished?"—strengthens the suspicion that Jacob is not another Joseph Andrews or Robinson Crusoe. In place of detailed descriptions about Jacob, readers are offered insipid and frequently truncated comments: " 'I like Jacob Flanders,' wrote Clara Durrant in her diary. 'He is so unworldly. He gives himself no airs and one can say what one likes to him, though he's frightening because . . .' " (71).

The moments of curiosity and insight Woolf relished in Jane Austen would no longer hold true for her own fiction. Writing one year after *Jacob's Room*, Woolf's assessment of Austen speaks to a different literary world, evoking a sense of change and the nostalgia that so often accompanies it:

> Always the stress is laid upon character. How, we are made to wonder, will Emma behave when Lord Osborne and Tom Musgrave make their call at five minutes just before three, just as Mary is bringing in the tray and the knife-case? It is an extremely awkward situation. The young men are accustomed to much greater refinement. Emma may prove herself ill-bred, vulgar, a nonentity. The turns and twists of the dialogue keep us on the tenterhooks of suspense. Our attention is half upon the present moment, half upon the future.[44]

That delight in character-building and situations involving intricate and palpable individuals clearly remain very real for Woolf. But the pleasure of character belongs elsewhere—in the fictional world before World War I. Indeed, in a chapter of Winifred Holtby's 1932 critical memoir of Woolf titled "Virginia Woolf is not Jane Austen," Holtby remarks of the ease with which Austen was able to set aside the matter of the Napoleonic Wars in her novels, even though she resolutely opposed them. "But the England of 1918 was not the England of 1818," notes

Holtby. "The difficulty of a novelist during the twentieth-century war lay in its all-pervading influence. It affected every personal as well as every impersonal problem."[45]

If, after the war, one's "attention is half upon the present moment, half upon the future," this dual focus extends beyond the novel's narrative frontiers. Now, the challenge of living between present and future exists not only within the story and its characters; it reaches beyond the text and becomes an ethical imperative to restructure the world. For the story of the war, as Woolf well knew, exceeded the suspense created by dialogue and character. It was reflected in the faces of the wounded soldiers who had returned from the Somme, Passchendaele, and Gallipoli. These soldiers called attention not only to the present and the future; one's attention was no longer neatly split into the temporal divisions of an Austen novel. The soldiers returned as painful reminders of a past that had not been fully reconciled, one that drove a stubborn wedge into the present. "The eighteenth century has its distinction," Woolf insists—a distinction, among other things, between present and future which, with a clever twist of plot, could be resolved to everyone's satisfaction. But in a postwar world, where absent soldiers and nonexistent funerals left the past unmastered, responsible writing required more than tying plot to the old strategy of expectation. Novels now had to be restructured by triangulating past, present, and future, a reorganization that would not evolve in any clear, plot-driven fashion. Novelists would have to feel their way toward a new literary process; like England itself, they needed to respond to changes that the physical world would not bear out: the estrangement felt by returning soldiers—and the memory of those who were not lucky enough to be counted among them.

Though she knew that abandoning the traditional focus on character would court criticism, Woolf maintained a steadfast resolve: "People, like Arnold Bennett, say I can't create, or didn't in *Jacob's Room,* characters that survive. My answer is . . . that character is dissipated into shreds now, the old post-Dostoievsky argument."[46] A shred of character, a shadow of a former self: it is only fitting, in light of these historical and literary upheavals, that Jacob's life comes to an end in a manner altogether unheroic, in a death indistinguishable from thousands of others. His death is denied its own narrative not because it is not worth narrating but because it cannot be seen by those who survive him. The reader infers his death from Woolf's descriptions of war, which appear before we learn of his death and thus serve to foreshadow it:

The battleships ray out over the North Sea, keeping their stations accurately apart. At a given signal all the guns are trained on a target which . . . flames into splinters. With equal nonchalance a dozen young men in the prime of life descend with composed faces into the depths of the sea; and there impassively (though with perfect mastery of machinery) suffocate uncomplainingly together. Like blocks of tin soldiers the army covers the cornfield, moves up the hillside, stops, reels slightly this way and that, and falls flat, save that, through field-glasses, it can be seen that one or two pieces still agitate up and down like fragments of broken match-stick. (155–56)

Here we encounter Austen's "injured body" in its most corporate and anonymous form: in official language that obstructs any sense of how an individual experienced the last moments of his life. Even the most assiduous observer—the viewer who witnesses the scene through field-glasses—cannot report these deaths in any personal, intimate way.

Woolf identifies this dehumanizing rhetoric with official pronouncements that explain these deaths as necessary losses, sacrifices made in the interest of progress or victory. Underneath this official language of inevitability and necessity, Woolf detects an unrelenting internal pressure:

These actions, together with the incessant commerce of banks, laboratories, chancellories, and houses of business, are the strokes which oar the world forward, they say. And they are dealt by men as smoothly sculptured as the impassive policeman at Ludgate Circus. But you will observe that far from being padded to rotundity his face is still from force of will, and lean from the efforts of keeping it so. When his right arm rises, all the force in his veins flows straight from shoulder to finger-tips; not an ounce is diverted into sudden impulses, sentimental regrets, wire-drawn distinctions. The buses punctually stop. (156)

In the figure of the impassive policeman, the novel's most straightforward representation of justice, law, and order, Woolf undercuts those "official intuitions" and calculated risks that underwrite everyday life. "They" may say that such losses are necessary costs of progress. And yet the price of such an insistence turns out to be emotion itself, which is kept at bay through the mechanical, practical work of maintaining order. Even the most resolute determination, however, cannot silence the persistent pulse of emotion underneath the order it safeguards—and Woolf's novel can be understood as an attempt to reach these "sudden impulses" by other, unauthorized means.

The official language used to represent and, more often, to obscure the war does not grant even the bravest soldiers a more distinguished death—and thus

we do not have the luxury of seeing Jacob in his final moments. Woolf withholds this scene from her readers, staying true to the manner in which death was
presented to an anxious public through the news wires, which reported on the
war in the most guarded, anodyne fashion. *Jacob's Room* offers its own version
of these reports, reinforcing their capacity to keep the war—and all upheavals
beyond England's borders—at a safe distance:

> The wires of the Admiralty shivered with some far-away communication. A voice kept
> remarking that Prime ministers and Viceroys spoke in the Reichstag; entered Lahore;
> said that the Emperor travelled; in Milan they rioted; said there were rumours in
> Vienna; said that the Ambassador at Constantinople had audience with the Sultan;
> the fleet was at Gibraltar. The voice continued, imprinting on the faces of the clerks
> in Whitehall . . . something of its own inexorable gravity, as they listened, deciphered,
> wrote down. Papers accumulated, inscribed with the utterances of Kaisers, the sta-
> tistics of ricefields, the growing of hundreds of work-people plotting sedition in back
> streets, or gathering in the Calcutta bazaars, or mustering their forces in the uplands
> of Albania, where the hills are sand-coloured, and bones lie unburied. (171–72)

The declarations of public knowledge, articulated in the crisp but disembodied
sound of the news wires, are shattered in the novel's final chapter by a voice that
communicates nothing at all: outside Jacob's room, "[a] harsh and unhappy voice
cried something unintelligible" (176). The outside world, the language of the press,
cannot make sense of this moment; all that can be grasped from this voice is its
tenor—the tremor of its emotions rather than the information of its message.[47]

An indecipherable voice, an undistinguished life, a death indistinguishable
from those of others, a novel presenting itself not as the character of Jacob Flanders
but as locations both remote and intimate, Flanders Fields and Jacob's room: in
these anonymous and indecipherable conditions, what is the place of distinction?
What distinguishes Woolf's literary and historical present from the eighteenth-
century past, a past that, as Woolf reminds us throughout *Jacob's Room*, "has its
distinction"?

Woolf's changing sense of distinction, I would argue, ultimately poses a challenge that had yet to be broached in law, a call for new forms that would only be
answered after World War II, with the unprecedented formation of the Nuremberg
War Crimes Tribunal. For Woolf attempts to register the sense of change when
injury remains invisible. Distinction, for her, is no longer an adjective used to assess character; it is transformed into the necessary task of *distinguishing*: of distinguishing life as it was from one's present existence—an existence ravaged by

the loss, the death, inflicted by war. This process, moreover, also means that one must abandon the distinctions that recall the war dead solely in heroic terms, glorifying them for making the "ultimate sacrifice." Telling a story without such distinction means, ultimately, narrating it in all of its facets—even those painful details that offer very little solace.

To recall Benjamin's conclusion in "The Storyteller," "His gift is the ability to relate his life; his distinction, to be able to tell his entire life."[48] The storyteller's distinction, in other words, is precisely that he does *not* distinguish—does not extract only those elements that cohere with one's expectations of the world. What counts as relevant, in other words, has changed as a result of historical circumstances; even the most seemingly irrelevant details, those voices and visions that do not corroborate the official version of the past, figure in the telling of a life. It is this difficult task of distinguishing the postwar world by narrating it in all of its indistinction, in its trivial or unheroic details, that marks Woolf's achievement in *Jacob's Room*. Woolf's prose, unlike legal language, can make do without the conventions that shape the law. "After all, what laws can be laid down about books?" she writes in her essay "How Should One Read a Book?" "To admit authorities, however furred and gowned, into our libraries and let them tell us how to read, what to read, what value to place upon what we read, is to destroy the spirit of freedom which is the breath of those sanctuaries. Everywhere else we may be bound by laws and conventions—there we have none."[49] Woolf's claims for reading would be enacted in her writing, in which she abandons law and convention to make her case in *Jacob's Room*.

"He left everything just as it was"

In order to understand Woolf's point, her reshaping of distinction, I turn now to what is perhaps the most remarkable, indeed the revolutionary moment of *Jacob's Room*: its fourteenth and final chapter—a chapter only one page in length, but one that transforms the novel into a work which is highly critical of the effort to make sense of the present through the structures of the past. Woolf anticipates in this chapter the very problems that will emerge in the wake of World War II, when existing systems of justice would be called upon to revolutionize themselves in the face of unthinkable atrocities.

One might expect that Woolf, in a chapter of such brevity, would break away from her narrative and take her readers in a radically new direction. But nothing

on this page resembles such a dramatic rupture. Instead, the chapter turns out
to be a reiteration of other passages from the rest of the novel, a series of reflections cobbled together from sentences that Woolf had scattered throughout the
pages of *Jacob's Room*. Readers are reminded of Jacob not through his qualities,
but through the spaces he inhabited: "The eighteenth century has its distinction.
These houses were built, say, a hundred and fifty years ago. The rooms are shapely,
the ceilings high; over the doorways a rose or a ram's skull is carved in wood.
Even the panels, painted in raspberry-coloured paint, have their distinction" (70,
176). This description, which revisits word for word the novel's earlier account of
Jacob's room in London, is followed immediately by another repetition, this time
of his room in Cambridge: "Listless is the air in an empty room, just swelling
the curtain; the flowers in the jar shift. One fibre in the wicker arm-chair creaks,
though no one sits there" (39, 176). The emptiness of these spaces speaks to the
wider emptiness of a nation that had lost ten percent of its young male population, suggesting that this scene is one that would be repeated in countless homes
throughout England—and indeed, all of Europe.[50]

Gathering the novel's fragments together, the chapter underscores the frus-
trating labor of coping with a fundamentally altered reality that, on the surface,
does not appear to have changed. "He left everything just as it was," marvels
Jacob's friend Bonamy in the chapter's opening words. This, of course, is a measure of the novel's—and the war's—bitter irony: everything *looked* the same, but
it *felt* altogether different. It is this apparent sameness that lies at the root of the
sorrow, the inconsolability, of the living, who want the world to bear their sor-
rows physically, to betray the signs of an existence that will never be restored:
"He left everything just as it was," Bonamy marveled. "Nothing arranged. All
his letters strewn about for anyone to read. What did he expect? Did he think
he would come back?" (176). Yet a chapter that leaves so much "just as it was,"
rehearsing its language and invoking its novelistic forebears in a way that mim-
ics, on a literary level, the legal practice of stare decisis—following precedent—is
unable ultimately to offer a satisfying sense of closure. For in spite of the sameness of Jacob's room, the fact of change registers itself internally, psychologically,
as a question. The question comes from Jacob's mother, who enters the room as
the novel closes and addresses herself to her son's friend: "'What am I to do with
these, Mr. Bonamy?' She held out a pair of Jacob's old shoes" (176).

Jacob's shoes enter the narrative precisely in order to break off the empty repetitions in the equally empty room. Like the old novelistic templates and the

repeated idioms of consolation or heroic purpose, these repetitions come up short, interrupted by the solid object that fills this empty space. As material reminders of Jacob's body, the shoes serve as a homely metonym for his injury—a surprising, unfitting "symptom" for a body whose injuries will never be witnessed or described. An image that chillingly presages the horrors to come in the next war—one thinks here of the shoes from thousands of anonymous victims of the Holocaust displayed at the United States Holocaust Memorial Museum—the shoes gesture towards, without fully recalling, the individual who once filled them.

Indeed, there is something searing about these artifacts, which contain their owner's bodily imprint and so call up something of his uniqueness—the proverbial impossibility of "filling his shoes." It is this powerful but inarticulate poignancy, echoed in Betty Flanders's question, which casts the shoes as a private memorial. As a new figure for injury—tangible but not altogether bodily, precious but useless—the shoes allow private grief to pierce the public discourse that sought to find meaning and justice in the war. One might think here of the last line of Wilfred Owen's 1917 poem "Anthem for Doomed Youth": "And each slow dusk a drawing-down of blinds."[51] Owen's image of the private process of mourning, separated resolutely from the outside world, finds its alternative at the end of *Jacob's Room*. Woolf, in the novel's last moments, lifts these blinds, bringing private grief out of its isolation and turning it into a public, practical and—in its practicality—normative question.

Betty Flanders's unspecific language—"What am I to do with *these*, Mr. Bonamy?"—coupled with her specific gesture of holding up the shoes, *these* shoes, returns us to the law's struggle with invisible injuries. The fatal injury inflicted on Jacob is, in this moment, passed on in a different form—as a question—to his mother. The injury to the dead becomes the injury to the living: the individual on the home front who survives the war with no physical scars, but whose emotional wounds leave open the question of how, practically speaking, one should carry on in the world. It is along the lines drawn by law that we can begin to understand the urgency of Mrs. Flanders's question, which becomes more than just a way to conclude a text without closing it off. Rather, it leaves us in suspense—suspended between the question and its answer—because it is a challenge, demanding both an existential and a normative response: absent a visible injury, a body, "what am I to do" with these shoes? It is important in this context that the question has a specified referent: it is not the open-ended cry of anguish—not "What am I to do?"—but the task-focused question of someone who, from the depths of her grief, sees the pressing need to order her world anew.

Significantly, the earlier version of this chapter suggests that Woolf made a conscious choice to end on a practical note. Originally, a more explicitly grief-laden scene followed Mrs. Flanders's question: "They both laughed. The room waved behind her tears."[52] Instead of this ending, Woolf opts for something less declarative, less direct in emotional content. "Left at the end the tears would have provided a resolution of the action, shifting the focus to the mother's grief. By breaking in mid-action, Woolf emphasizes the impossibility of making sense of such a death," writes Edward Bishop.[53] But she also, I would add, asserts her commitment to the practical business of reordering the world in the wake of this senselessness—a practicality that translates into the response and responsibility that the living owe to the dead.

Where one might expect the war's conclusion to involve soldiers returning to a landscape changed beyond recognition, World War I presented a profoundly different set of circumstances: Jacob Flanders does not return—and everything is *not* different. The sorrow of leaving everything "just as it was" suggests, then, that it is *our* responsibility—the responsibility of the living—to alter the physical world, to make it cohere with the feeling that nothing will ever be the same. Betty Flanders's question is ultimately a normative one, reflecting not the world "as it is" but asking instead how it *ought* to be. It is in this sense that Woolf pursues the notion of distinction, finds it insufficient as an adjective describing character, and recasts it as the basis for her final, normative question. Distinction is transformed into its active sense—*to distinguish:* a verb conveying grief for Woolf, but also responsibility: the responsibility of the living for the dead. How, Woolf asks, ought we distinguish life as it is from life as it was? How do we register irreversible injury when that injury, because it cannot be seen, does not register itself?

It would take another world war, with atrocities still inconceivable in Woolf's time, to make this process urgent and necessary on a legal scale. *Jacob's Room,* through its literary stare decisis and its unsettling of our conceptual and literary inheritance, inaugurates a process that would culminate in the unparalleled legal events following World War II. Addressing Benjamin's "profound perplexity of the living," Woolf's insistence on change, distinction, and responsibility calls upon us—in a way reminiscent of but fundamentally different from Jane Austen—to address the injury in our midst: the injury of the dead which becomes, with a painful difference, the injuries to the living. What Woolf once attributed to Austen supplies a fitting description, though in a drastically different way, of her own work: "Our attention is half upon the present moment, half upon the future."[54] It is her question to the living which keeps us "on the tenterhooks of suspense," preventing us from deserting one another and, at the same time, demanding from us an answer. As the next chapter will show, Woolf responds to this demand with her subsequent novel, *Mrs. Dalloway,* following the effort to transform her fiction in the face of war's injuries with her search for a narrative response to these injuries. Moving from the individual's quiet room to the loud, busy streets of London, she would carve out an ethical landscape that made sense in the postwar city, where the anonymity of Jacob Flanders and others like him posed no impediment to social responsibility.

CHAPTER TWO

The Strange Character of Law

The result of Tuesday's destruction is that we have been given a privileged glimpse into the interior of one family after another. It is like walking down the block and being able to see for a moment through the walls of some of the houses. The emotional architecture looks familiar. It is the act of seeing that seems strange.

—*New York Times*, September 16, 2001[1]

Ignorance, far more than knowledge, is what can never be taken for granted. If I perceive my ignorance as a gap in knowledge instead of an imperative that changes the very nature of what I think I know, then I do not truly experience my ignorance. The surprise of otherness is that moment when a new form of ignorance is suddenly activated as an imperative.

—Barbara Johnson, *A World of Difference*[2]

If tort law raises the question of how we deal with accidents and injuries, it also invites us to imagine the people these calamities involve. The world that tort law conjures beyond the courtroom—its normative effect—presents us with both a reassuring and a distressing face. In its reassuring guise, the law acts as a steady presence, enabling judges and ordinary citizens alike to tell the difference between an injured party and a legitimate plaintiff. But in a less predictable world, every encounter becomes a potential accident and every person a prospective plaintiff. In this more threatening reality, duty of care becomes a duty to be careful, and people move from being mindful of others to avoiding them. The social imaginary that tort law incites thus represents a much more expansive dimension of what its legal opinions dictate, setting out a set of implied directions that conceivably structure every random encounter. These directions appear to have the social world at their core but simultaneously, and ironically, also seem to reward antisocial behavior. What we do with these unspoken normative guidelines tells us a great deal about what it means to be part of an ethical community under modernity.

It is at the edge of this ethical community that Virginia Woolf closes her first postwar novel *Jacob's Room*. Ending with the practical question of what to do with Jacob's shoes, Woolf turns her attention three years later in *Mrs. Dalloway* from *what* to *who:* Who will take responsibility in the aftermath of war? Her focus, in contrast to the individual imagined in much of tort law, is not on who will be injured but who will take care—and of whom. At first glance, *Jacob's Room* seems to offer a straightforward answer. The dead, and the life they left behind, will be cared for by those closest to them: by their mothers, the Betty Flanderses of the world, and their good friends, the Bonamys (*bons amis*). But Woolf postulates yet another kind of relationship in *Mrs. Dalloway,* one that had already begun to make its presence felt in the modern postwar city. Revisiting her own normative question in *Jacob's Room,* she imagines a new kind of social responsibility, one that not only takes accidental encounters with strangers into account but actively seeks them out. These encounters noisily intrude upon home and disturb the sense of being at home, showing that sense to have been premature. But in an estranged and anonymous postwar world, these encounters offer the rarest and yet most productive of opportunities: the possibility of unexpected ethical obligation to someone outside the sheltering orbit of one's mind and one's enclosed social world.

Before turning to Woolf, I want to consider the salient place of strangers in tort law, the body of law that developed, as we saw in Chapter 1, in response to a changing world in which injury was no longer the result of a person's intentional criminal act but an outcome of accidents and negligence—and often simply of being in the wrong place at the wrong time. Tort law, however, is not just the law of accidents but also of strangers. For the injuries it addressed were not the kind that happened among individuals who knew one another, who lived in the same small village and saw each other on a daily basis. In an era of crowded cities, industrial expansion, frequent train travel, and population growth, accidents increasingly occurred among strangers, people who owed nothing to each other and stood to gain nothing by helping each other. To understand how Woolf's literary sensibility speaks to these concerns generally and to those of tort law specifically, it is important to grasp the complicated way that strangers both create and are created by legal narrative. In detailing the human shape of responsibility through these figures, I place Woolf's *Mrs. Dalloway* alongside one of the most famous cases in American tort law, *Palsgraf v. Long Island Railroad,* and consider how these texts offer a vision of the social world where the anonymity of strangers serves as the guiding principle.

Legal Impersonality: Retelling *Palsgraf v. Long Island Railroad*

It is out of concern for the law's concrete relationship to people, rather than its reliance on abstract theories of justice, that Judge John Noonan wrote *Persons and Masks of the Law.* What began as a study of legal history became, instead, a project consumed by personal—in law, trivial—concerns:

> As I reached what seemed to me the heart of law's dependence on history, however, I became increasingly conscious of the neglect of the person by legal casebooks, legal histories, and treatises of jurisprudence. Only in the response of person to person, so it seemed to me, did history have a significance to law. Neglect of persons, it appeared, had led to the worst sins for which American lawyers were accountable.[3]

This neglect of law's human subjects compels Noonan to consider the decisions of judges like Benjamin Cardozo and Oliver Wendell Holmes, Jr., in light of what their opinions leave out and how irrepressible and potent this expunged content turns out to be. In the process, he notes the impersonal language that law uses to make sense of private human circumstances, a rhetoric that may benefit dispute resolution but ultimately turns unique individuals into strangers, casting them as faceless plaintiffs and defendants.

What Noonan does not note, however, is the irony of this estrangement. The law may create strangers by turning particularity into anonymity, stripping people of their specificity in order to find the common principles connecting one case to another. But law also exists precisely to deal with the problems that arise among strangers: even as it creates these strangers through rhetoric and principle, their existence constitutes a crucial raison d'être of law, and particularly tort law. In fashioning a unified system for adjudicating accidents and assigning responsibility, tort law also developed a doctrine for dealing with incidents involving strangers which, in an industrializing world, were becoming more rules than exceptions. As legal scholar G. Edward White explains, "The modern negligence principle in tort law seems to have been an intellectual response to the increased number of accidents involving persons who had no preexisting relation with one another—"stranger" cases."[4]

The importance of these "stranger cases" cannot be underestimated. Whereas it was once believed that a person only owed duties of care to those with whom one had a previously defined relationship, the rise of industrial accidents demanded that these duties extend to people one had never met. These stranger cases meant that people who had no prior relationship—and hence no defined duties toward each other—were nonetheless accountable for their behavior before the fact. There is, to be sure, a limitless potential here, a duty that could expand theoretically to encompass all people in all manner of circumstances. As Oliver Wendell Holmes framed the matter when speaking of potentially hazardous activities, the duty to use ordinary care is one "of all the world to all the world."[5] At the heart of this claim is a fundamental assumption of tort law—one of those "felt necessities" or intuitions that Holmes saw as the anvil upon which law is shaped: the feeling that one wants to take responsibility for everyone, to keep faith with this sprawling duty owed—at least in principle—to the entire world, despite the understanding that in practice, one cannot fulfill this duty each and every time. Implicit in this sensibility is the vision of a world full of strangers, coupled with the recognition that law needs a systematic way of adjudicating accidents occurring among them. In order to shape this practical legal response, however, tort law prevails on legal subjects to take a conceptual leap: to imagine the existence of individuals one may never meet and to determine concretely the duties one owes them. In the torts process, one continually asks what strangers owe to each other and how one distributes justice among parties who might never have known of one another's existence but for the accident that brought their lives together violently and unpredictably. When these paths intersect, the question of responsibility comes down to who owes what to whom: duty of care between the parties needs to exist to establish a basis for negligence. Where these duties were once clear, they became harder to define in an industrializing, increasingly anonymous era.

This is precisely the issue at stake in the landmark torts case *Palsgraf v. Long Island Railroad* (1928), which set limits on who counts as a foreseeable plaintiff. We saw in the previous chapter that in the case of *Smith v. Johnson* and subsequent opinions, courts sought to limit the claims of injury when dealing with strangers. Strangers directly affected by an accident could recover, whereas those in near proximity who suffered emotional distress could not. The question in *Palsgraf*, however, turns not on the distance between two individuals but on the distance between the present and future—that is, on the limits of predictability. In setting limits on potential plaintiffs, the *Palsgraf* court had to determine what one party owed to another when the unpredictable happens; in this case, what the Long Island Railroad owed to one passenger, Helen Palsgraf.

The circumstances of the case were famously and sparingly narrated by Justice Benjamin Cardozo, whose opinion opens with the simple story of a woman in the wrong place at the wrong time:

> Plaintiff was standing on a platform of defendant's railroad after buying a ticket to go to Rockaway Beach. A train stopped at the station, bound for another place. Two men ran forward to catch it. One of the men reached the platform of the car without mishap, though the train was already moving. The other man, carrying a package, jumped aboard the car, but seemed unsteady as if about to fall. A guard on the car, who had held the door open, reached forward to help him in, and another guard on the platform pushed him from behind. In this act, the package was dislodged, and fell upon the rails. It was a package of small size, about fifteen inches long, and was covered by a newspaper. In fact it contained fireworks, but there was nothing in its appearance to give notice of its contents. The fireworks when they fell exploded. The shock of the explosion threw down some scales at the other end of the platform, many feet away. The scales struck the plaintiff, causing injuries for which she sues.[6]

Cardozo reasoned that negligence is "a term of relation" (P 345), which can only be determined by relating an act to its reasonably foreseeable outcome. Moreover, because "[n]othing in the situation gave notice that the falling package had in it the potency of peril to persons thus removed" (P 341)—here, to an unrelated passenger—Mrs. Palsgraf cannot recover for her injuries. No reasonable person could have anticipated that an apparently harmless package contained fireworks; that they would explode; that the explosion would dislodge the scales and that the scales would fall on the plaintiff. It would have been impossible, Cardozo reasoned, to anticipate the plaintiff's injuries. "Life will have to be made over, and human nature transformed, before prevision so extravagant can be accepted as the norm of conduct, the customary standard to which behavior must conform" (P 343). The court holds that Helen Palsgraf is an unforeseeable plaintiff and reverses her case. She will receive no compensation for her injury.

The opinion's literariness—its terse, bare-bones rhetoric emphasizing only the legally relevant particulars and leaving the rest to the mind's eye—has much to do with its enduring hold on the legal imagination. From its alliteration ("potency of peril to persons thus removed") to its imagery, it reads like a well-crafted narrative. If one were to locate the opinion in a particular literary tradition, one might be tempted to place it within realism for its commitment to objective, omniscient narration and its adherence to unadorned fact. Along these lines, one might note Cardozo's emphasis on the physical world, the weight he gives to visibility in determining who counts as a potential plaintiff. The "prevision so extravagant" that law is unable to accommodate it ultimately turns not on the possibility of *imagining* the future, but on the more literal experience of *seeing* it. The task of imagining injury only extends as far as the eye can see; the package might well have contained explosives, but since "there was nothing in its appearance to give notice of its contents," there is no obligation to handle it with special care. "To the eye of ordinary vigilance, the bundle is abandoned waste, which may be kicked or trod on with impunity" (P 342), Cardozo insists, rephrasing his sense of the visual world only slightly in declaring that "the orbit of danger as disclosed to the eye of reasonable vigilance would be the orbit of duty" (P 343).

It is strange that an opinion so steadfast in its observance of the physical should be so difficult to imagine. Yet one of the very reasons for Cardozo's legal legacy in *Palsgraf* is his concise language, which sets out just enough details to trace his own reasoning but not enough to make clear the specifics of the accident. Other than the exploding package, the discrete links in the accident's chain of events prove difficult to pin down with any specificity. There is no description of the scales that were thrown down, nor of how they struck the plaintiff or of the injuries she suffered. The most precise piece of description has to do not with the accident or the people involved, but with the mysterious package itself, "a package of small size, about fifteen inches long, and . . . covered by a newspaper." The description is precisely of that which, to all appearances, cannot be described— of the explosives no one could have anticipated.

Caring little for predictability, Justice William Andrews writes an eloquent dissent in the case, arguing that law cannot look forward to assess the future of an act. If the law has a sense of vision, it is only a belated one: "We look back to the catastrophe, the fire kindled by the spark, or the explosion. We trace the consequences—not indefinitely, but to a certain point. And to aid us in fixing that point we ask what might ordinarily be expected to follow the fire or the explosion" (P 355). Under ordinary circumstances, an explosion on the railway tracks would likely injure a person waiting for a train. Although this seems to suggest a measure of foreseeability, Andrews believes otherwise, building his argument around the principle of a necessary cause—in law, a but-for cause—rather than upon duty of care: "Except for the explosion, [Mrs. Palsgraf] would not have been injured . . . The only intervening cause was that instead of blowing her to the ground the concussion smashed the weighing machine which in turn fell upon her. There was no remoteness in time, little in space" (P 356). The difference between decision and dissent in *Palsgraf* thus turns on the difference between future and past: in the former (Cardozo), we must be able to predict who will be injured by an act in order to determine negligence; in the latter (Andrews), we can only establish such relationships retrospectively. Caught in this tension between past and future, between Cardozo's majority opinion and Andrews' dissent, is Mrs. Palsgraf herself, who stands as the mute voice, the blank spot on the canvas of legal time.

The glaring emptiness of this faceless plaintiff offers a stark reminder of the way Cardozo and Andrews succeed in eliminating all traces of the personal, dramatic, or unwieldy. Their ellipses constitute the opinion's profound irony: to determine who is responsible—and to adhere to what Cardozo calls the "eye of reasonable vigilance"—both judges effectively render the plaintiff invisible, making the *who* closer to a *what*. She becomes, in effect, a stranger, and the legal account becomes not a story but a syllogistic explanation. Indeed, part of what has made *Palsgraf* so celebrated and timeless is the scarcity of personal, human details in the case—particulars like Mrs. Palsgraf's first name (Helen), her age (forty-three), profession (cleaning woman), family circumstances (married but possibly separated, with three children, two of whom were with her during the accident).[7] In its omissions and its neutral tone, *Palsgraf* may well be the perfect legal opinion, setting out just the facts with minimal legal jargon, embellishment, or distracting superfluities. The opinion's legal force issues from a rhetorical strategy that Pierre Bourdieu identifies as part of law's authority more generally: the appropriation of ordinary speech set in the context of legal impersonality and neutrality.[8]

Decades later, these omissions send John Noonan back to the trial transcripts to fill in the personal details that Cardozo and Andrews left out. These apparent minutiae, Noonan suggests, may well have had a bearing on the case; instead, they remain hidden in the blind spot of legal reasoning. But what further intrigues Noonan is that this impersonal stance, one of principles over people, extends well into the decades following *Palsgraf*. For while the literature on the case is vast and varied, most of it deals in the broad language of the majority and dissent; few scholars offer descriptions of the individuals whose lives became intertwined as the case made its way through the courts. There is a surprising lack of curiosity about the case's human dimensions.[9]

In addition to the rather opaque description of the accident itself, one of the most obscure and least-discussed particulars of the case remains Helen Palsgraf's injuries. The trial record indicates that they were traumatic in nature, resulting in her stammering and stuttering; as one doctor testified, "it was with difficulty that she could talk at all."[10] Reinforcing the neutral language that, in Andrews's dissent, effaces even her gender, the record of the court proceedings—presumably the product of an over-zealous stenographer—eliminates Helen Palsgraf's stammer from her testimony. Significantly, however, this stammer was not just the result of her accident but was exacerbated, as her doctor testified, by the trial itself. "While her mind is disturbed by litigation she will not recover," the physician explained: "but after litigation—I don't mean by that her getting any verdict but as soon as the worry of the trial is over and she knows she doesn't have to go here on the witness stand and undergo cross-examination she should make a fairly good recovery in about three years."[11]

It is not clear whether Helen Palsgraf ever recovered. But in a striking way, her injuries are replicated and embedded in the history of the opinion itself, which adds very little to the human dimensions of the case. The more the opinion is mentioned in the literature, the more its principled reasoning is extended at the expense of all else. In spite of its judicial clarity, *Palsgraf* continues to stutter and stammer its way through the terrain of the personal. Each time the case is repeated in the annals of law, and each time these retellings routinely pass over the intimate facts of the case, we are reminded of Helen Palsgraf's presence on the stand—and on the platform of the Long Island Railroad. And we are reminded, too, of how little we know about either of these positions, save how they fit the hard-edged contours of legal reasoning.

Such incontrovertible, impersonal lines of jurisprudence are precisely what Oliver Wendell Holmes, Jr. took to be the key to good lawmaking. For him, an opinion like Cardozo's, which strips an incident of its negligible details, is the ideal language for which judges should strive:

> The process is one, from a lawyer's statement of a case, eliminating as it does all the dramatic elements with which his client's story has clothed it, and retaining only the facts of legal import, up to the final analyses and abstract universals of theoretic jurisprudence. The reason why a lawyer does not mention that his client wore a white hat when he made a contract, while Mrs. Quickly would be sure to dwell upon it along with the parcel gilt goblet and the sea-coal fire, is that he foresees that the public

force will act in the same way whatever his client had upon his head. It is to make the prophecies easier to be remembered and to be understood that the teachings of the decisions of the past are put into general propositions and gathered into text-books, or that statutes are passed in a general form. The primary rights and duties with which jurisprudence busies itself again are nothing but prophecies.[12]

The more one clutters law with description, Holmes suggests, the less efficient it becomes. The colorful details that make for good storytelling distract from the bigger legal picture, making it difficult to grasp—and thus to remember—the law in its abstract sense. As one of the most powerful examples of Holmes's vision, *Palsgraf* drove home the force of pared-down legal reasoning, becoming a legal tour de force built on just the bare necessities.

I would suggest, however, that *Palsgraf*'s high polish is not the only reason for its enduring hold on the legal imagination. For beneath the smooth surface of Cardozo's terse prose, in which the personal never tarnishes the principle, is a sense of mystery: the mystery of Helen Palsgraf—plaintiff, passenger, cleaning woman, mother, stammerer. Stripped of these attributes in law, her blank existence haunts the case, inviting readers to imagine, embellish, and respond. The blankness, which casts *Palsgraf* as a Rorschach inkblot of legal narrative, inspires the very details that Holmes saw as irrelevant to the legal process. It is in response to the stranger created by Cardozo and Andrews that Noonan returns to the case fifty years later, reopening it, filling in details, and retelling the story to consider whether these missing facets would have made for a different decision (he thinks they would have). Helen Palsgraf haunts Noonan—and haunts law more generally—because she confronts us as a stranger. Her persistent presence speaks to that "felt necessity" that Holmes suggested was embedded deep within the law—an intuition that he would crystallize with his pronouncement that duty of care was a duty "of all the world to all the world." *Palsgraf*'s carefully wrought language is an attempt to make such an intuition manageable. Practically speaking, it reminds us that we cannot take responsibility for everyone: law, to function properly, cannot account for all accidents. Less practically, however, *Palsgraf*'s estranging prose also demands a response: a filling in of details, an arousal of curiosity—and, as Noonan's own competing account suggests, a creation of new narratives.

But *Palsgraf* also reminds us that in its attempt to set out principles for what people owe to each other, tort law often creates the very strangers it addresses. Ultimately, some of them fall outside the law's protection, their anonymity formed and amplified by legal narrative. The figure of the stranger directs us to the law's very limits by suggesting that the opportunity for responsibility often presents itself at the very moment when legal reasoning holds that no one is responsible. For Virginia Woolf, I will be arguing, this moment is the very basis of ethics. The most radical potential for remaking a normative world, *Mrs. Dalloway* suggests, lies in the capacity to extend a duty of care to strangers who might otherwise fall between the cracks of "official" responsibilities—to take responsibility, in other words, when one does not know the person on whose behalf one acts.

Strange Homecomings

If *Palsgraf v. Long Island Railroad* was concerned with setting limits on predictability, the issue was not far from Virginia Woolf's mind at the time. Less than one year after Helen Palsgraf's accident, Woolf came home from a trip to France and recorded the following event in her diary:

> I am under the impression of the moment, which is the complex one of coming back home from the South of France to this wide dim peaceful privacy—London (so it seemed last night) which is shot with the accident I saw this morning—a woman crying oh, oh, oh, faintly, pinned against the railings with a motor car on top of her. All day I have heard that voice. I did not go to her help; but then every baker and flower seller did that. A great sense of the brutality and wildness of the world remains with me—there was this woman in brown walking along the pavement—suddenly a red film car turns a somersault, lands on top of her and one hears this oh, oh, oh.[13]

The peacefulness of London is shattered for Woolf by the hard fact of accident, by the unexpected sight of a stranger being injured and the guilt of one who "did not go to her help." Woolf, as an eyewitness, does not convey a sense of who is at fault in the accident—nor, of course, is the question of fault the reason she is so struck by it. Unlike the juridical attentiveness that Holmes saw as necessary and sufficient for law, Woolf takes note of the trivial details that leave an impression, though not necessarily a judgment: the woman in brown, the red film car. Her account, moreover, is marked by a notable disjunction: she sets out to record "the accident I *saw* this morning," but is haunted instead by its sound—"All day I have heard that voice." In a manner reminiscent of Helen Palsgraf's stutter, the woman's pained "oh, oh, oh" stammers its way through Woolf's consciousness, a reminder not only of "the brutality and wildness of the world" but also of her own inaction in the face of such violence.

It is perhaps no surprise that Woolf pays such attention to this injured stranger, since she witnesses the accident one month before the publication of *Mrs. Dalloway,* a novel preoccupied with the issue of responsibility to strangers. Three years after *Jacob's Room,* Woolf would answer her own suspended question— "What am I to do?"—by positing an ethic of responsibility based neither on foreseeability nor on proximate cause. *Mrs. Dalloway's* normative world is founded, rather, on the unanticipated encounter with strangers, both seen and unseen— and above all, heard, acknowledged, and felt.

To understand Woolf's move from the problem of accidents to the figure of the stranger, one need only consider the circumstances in London in the years following World War I. London was a city reeling from the war, still trying to make sense of the staggering death toll and of soldiers who were killed inexplicably, anonymously, and indiscriminately. Because the war had not been fought on British soil, it was also a city struggling to square its unchanged contours—an urban landscape without shell fragments, trenches, graves—with a population of strangers, the soldiers who could not simply fall into step with their old selves or with life as it had been in 1914. A painful gap had formed between altered feelings and untouched surroundings—and by extension, between those who had fought in the war and those who had not.

This disparity between soldiers and civilians was not just a postwar phenomenon: the divide between home front and war front had grown sharper and wider with each year of the conflict. The years between 1914 and 1918 brought those who waited at home no closer to understanding the experiences of those who fought in the trenches. As Paul Fussell observed:

> [E]ven if those at home had wanted to know the realities of the war, they couldn't have without experiencing them: its conditions were too novel, its industrialized ghastliness too unprecedented. The war would have been simply unbelievable. From the very beginning a fissure was opening between the Army and civilians. Witness the *Times* of September 29, 1914, which seriously printed for the use of the troops a collection of uplifting and noble "soldiers' songs" written by Arthur Campbell Ainger, who appeared wholly ignorant of the actual tastes in music and rhetoric of the Regular Army recently sent to France.[14]

After the war, this gap in experience hardened into an impenetrable barrier, reified in the countless memorials erected throughout the country. These monuments, which spread like brush fire throughout the country, seemed to eclipse the task of caring for the war's veterans, an ordering of priorities that certainly seemed to make sense to a generation struggling to come to grips with its losses.[15] But the no less difficult question of what one owed to those who returned cast its shadow over the impulse to memorialize the dead. Often, in fact, the two gestures accompanied one another, as they did in the Borough of Shrewsbury's deliberations over its war memorial:

> At the War Memorial meeting . . . the Mayor . . . made the gratifying announcement that when peace rejoicings take place in the borough it was his intention to call all the returned local soldiers together and let them have a royal welcome from the people of Shrewsbury. This intimation from his worship will help to remove the impression, which has aroused no small amount of indignation, that demobilised soldiers at Shrewsbury were not to receive the recognition to which they are so justly entitled.[16]

Such fleeting welcomes, however warm, were bound to leave unsatisfied those who wanted to honor returning soldiers in more permanent ways and who saw memorials as potential tributes to both living and dead. While some people took up the question of what forms these memorials should take—ornamental or practical, simple or elaborate—others expressed concern that not enough was being done to recognize the soldiers who had come home. Consider the remarks of a Letter to the Editor of the *Shrewsbury Chronicle*:

> Sir—I notice, and have done so for some time, in the various war memorials raised to men who fell in the war belonging to various churches and parishes, that they give (which is very proper) the names and numbers of men who fell, belonging to the parish, but nothing whatever seems to be said about those who went out to war and returned safely; this doesn't seem to be recognised in any way. I think at the foot of the tablet, or whatever they choose for their memorials, should be added the words "In gratitude also for the safe return of those who served in the war"—giving in one total number the men, of course, from the parish, and their names should be inscribed in a handsome leather bound vellum book, kept we will say, on a shelf provided for that purpose.[17]

The act of inscribing the names of the living into a book that would soon after be relegated to a dusty, forgotten shelf would likely have disappointed Virginia Woolf. For the question of what is owed to the living after the war is answered in dramatically different fashion in *Mrs. Dalloway*, exceeding short-lived rites or forgotten inscriptions and demanding instead that people reshape the social world through ordinary rather than ceremonial acts: walking down a street, riding a bus, hosting a party. Woolf returns in 1925 to the question she left open in *Jacob's Room* with Betty Flanders's practical appeal: "What am I to do?" Her answer to this question, I argue, is *Mrs. Dalloway,* which posits a world motivated rather than ruptured by social accidents and encounters with strangers.

An Ethic of Social Accidents

Mrs. Dalloway tells the story of plans come undone. Clarissa Dalloway spends one day in June, the day on which the novel is set, preparing for a party, only to have her hopes for the evening dashed by the news of a suicide. The dead man, whose name she never learns, turns out to be Septimus Warren Smith, a soldier whom Clarissa does not know but whose doctor, Sir William Bradshaw, is among her guests. The novel's tragic moment appears as something of an anticlimax: a spoiled evening may qualify as bourgeois disappointment but seems an unlikely candidate for a site of ethics. Yet in a novel whose narrative rhythms are composed of anonymous individuals, fleeting interactions, and social misreadings, the strange meeting between Septimus and Clarissa becomes a culmination of missed encounters: a testament to the force of strangers. Critics have long pointed to the role of anonymity in the novel, from which it derives its sense of modern London and its creative process.[18] This anonymity, however, does more than offer an explanation for creativity; it forms the basis for the novel's ethical purchase, laying the foundations for the unlikeliest and most potent encounters.

We find the stranger in *Mrs. Dalloway* not in a court of law but on the streets of London, in the doctor's office, and finally, as the uninvited ghost at Clarissa Dalloway's party. The novel begins by reminding us that appearances to the contrary, everyone in London had been touched by the tragedy of the war.

> For it was the middle of June. The War was over, except for some one like Mrs. Foxcroft at the Embassy last night eating her heart out because that nice boy was killed and now the old Manor House must go to a cousin; or Lady Bexborough who opened a bazaar, they said, with the telegram in her hand, John, her favourite, killed; but it was over; thank Heaven—over. It was June. The King and Queen were at the Palace.[19]

This restoration of order and apparent tranquility is undone moments later by the presence of death in the midst of reconstruction, the memories of "nice boys" and favorite sons whose absence haunts the world of the living. The war's resolute end unravels further when moments later a car carrying an unknown but presumably important person cuts through the streets of London. Suddenly, waves of speculation break through the city's placid surface, as passersby attempt to guess the identity of the passenger in the distinguished-looking vehicle. In this moment of urban upheaval, the comfort of carrying on is shattered by the recognition of strangers.

> Something so trifling in single instances that no mathematical instrument, though capable of transmitting shocks in China, could register the vibration; yet in its fullness rather formidable and in its common appeal emotional; *for in all the hat shops and tailors' shops strangers looked at each other and thought of the dead; of the flag; of Empire.* In a public house in a back street a Colonial insulted the House of Windsor which led to words, broken beer glasses, and a general shindy, which *echoed strangely* across the way in the ears of girls buying white underlinen threaded with pure white ribbon for their weddings. For the surface agitation of the passing car as it sunk grazed something very profound. (18, emphasis added)

Strangers crowd this urban scene, disrupting the move from concreteness to abstraction in the transitions between the dead, the flag, and Empire. There is something law-like about this movement, absorbing as it does the particular into the general in a rhetorical rendering of Oliver Wendell Holmes, Jr.'s legal ideal of "abstract universals," "general propositions," "general forms."[20] The distinctiveness of the soldiers who would never come home is replaced incrementally by the symbols for which they had fought: the British flag, followed by the all-encompassing (and resolutely undetailed) notion of Empire. But before it is possible to take too much shelter in the baggy symbols of nationalism, the impulse toward abstraction is ruptured by yet another stranger: the Colonial, the strange face of a British subject from elsewhere, who cannot possibly understand what the House of Windsor means to England. It is the face of this stranger that brings the lofty ambitions of symbolism crashing down, sparking a bar-room brawl and returning people to bitter reality: all was *not*, after all, right with the world; Londoners—to say nothing of the British or Europeans—had endured unimaginable losses that would countenance no conclusion.

The moment of upheaval exposes this ongoing grief not as part of the visible world, but rather as sound, which "echoed strangely" and haunts the living—not unlike Woolf's memory of the "oh, oh, oh" of the woman whose accident she witnessed. This echo evokes too the conversations that had gone silent, the communicable experience that Walter Benjamin insisted was no longer expressed. The strange echo that reverberates in these opening moments of *Mrs. Dalloway* gestures toward this unspoken experience, to "something very profound" that can only be hinted at obliquely yet whose force is as undeniable as an earthquake. Its public rather than private appearance, moreover, affirms Woolf's commitment to the public world, a sense of obligation that has often been overlooked in favor of a more subjective, psychological reading.[21] Such critical focus on interiority, however, elides the way in which Woolf's depiction of inner worlds is intimately bound to public events, in which even the most private experiences issue from collective urban scenes that draw together an array of private worlds.

It is no accident that *Mrs. Dalloway's* central images of industrial progress, resonating as they do with the industrialized warfare, also turn out to be symbols of opaqueness and illegibility. The city's rapt attention to the car and its mysterious passenger thus gives way to its mechanical companion piece, the airplane, as it writes a series of letters in the sky. But rather than sending a clear message to the mesmerized onlookers, the airplane holds their gaze with no message at all, disappearing and reemerging seconds later as yet another symbol of industrialization:

> Then suddenly, as a train comes out of a tunnel, the aeroplane rushed out of the clouds again, the sound boring into the ears of all people in the Mall, in the Green Park, in Piccadilly, in Regent Street, in Regent's Park, and the bar of smoke curved behind and it dropped down, and it soared up and wrote one letter after another—but what word was it writing? (21)

If the airplane's message, like the passenger's identity in the motor-car, is not meant to be known—if its message proves inconsequential within the broader scheme of *Mrs. Dalloway*—this is because Woolf cares little for the clear, quantifiable answer which, were it to be given, would remove all sense of suspense and return the spectators to the private contours of their own lives.

The airplane's intrusion as sound rather than sight, "boring into the ears of all the people in the Mall," is extended and amplified by the motor car's entrance. For the car interrupts the early scenes of the novel not merely as the industrial noise of an engine and a propeller, but as the sound of an accident:

> The violent explosion which made Mrs. Dalloway jump and Miss Pym go to the window and apologise came from a motor car which had drawn to the side of the pavement precisely opposite Mulberry's shop window. Passers-by who, of course, stopped and stared, had just time to see a face of the very greatest importance against the dove-grey upholstery, before a male hand drew the blind and there was nothing to be seen except a square of dove grey. (14)

For Paul Saint-Amour, the backfiring car and the skywriting airplane together illustrate how the war continued to traumatize civilians, whose fears of aerial bombings are reactivated in the moment as "a pre-traumatic stress syndrome whose symptoms arose in response to an anticipated rather than an already realized catastrophe."[22] To which one might add that in rehearsing the war thus, the scene also makes clear that not only the grief but also the *potential* of common experience could still be had even when "the war was over." Rather than a private world shuttering out a public reality—the image conveyed so forcefully in Wilfred Owen's final line of "Anthem for Doomed Youth,"—"And each slow dusk a drawing-down of blinds"[23]—the act of turning away is initiated here by official channels. Woolf forcefully exemplifies the power of accidents to draw people together, as a moment of confusion diverts attention from people's individual pursuits toward one common experience.

"Strangers looked at each other and thought of the dead"; "a Colonial insulted the House of Windsor"—in a city full of strangers wanders the man whose suicide will ruin Clarissa Dalloway's party later that evening. Septimus Warren Smith, who has returned from the war shell-shocked and suicidal, is also part of the London street scenes that begin *Mrs. Dalloway*. As the human counterpoint to the novel's exuberant beginning, he remains trapped in his wartime past and in the death of a fellow soldier, a man known only as Evans. The unshakable memory of his friend, which figures more heavily than the lofty concepts of the flag or Empire, prevents Septimus from entering fully the bustle of London's streets, where he finds himself "unable to pass" (14). In the trenches of his past, his wife Rezia finds a stranger—"Septimus, who wasn't Septimus any longer" (65). Her husband's worrying alienation, she believes, issues from the terrible thoughts to which he constantly returns, in stubborn adherence to his war experience: "But Septimus let himself think about horrible things, as she could, too, if she tried. He had grown stranger and stranger. He said people were talking behind the bedroom walls" (66).

But Septimus, it turns out, is just one stranger among many in *Mrs. Dalloway*. Woolf's London is a city full of strangers—people like Peter Walsh, Clarissa's former lover who has just returned from India, or Maisie Johnson, a recent arrival from Edinburgh. These strangers continually pass each other and, in the large and teeming cityscape, misread each other—as Peter Walsh does when he passes by Septimus and his wife and takes the couple to be in the thick of a lovers' quarrel: "And that is being young, Peter Walsh thought as he passed them. To be having an awful scene—the poor girl looked absolutely desperate—in the middle of the morning" (70). In this cityscape of chance collisions, the potential for genuine interaction always exists. Like the situation to which tort law responds, the capacity to engage with a perfect stranger is limitless. But in *Mrs. Dalloway,* the potential for such intimacy turns out to be something of a mirage: it is never ultimately realized, hovering over the city as a promise unfulfilled.

This promise of intimacy plays itself out most painfully in Septimus's visit to Sir William Bradshaw, the renowned physician whose expertise seems to promise a cure. But Septimus enters the doctor's office determined not to describe his symptoms but to confess to a crime. "He had committed an appalling crime, and had been condemned to death by human nature" (96). He is guilty, in his own mind, not for his act but for his omission: "[W]hen Evans was killed, just before the Armistice, in Italy, Septimus, far from showing any emotion or recognizing that here was the end of a friendship, congratulated himself on feeling very little and very reasonably" (86). After the war, this indifference grew increasingly impenetrable; "now that it was all over, truce signed, and the dead buried, he had, especially in the evening, these sudden thunder-claps of fear. He could not feel" (87). Desperate to break through the frozen surface of his apathy, Septimus confesses to his crime:

> "I have—I have," he began, "committed a crime—"
> "He has done nothing wrong whatever," Rezia assured the doctor. (96)

Rezia interrupts her husband's outburst by pointing out the obvious: Septimus is not a criminal but a decorated war hero.[24] Yet his pleas point us toward the larger question of justice at the heart of *Mrs. Dalloway.* For if his self-confessed crime is indifference, this crime is perpetrated upon him by the dismissive response of those people who are in the very position to help him. Dr. Bradshaw turns away from Septimus's pleas and prescribes plenty of bed rest in the country. "Try to think as little about yourself as possible" (98), he tells his patient. What Septimus wants is to be judged, to make sense of his impassiveness in some ethical way. What he receives instead is a diagnosis.

The directive not to think, Woolf implies, is prescribed not only to banish torturous images from Septimus's mind but also to instruct him in the finer points of postwar silence. "Was it not noticeable at the end of the war that men returned from the battlefield grown silent?" Benjamin would ask over a decade later in

"The Storyteller." But Woolf's novel suggests not only that these soldiers had grown silent but that they had been *reduced* to silence, their attempts at communication actively deflected by individuals unable or unwilling to make sense of their confessions. The psychiatrist W. H. R. Rivers, who treated shell-shocked patients like Siegfried Sassoon and Wilfred Owen at Craiglockhart War Hospital, saw in this imposed silence cause rather than remedy. Addressing the Royal Society of Medicine in 1917 in a lecture entitled "The Repression of War Experience" (which would inspire Sassoon's poem of the same name), Rivers explained:

> [M]any of the most trying and distressing symptoms from which the subjects of war-neuroses suffer are not the necessary results of the strain and shocks to which they have been exposed in warfare, but are due to the attempt to banish from the mind distressing memories of warfare or painful affective states which have come into being as the result of their war experience.[25]

Disregarding this alternative, Dr. Bradshaw becomes less respectable as a physician and far more convincing in his role as a gatekeeper, embodying Freud's human metaphor for the process through which mental impulses are censored.[26] As the expert who takes it upon himself to keep his patients' emotions at bay, Dr. Bradshaw functions as more than the novel's dubious authority figure. He is, above all, its figure for a particular brand of justice, reminding his patients of the balance that proper health—and, one might add, law—demands. "Sir William said he never spoke of 'madness'; he called it not having a sense of proportion" (96). The equilibrium privileged by this proportion calls to mind one of the law's most time-honored symbols, the scales of justice. Woolf's language invokes Aristotle's in *The Nicomachean Ethics,* where he set out the notion of law as equilibrium: "Justice then is a sort of proportion . . . That which is just then . . . is that which is proportionate, and that which is unjust is that which is disproportionate."[27] Reinforcing this sense of balance, Dr. Bradshaw prescribes isolation in the country for Septimus: "He had threatened to kill himself. There was no alternative. It was a question of law" (96–97). Faced with the authority of these unequivocal pronouncements, it is only natural that Septimus feels himself to be less a patient in a doctor's office and more a "criminal who faced his judges" (97).

In Bradshaw's idea of proportion, Woolf details the very attitudes that her novel labors against: the exacting, measured division of the world, the drive to fit everything into its proper place and time. Patients receive no more or less than three-quarters of an hour: a sensible allotment that is of a piece with a mind that neatly separates the world into useful categories: healthy and ill, proportionate and disproportionate.

> Health we must have; and health is proportion; so that when a man comes into your room and says he is Christ (a common delusion), and has a message, as they mostly have, and threatens, as they often do, to kill himself, you invoke proportion; order rest in bed, rest in solitude, silence and rest; rest without friends, without books, without messages; six months' rest; until a man who went in weighing seven stone six comes out weighing twelve. (99)

Justice, expressed here in the textbook-inflected voice of the physician, strikes a posture not unlike that in Cardozo's *Palsgraf* opinion, extending only as far as the eye can see. If "the eye of reasonable vigilance" (and, of course, the scale) registers that a patient has gained weight, then it would not be unreasonable to assume that the patient has been cured. If this unforgiving remedy is the novel's vision of law and order, *Mrs. Dalloway* does more than simply reproach it as flawed justice. Rather, Woolf seeks out other possibilities for response, alternative modes of redress that would do justice without callousness and take responsibility without calibrating its appropriateness.[28] This redress, however, would come too late for Septimus, who takes his own life by leaping out a window. As in many of her works, *Mrs. Dalloway* contains no death scene: Septimus's death, like Jacob Flanders's before him, is presented only indirectly.[29] His posthumous appearance at the end of the novel poses the wider social question of mourning after the war: How is it possible to take responsibility for the deaths of anonymous individuals across vast distances? What does one owe to them if one does not even know who they are?

Septimus's suicide does not merely interrupt the party; it reaches back to the novel's opening scenes, offering a belated commentary to the way that Londoners pass each other in the city streets without diverging from their paths in the slightest. Woolf had already hinted at the possibility of an alternative course in *Jacob's Room*: "The streets of London have their map," her narrator observes in that novel, "but our passions are uncharted. What are you going to meet if you turn this corner?"

> "Holborn straight ahead of you," says the policeman. Ah, but where are you going if instead of brushing past the old man with the white beard, the silver medal, the cheap violin, you let him go on with his story, which ends in an invitation to step somewhere, to his room, presumably, off Queen's Square, and there he shows you a collection of

birds' eggs and a letter from the Prince of Wales's secretary, and this (skipping the intermediate stages) brings you one winter's day to the Essex coast, where the little boat makes off to the ship, and the ship sails and you behold the skyline of the Azores; and the flamingoes rise; and there you sit on the verge of the marsh drinking rum-punch, an outcast from civilization, for you have committed a crime, are infected with yellow fever as likely as not, and—fill in the sketch as you like.

As frequent as street corners in Holborn are these chasms in the continuity of our ways. Yet we keep straight on. (JR 95–96)

The punishment that ends this passage—"for you have committed a crime"—echoes in Septimus's self-accusation: "I have committed a crime." These crimes, however, are of a vastly different order. For the offense that ends in excommunication in *Jacob's Room* is that of throwing the social order off balance, of following a stranger home and indulging in his stories. Indeed, this is the very deviance—telling senseless stories when he should be listening to the doctor's orders—of which Septimus, in his futile attempt to confess, stands accused in Bradshaw's office. The transgression of upsetting life's proportion is transformed, in Septimus's mind, into the crime of indifference, of keeping his emotions appropriately balanced, "feeling very little and very reasonably." Setting these offenses alongside each other, Woolf suggests their interrelation: to maintain social order, one needs a measure—and an agent—of impassiveness: the indifferent policeman of *Jacob's Room* who becomes in *Mrs. Dalloway* the figure of the doctor. The "chasms in the continuity of our ways" are wider not only for maintaining social order, but also for invoking one crime, indifference, to control another: the "offense" of straying from life's course.

The chasms left open in *Jacob's Room* are bridged in *Mrs. Dalloway* by Septimus's death, which interrupts Clarissa Dalloway's festivities as the very deviation that breaks apart life's continuity and forces strangers together:

Lady Bradshaw (poor goose—one didn't dislike her) murmured how "just as we were starting, my husband was called up on the telephone, a very sad case. A young man (that is what Sir William is telling Mr. Dalloway) had killed himself. He had been in the army." Oh! thought Clarissa, in the middle of my party, here's death, she thought. (183)

Septimus enters the party as the absent subject of conversation and as the ghostly presence that had signaled itself earlier in the novel in the pealing bells of St. Margaret's. These bells, which sound throughout the opening scenes, are refigured in this moment, recalling the sound (rather than the sight) that jars

Londoners out of the comfortable, unbroken rhythms of a city desperate to forget its recent past. The bells of St. Margaret's undo the sense of proportion maintained by Big Ben, which tolls precisely on the hour in an audible reinforcement of Bradshaw's proportion.[30] The less punctual bells cut through this order, creating a dissonance that recalls life's more permeable boundaries, "the sudden loudness of the final stroke tolled for death that surprised in the midst of life" (50)— a death made literal on a June night in the Dalloway home.

Her party ruined, Clarissa finds herself inexplicably drawn to think about Septimus's death not by reflecting on its details but by sensing it: feeling his suicide by literally, physically, taking it personally. "He had killed himself—but how? Always her body went through it first, when she was told, suddenly, of an accident; her dress flamed, her body burnt. He had thrown himself from a window" (184). Her unexpected response extends the imperceptible but palpable sense at the novel's beginning, in which the car passing through London hints at "*something* so trifling" that, in spite of its apparent triviality, strikes an emotional vein and so forges a temporary affective community. This "something" precipitates a moment in which "strangers looked at each other and thought of the dead," setting off a "surface agitation [that] grazed *something* very profound." The inability to specify this "something" beyond the vague, repeated word only reinforces its acuteness; it is powerfully felt, one is tempted to add, precisely because it is inarticulate.

It is also this nonspecific "something," I would suggest, that ties Clarissa and Septimus together in *Mrs. Dalloway's* final scenes. No fitting word or phrase exists to describe their connection; it is not enough to call them British subjects, Londoners, or neighbors. Their relationship needs to be narrated precisely because it cannot be named. Depicted as an act, their association might best be described as a moment in which Clarissa Dalloway takes responsibility for Septimus Smith through a surfeit of feeling; she does not want to see the accident so much as to *sense* it. "He could not feel," the narrator says of Septimus; but Clarissa, in these moments after learning of his death, is moved to do just that. Their connection does not emerge, moreover, only because Clarissa learns of his suicide, nor is it reducible to the fact that Woolf had intended Clarissa and Septimus as *doppelgangers*. The tie between them forms because the story of his suicide catches her unaware, interrupting the gathering she had worked to bring together. And it is cemented because she allows herself to diverge from her best-laid plans, leaving her party and going upstairs to feel for this strange, dead man. It is only here, in abandoning her own party—her sole purpose in the novel and the one thing for which she felt responsible—that Clarissa can recognize the existence of a person she will never meet and, in this act of recognition, take responsibility for him.

Retreating to an empty room, Clarissa walks to the window in a gesture that rehearses Septimus's death earlier that evening. Here, in an unanticipated moment of solitude—and an encounter with yet another stranger—she sees clearly for the first time:

> She parted the curtains; she looked. Oh, but how surprising!—in the room opposite the old lady stared straight at her! . . . She was going to bed, in the room opposite. It was fascinating to watch her, moving about, that old lady, crossing the room, coming to the window. Could she see her? It was fascinating, with people still laughing and shouting in the drawing-room, to watch that old woman, quite quietly, going to bed. (186)

Clarissa's gesture counters Owen's "drawing down of blinds" enacted by the anonymous passenger in the car at the novel's beginning, who draws the shade to shut out the city's crowds. Indeed, her contact with the old woman is defined solely by vision, which becomes possible only once the veil of isolation has been rent by Septimus's death. The interruption this death produces sets off a kind of chain reaction—perhaps the only linear, causal thread in the novel's tangled web of associations. It is Septimus's position as the strangest of strangers that sets in motion Clarissa's encounter with the old woman, which in spite of her surprise, she seems to have actively sought out—"She parted the curtains; she looked." In pursuing this experience, she shifts her focus and responsibility from the people at her party to those outside her familiar social world.

Yet the clarity of her vision as she looks at the old woman neither begins nor ends in knowledge: Clarissa knows nothing about this woman except what she sees through the window. In this act of seeing, the woman becomes the visual counterpart to the death she has just heard about, the death of a man she might have passed on the streets of London but had never laid eyes on.[31] This moment of seeing clearly ultimately transports the action of *Mrs. Dalloway* from a world in which people pass by each other to one in which they encounter each other. And this modern encounter, defined by strangeness rather than knowledge, suggests that to see clearly—to understand, to respond—is to feel rather than to know. Knowledge, Woolf seems to imply, is neither the ends nor the means of ethical action. Indeed, *Mrs. Dalloway* suggests that this feeling reaches its greatest potency the *less* one knows, that it is at its most far-reaching when one takes a complete stranger into account.

For Woolf, the encounter between individuals who know nothing at all about each other becomes the ideal circumstance under which to imagine connections founded solely upon responsibility, relationships untainted by old assumptions or debts and freed from the burden of knowledge. Her vision of social ethics is thus profoundly different from the one Emmanuel Levinas saw as the very basis of responsibility. For Levinas, ethics takes root in "the face to face encounter with a substantial interlocutor . . . a thou, springing up inevitably, solid and noumenal, behind the man known in that bit of absolutely decent skin that is the face."[32] In "the pure vis-à-vis of the interlocutor,"[33] we find the condition of ethics. *Mrs. Dalloway,* however, contains no face and no locution. Instead, ethics is grounded in an act of imagination, a fictive encounter where one feels for, rather than faces, a stranger. The novel's nomos thus shares certain elements with the normative universe defined by tort law. But in casting the net of responsibility as widely as possible, it makes a different—and a legally impossible—normative claim.

Woolf's insistence that one does not need to know individuals intimately, or at all, to be responsible for them recasts the question of accountability, extending its temporal and physical boundaries in a way that tort law, with its emphasis on proximity and causality, cannot. The normative encounters with strangers in *Mrs. Dalloway* suggest that responsibility exceeds temporal limits, and that one owes a duty of care—which is also a duty *to* care—not only to strangers in the present, but also to those in the past and the future. Law cannot do without a very practical sense of time: practically speaking, cases must be closed, decisions made, if a legal system is to function at all. Woolf's sense of responsibility, however, expands the limits of the "stranger cases" from which tort law developed, undoing the confines of time and place, causality and foreseeability, upon which torts insists.

"There was no remoteness in time, little in space," writes Justice Andrews of the events on the Long Island Railroad in his *Palsgraf* dissent. But *Mrs. Dalloway* and Helen Palsgraf point to the potential of strangers across temporal divides, across the gulf between the dead and the living. This is why Helen Palsgraf matters long after her case has been closed, and why Septimus Smith's life is woven into Clarissa Dalloway's although they would never meet. These strangers call upon us to act through rifts that may appear unbridgeable, those fractures that divided the world of London from the trenches of World War I. The strangers who came home, it turns out, became both reminders of this divide and invitations to recast the human shape of responsibility.

Discomforts of Home

It is this very responsibility that I believe Woolf is still after when the next world war once again makes it difficult to feel—and to respond—to the people with whom she shares the city of London. On a stray page in a notebook devoted to her last novel, *Between the Acts,* Virginia Woolf records the following thoughts, concerns that suggest that, with the onset of another war, her hopes for a different postwar world had not come to pass. Titled "London in War," her reflections note how social relations had dissolved into a sense of undifferentiated purpose:

> The sensation of fear very soon evaporates. Everybody is feeling the same thing: therefore no one is feeling anything in particular. The individual is merged in the mob. That is why after the first three nights one's ears become stopped. They were acute the first night. Everyone is on business. Their minds are made up. It is extremely sober. The streets are (?) lit. They have gone back to the 18th Century. Nature prevails. I suppose badgers and foxes wd. come back if this went on, & owls & nightingales. This is the prelude to barbarism. The City has become merely a congeries of houses lived in by people who work. There is no society, no luxury no splendour no gadding & flitting. All is serious & concentrated. It is as if the song had stopped—the melody, the unnecessary the voluntary. Odd if this should be the end of town life.[34]

What might well be taken as Woolf's snobbery—as a desire for luxury and for the frivolous pleasures of London's social scene—might also, if one draws from *Mrs. Dalloway,* be set within the terms of the broader social obligations that Woolf lays out after World War I. These obligations are not desperate attempts to forget the past by cloaking it in opulent parties and mindless social chatter. They insist, rather, on the responsibility of the postwar world to create as many encounters with as many individuals as possible—to avoid the atomization that occurs when people retreat into the comfort of their houses after a long, isolated day of work. "It is as if the song had stopped"—the hum of conversation, the storytelling that catches someone off guard and connects one person's life to another's. The unpredictable capacity of sounds and echoes to cut through indifference, setting off potent feelings that cannot be measured—the "oh, oh, oh" of the woman whose accident Woolf witnesses in 1925, the tolling of St. Margaret's bells that become, with a shade of difference, the story of Septimus's suicide: these unexpected intrusions threaten once more to fall into a pattern of measured and strategic behavior. And it is this behavior—one that in its proportion, spare details, and sobriety is reminiscent of law—that Woolf wants to avoid.

For her, the inconvenient interruptions that take place when unacquainted lives intersect need to happen of their own accord—in a manner "unnecessary and voluntary," in the most unpredictable of ways. Through this sensibility, we can understand why, in the midst of an air raid in 1940, Woolf seems to relish an unexpected moment of intimacy with a couple she meets in a makeshift bomb shelter. She writes in her diary:

> Pouring. Guns in the distance. Saw a pink brick shelter. That was the only interest in our journey—our talk with the man, woman and child who were living there. They had been bombed at Clapham. Their house unsafe, so they hiked to Wimbledon. Pre-ferred this unfinished gun emplacement to a refugee over-crowded house. They had a roadman's lamp; a saucepan and could boil tea.[35]

The unanticipated moment, in which Virginia and Leonard Woolf find them-selves thrust into a confined space with another couple (and taking tea, or imag-ining taking tea, with them), is precisely the kind of "ethical accident" that Woolf fears is vanishing—and vanishing at the very moment when it is needed most. It is disappearing, she implies, because people are once more making sharp distinctions—eighteenth-century distinctions that so troubled her in *Jacob's Room*—that separate individuals into the discrete contours of their private lives and compel them to guard the boundaries of those lives with a disappointing measure of vigilance.

For Woolf, the comforts of home that these behaviors safeguard may be reassuring—but they are not contemporary, and they are decidedly not just. What she ultimately creates in bringing together Clarissa Dalloway and Septimus Smith is a sense of homecoming that challenges the consolation of these private spaces, inviting individuals to inhabit them as more than shelters from the sor-rows of history. *Mrs. Dalloway*, it turns out, returns to these places and fills them with strangers, disappointments, and immeasurable, inconsolable feelings. And in doing so, the novel offers a vision of how to make one's home less a home of one's own: a less comfortable, possibly even painful, but always a more ethical place.

Woolf, we come to understand, positions her sense of home not against the public sphere but as an extension of it—indeed, as the optimal place to test our most public commitments. If we can take responsibility for strangers here, where such responsibility is least expected, then we can foster a nomos that makes sense in a world where neighbors no longer know each other and where a novel's main characters never meet. In her next novel, *To the Lighthouse,* Woolf would come home once again to work through the grief of her war-torn generation in yet another way. As the next chapter shows, she would do so through questions of inheritance historically shaped in law. If the English jurist Sir Edward Coke suggested in the seventeenth century that a man's home is his castle, Woolf would rebuild this home as a site of public grief, a place to ask how inheritance becomes possible when nothing is left to inherit.

CHAPTER THREE

Property and Carrying On

Where have they gone to, brother and sister, mother and father? Off along
the shore, perhaps. Their clothes are still on the hangers . . .

—Margaret Atwood, "Morning in the Burned House"[1]

For there were clothes in the cupboards; they had left clothes in all the
bedrooms.

—Virginia Woolf, *To the Lighthouse*

In her 1933 memoir *Testament of Youth,* Vera Brittain, the war nurse who became
one of the most prominent chroniclers of her times, relates how World War I
shattered her life and the lives of everyone in her generation beyond recognition.
The war saw the deaths of her brother Edward, her friends, and her fiancé Roland
Leighton, who was killed in 1915 and buried abroad at Louvencourt. Because
the war dead were not repatriated, the delivery of a soldier's kit often served as
the final reminder that the owner of its contents would never come home. This
collection of supplies—stained uniforms, identification papers, the occasional
diary—grimly announced, in material form, the loss of a life. Brittain recalls a
profound sense of helplessness when Roland's kit was delivered:

> I had arrived at the cottage that morning to find [Roland's] mother and sister stand-
> ing in helpless distress in the midst of his returned kit, which was lying, just opened,
> all over the floor. The garments sent back included the outfit he was wearing when he
> was hit. I wondered, and I wonder still, why it was thought necessary to return such
> relics—the tunic torn back and front by the bullet, a khaki vest dark and stiff with
> blood, and a pair of blood-stained breeches slit open at the top by someone obviously
> in a violent hurry.[2]

Overcome by the sight of her son's possessions, Roland's mother turns in her devastation to her husband: "Robert, take those clothes away into the kitchen and don't let me see them again: I must either burn or bury them. They smell of death; they are not Roland; they even seem to detract from his memory and spoil his glamour. *I won't have anything more to do with them.*"[3] Brittain's depiction of this scene speaks to the complex, emotional nature of material objects during and after World War I—and not simply as symbols of the war's destruction or as macabre, material "relics," to use Brittain's term, but as possessions. The delivery of Roland's kit points to the difficult situation that unfolds when things become property—when legal or official channels intervene to assign ownership—and when property is transferred from the dead to the living. Like the stories of so many individuals during and after the war, Brittain's story is one of inheritance: not only of the postwar generation inheriting the burden of history, but quite literally of inheriting property, of coming to possess ordinary objects that never seemed to matter enough to their original owners to be included in a will. Now, however, these all-too-ordinary possessions became the matter of memory, of sorrow, and—as Mrs. Leighton's response powerfully reminds us—of helplessness.

It is with this problematic inheritance in mind that I would like to consider how property—both the private property of individuals and the public property of memorials—functioned after World War I, and how the experience of inheriting this property challenged people to relate to their past differently by refiguring traditional notions of inheritance. What difference does property, and by extension inheritance, make? What difference does the war make in these experiences? How is it possible to inherit something that was never willed—something, moreover, that one never even wanted to own in the first place?[4] In what follows, I take up these questions in order to show how World War I saw the widespread occurrence of a different form of inheritance, one that broadened this concept to ordinary, unwilled objects and that, moreover, cannot be accounted for in law. This process, which I call traumatic inheritance, emerges both as a public and a private phenomenon, taking shape as much from national posttraumatic grief as it does from personal spheres of mourning. Traumatic inheritance becomes a way to relate to these spheres and to understand how it is that memorials, whether large-scale, public monuments or personal, homely artifacts, together tell the story of how we live with—and go on living after—our most inconceivable losses.

To attribute emotional registers to property, however, is to recognize affective resonances that were in evidence long before World War I. Already at the start of the nineteenth century, Jeremy Bentham—a rather unlikely candidate for a theory of the emotions—wrote in *The Theory of Legislation* (1802): "Property is nothing but a basis of expectation; the expectation of deriving certain advantages from a thing which we are said to possess, in consequence of the relation in which we stand towards it."[5] He goes on to argue that property is not an innate attribute of objects but a relationship constituted by law, "a mere conception of the mind."[6] Without law, he insists, we can expect nothing from the material world—least of all the guarantee that we can derive any sort of benefit from it:

> I cannot count upon the enjoyment of that which I regard as mine, except through the promise of the law which guarantees it to me. It is law alone which permits me to forget my natural weakness. It is only through the protection of law that I am able to inclose a field, and to give myself up to its cultivation *with the sure though distant hope of harvest.*[7]

Bentham locates his sense of property within the larger context of time and history: to have expectations of property, one must have expectations of the future— in short, one must have *hope,* and law provides the assurance that this hope will be realized. Property speaks to our hopes for the future because it retains its value or meaning beyond the present moment, reassuring us that at some point in time, provided that the law protects what is ours, we will benefit from our possessions.

But property addresses the future in still another sense: because it outlives us, and thus can be willed, passed on from one generation to the next as an extension of our person. In its connection to mortality, the hope associated with property is inflected with a sense of the tragic, with the knowledge that because it outlives its owners, property presages their death. Perhaps one of the most explicit acknowledgments of an individual's mortality is a will, which documents, and in so doing anticipates, one's own death. A will, put simply, gestures not only to one's future, but also to the future of one's property.[8] To will something is thus to undertake a creative act: to imagine the fate of one's possessions and, in a legal effort to master that fate, to determine their place—their future owners—after one's death.

The process of engaging the imagination in protecting one's possessions extends to the expectation that Bentham posits as the very definition of property.

To say that property is a "basis of expectation" is to tell a story of the life to which that piece of property is bound. Bentham's insistence on expectation, it turns out, does not just explain the need to legally protect our possessions; it also imposes a kind of narrative continuity on the lives of property owners:

> It is hence that we have the power of forming a general plan of conduct; It is hence that the successive instants which compose the duration of life are not like isolated and independent points, but become continuous parts of a whole. *Expectation* is a chain which unites our present existence to our future existence, and which passes beyond us to the generation which is to follow. The sensibility of man extends through all the links of this chain.[9]

In a curiously narratological turn, Bentham imputes to expectation, and by extension to property, a remarkable capacity for coherence. Expectations, and the legal guarantee that they will be realized, impart a unifying sense of meaning to the disparate episodes of a life. And this meaning, presumably, extends to the way we tell the story of that life—a story of ambitions realized, hopes met or thwarted. As an organizing principle, it allows us to tell a story retrospectively by positing it as a future-oriented tale: the past as seen through the expectations we once held of it—that is, when it was still the future.

But the process of inheriting the possessions of those who die intestate, without making a will, poses a challenge to Bentham's conception of property. The example of receiving a soldier's kit suggests that in the case of ordinary possessions, the sort of property one comes to own in the absence of legal arrangements, one experiences not continuity but rupture. These impractical, unwilled objects do not affirm one's expectations for the future but, in confirming a soldier's death, foreclose them. In doing so, they invite us to rephrase a central question of trauma posed by Cathy Caruth: "Is the trauma the encounter with death, or the ongoing experience of having survived it?"[10] For those on the home front during World War I, the encounter with death, and thus its survival, was not part of the war experience; for them, the encounter would be mediated by property. We might thus recast Caruth's question to ask: Is the trauma for those at home the experience of *receiving* property, or the ongoing experience of *inheriting* it? How, precisely, are these experiences rooted in property—particularly when property becomes not a basis of expectation in Bentham's sense, but rather a source of its undoing? What do we do when experience overwhelms our expectations? How might we situate ourselves in relation to property we have not inherited through a will—through the legal transfer created by that will—but rather acquired through the unexpected events of history and, specifically, through a person's sudden, unanticipated death?

These questions, which weigh heavily on the scene of the Brittain family faced with Roland's military kit in *Testament of Youth,* are no less present in the postwar writing of Virginia Woolf. This body of her work, particularly *To the Lighthouse,* is deeply concerned with expectations—specifically, how individuals negotiate their unfulfilled expectations in a world unequipped to address these discrepancies. I would like to suggest that Woolf has something to offer in the problem of traumatic inheritance: those quotidian objects left behind or sent back, the things one never wanted to acquire, and more broadly, the unfinished business of the dead. Woolf initially addresses this problem in *Jacob's Room* (1922) but takes it up more fully two novels later in *To the Lighthouse* (1927).

In spite of the fact that in *Jacob's Room* Woolf casts aspersions on the "characters of Great Men" at the center of historical narratives, and in spite of the fact that she finds the notion of the distinguished or fully available character wanting, the last page of *Jacob's Room* still astonishes. For even in light of Woolf's assault on identity, the anticlimactic tenor of the novel's page-long final chapter nonetheless confounds expectations: character may have disintegrated, but does this mean that we can find no more fitting an image to convey the war's devastation than a pair of old shoes? Rather than offering a profound reflection on Jacob Flanders's life, Woolf concludes her novel with a seemingly mundane account of his things and with his mother's lingering question about his shoes: "What am I to do with these?"[11]

The preoccupation with the material world haunts Woolf's fiction and reappears—almost word for word—five years later in *To the Lighthouse.* Its repetition suggests that the problem of what to do with these ordinary possessions is, for Woolf, fundamental to facing life after unanticipated tragedy and suggests to her readers and critics, who tend to overlook her attention to material things, that these objects in fact demand closer examination.[12] *To the Lighthouse,* which depicts the Ramsay family's relationship through its vacation home in the Hebrides, extends the priority given to practical over philosophical matters at the end of *Jacob's Room* and sets up the conditions for inheriting property beyond official, legal means.

I would like to approach *To the Lighthouse* through its middle section, "Time Passes," in order to examine its depiction of the ten-year span between the novel's first and last sections, a transition that sets up the conditions of unofficial inheritance. I begin here, moreover, because it is the section about which critics in Woolf's time were most ambivalent. Arnold Bennett—never a great fan of Woolf's work—approved of the novel in general, but criticized it for this middle section, writing in the *Evening Standard* in 1927 that it "does not succeed. It is a short cut, but a short cut that does not get you anywhere. To convey the idea of the passage of a considerable length of time is an extremely difficult business, and I doubt if it can be accomplished by means of a device, except the device of simply saying 'Time Passes,' and leaving the effort of imagination to the reader."[13]

But Woolf is after something else in this section: not simply a depiction of the passage of time, but a transition at once psychological and material: the conversion of time into space and, with it, the creation of a kind of memorial. The novel's structure situates the ephemeral section "Time Passes" between the sections that name physical, architectural structures, "The Window" and "The Lighthouse." Yet "Time Passes," in spite of its purported ethereality, dwells not on the intangible movement of time but on its visibility in an architectural space, the decaying house. More broadly, it describes what happens to property once it is deprived of human life and given over to the forces of nature.

Mrs. Ramsay's death is reported briefly in brackets at the end of the third part of the section, and the narrative moves immediately from her death to the contours of the house:

[Mr. Ramsay, stumbling along a passage one dark morning, stretched his arms out, but Mrs. Ramsay having died rather suddenly the night before, his arms, though stretched out, remained empty.]

[IV]

So with the house empty and the doors locked and the mattresses rolled round, those stray airs, advance guards of great armies, blustered in, brushed bare boards, nibbled and fanned, met nothing in bedroom or drawing-room that wholly resisted them but only hangings that flapped, wood that creaked, the bare legs of tables.[14]

The description of Mrs. Ramsay's death initially seems matter-of-fact, even ironic: a small, parenthetical event swallowed up by the permanence of its domestic surroundings. Yet Woolf does more than just embed this moment in the description of the house, draining death of its emotional content by assuming a detached tone. Instead, she grafts this emotional content onto the physical world, describing the bodily contours through which death is recognized. Death, in this moment, is felt not purely on an emotional level, but is experienced physically—discovered because one stumbles upon it in the course of bodily habit: the habit of reaching for one's wife in the middle of the night. Mrs. Ramsay's death is presented precisely as the *interruption* of that habit: Mr. Ramsay stretches his arms out, as he might have done every morning, and feels not his wife's body but empty space. The form through which this narrative unfolds underscores this rupture of old patterns, breaking into the narrative not with the smoother contours of parentheses but with angular, jarring brackets—Woolf's textual reenactment of the interruption of physical habits.

It is in this sense that we can understand the narrative's turn away from any philosophical reflection on Mrs. Ramsay's death, the reason it loses itself in the minute details of the abandoned house. The jarring transition does not represent a move away from emotion but rather a return to the places of habit, and specifically the domestic space where habits take shape. At work here, I would suggest, is the relation between habit and habitation, the idea that the physical spaces we inhabit ultimately bind themselves to the repeated return, to the habit, of memory. "[T]he house we were born in is physically inscribed in us," Gaston Bachelard writes in *The Poetics of Space*. "It is a group of organic habits."[15] It is in this sense, then, that we might understand the haunting tour through the Ramsays' abandoned house as an attempt to locate these habits once more, all the while projecting a vision of what *un*inhabited space looks like.

In pursuing this space of habit and habitation, the narrative's next turn withdraws us further still from any lofty reflections on life and death, settling even more firmly on the everyday things left behind, those possessions that bring the ghostly world of the past back to the surface of the present. As if picking up where *Jacob's Room* left off, Woolf begins her inventory with the shoes in Betty Flanders' hands at the close of that novel:

> What people had shed and left—a pair of shoes, a shooting cap, some faded skirts and coats in wardrobes—those alone kept the human shape and in the emptiness indicated how once hands were busy with hooks and buttons; how once the looking-glass had held a face; had held a world hollowed out in which a figure turned, a hand flashed, the door opened, in came children rushing and tumbling; and went out again. (129)

This "world hollowed out" finds its most monumental shape in the image of the house itself which, like the skin "shed" by its former inhabitants, takes on dimensions of the natural world: "The house was left; the house was deserted. It was left like a shell on a sandhill to fill with dry salt grains now that life had left it" (137). One might say this of the lighthouse as well, with its winding staircase reminiscent of a shell's geometric coils.

With this image of the shell, Woolf offers another way to imagine the life that would no longer fill the Ramsays' home. For if there is something fascinating and mysterious about shells, argues Bachelard, it is not their physical form but the process through which this form is made. Borrowing from Valéry, he explains that it is not the geometrical intelligibility of the shell that captures the imagination; rather, "it is the *formation,* not the form, that remains mysterious," a process that calls our attention to "the mystery of form-giving life, the mystery of slow, continuous formation."[16] Explaining Valéry further, Bachelard surmises that in order for human beings to construct a shell, they would have to do so from the outside, in spite of the fact that a shell is formed from the inside out. This "inside formation" is what makes the shell so mysterious, what makes its formation impossible to replicate with human hands. I would suggest, however, that we replicate something of this formation by inhabiting a space. Building a house means constructing a physical husk from the outside; at this point, the structure is still only geometrical shape, form rather than formation. Creating a psychologically inhabited space, however, means building this structure from the inside, fitting the supple contents of a life within its solid, angular construction. We might note, along such lines, the implied distinction between "house" and "home," the former denoting the literal, geometrical object, the latter the lived-in, psychological one. Woolf invokes the shell, then, to recall the old habits that carved out the Ramsay home from the inside, and announces the end of these habits by filling this space with sand, blanketing over the uninhabited space.

The uninhabited, abandoned home may deteriorate—but perhaps the more poignant part of its story is that it remains at all. For its endurance, however dilapidated, make the journey home possible, extending the prospect of memory to those who come back to their old spaces of habit. The potential to retrieve both habit and memory, however, is always qualified by the sadness that accompanies these private memorials: it seems somehow unfair that these things should survive when their owners do not. More recently, the British writer Penelope Lively attested to the continued existence of such possessions by conducting a private memory experiment, thinking back through the various objects and rooms in her ancestral home so as to trace the broader contours of history:

> Objects had proved more tenacious than people—the photograph albums, the baffling contents of the silver cupboard, the children on my grandmother's sampler of

the house—but from each object there spun a shining thread of reference, if you knew how to follow it. I thought that I would see if the private life of a house could be made to bear witness to the public traumas of a century.[17]

This connection between private and public history is also at work in *To the Light-house,* a novel scarred as much by the inexplicable death of Mrs. Ramsay as it is by her son Andrew's death in World War I. "But every one had lost some one these years," reflects the housekeeper, Mrs. McNab, as she prepares for the Ramsays' return. "Prices had gone up shamefully, and didn't come down again neither. She could well remember her in her grey cloak" (136). That the private recollection of Mrs. Ramsay in her cloak flows directly from Mrs. McNab's thoughts about the public matters of war and economics is not surprising: for the shell that endures negotiates between the two realms, allowing one to unfold from the other.

Yet even as the narrative lays bare the contours of an empty house, recalling the life it once contained, it also appeals to something other than memory. As Mrs. McNab reminds us, these objects demand attention and work in the present:

> All those books needed to be laid out on the grass in the sun; there was plaster fallen in the hall; the rainpipe had blocked over the study window and let the water in; the carpet was quite ruined. But people should have come themselves; they should have sent somebody down to see. For there were clothes in the cupboards; they had left clothes in all the bedrooms. *What was she to do with them?* (135, emphasis added)

Mrs. McNab's question, a nearly verbatim repetition of the one Betty Flanders asks as she holds up the shoes at the end of *Jacob's Room*—"What am I to do with these, Mr. Bonamy?"—suggests that these abandoned possessions not only produce memory but demand concrete, practical work. They insist that someone *do* something and, in so doing, they offer a sense of memory that is active rather than passive. For the stuff of memory in Woolf, unlike that in Proust, does not give rise to surges of involuntary memory; memory in *To the Lighthouse* demands action, work—and ultimately, the will to take on these simultaneously menial and painful tasks.

Woolf thus recasts Mr. Ramsay's philosophy of "subject and object and the nature of reality" (23) into a scene of domestic labor, a transformation that Lily Briscoe anticipates at the beginning of the novel when she attempts to understand Mr. Ramsay's work.[18] "Think of a kitchen table when you're not there" (23), Andrew Ramsay advises her. But rather than conjuring up a kitchen table on its own, Lily envisions "a scrubbed kitchen table," dislodging the solid object from its position as a philosophical example and projecting it into the web of domestic space, placing it in relation to one who cleans it: A table tended to and cared for by someone. In tampering with the "pure" philosophical example of the table, Woolf manipulates Mr. Ramsay's rational severity in order to address its practical import: what, indeed, becomes of the kitchen table when you're not there? Her answer, like Lily's image of the scrubbed table, is a decidedly practical one: The table, like the house and everything it contains, decays—and so to think of this table or house is already to put oneself into a practical relationship with it, to dust it off, scrub it, care for it. It is, in short, to ask, "What am I to do with these?"—and to set about doing something in the most practical, least philosophical of ways.

But if these ordinary things demand an active, practical response, they also signify the shattering of expectation. Returning once more to the shoes, and to Bonamy's question in *Jacob's Room*—"What did he expect? Did he think he would come back?"—Mrs. McNab continues her lament:

> There were boots and shoes; and a brush and comb left on the dressing table, for all the world *as if she expected to come back tomorrow* . . . they had never come all these years; just sent her money; but never wrote, never came, and *expected to find things as they had left them*. (136, emphasis added).

Material possessions here become not only an occasion for work, a demand to "do something." They also point to the expectations of the living that the world, even in their absence, will remain unchanged, that life will go on as it always has. Yet even as these possessions recall the habits that made up this world, "how once hands were busy with hooks and buttons; how once the looking-glass had held a face," they also undo the expectations associated with those habits. The abandoned property—the empty house, the lifeless objects it contains—thus becomes a literal reminder, a memorial to the expectations that no longer hold. Mrs. Ramsay did not come back; the Ramsay family will not find things as they had left them. But because these things endure and outlive their owners, they will find them nonetheless. What, then, does one do with these useless things—other people's possessions that one acquires but that no longer serve a purpose? How does one inherit these impractical reminders of the past?

Unofficial Inheritance: Memory and The Cenotaph

In order to conceptualize the house, its contents, and the habits and expectations they create as figures for both memory and inheritance, I would like to extend the sense of property and to situate it in a more public, social rubric of inheriting. In doing so, I turn from the private, domestic realm of the home to the public, but still architectural, construction of memorials—and to one memorial in particular, which is itself a kind of shell, but in a dramatically different way from the one that Woolf invokes to describe the Ramsays' home. The years following World War I saw the dedication of countless memorials throughout England commemorating the war dead; the National Inventory of War Memorials at the Imperial War Museum notes that "the construction of war memorials after the First World War was the largest series of public works of art ever undertaken in Britain."[19] I would like to consider the particular case of the Cenotaph, which became, quite by accident, England's most prominent national war memorial. The story of the Cenotaph offers a striking model for how property—in this case, public property—becomes a permanent part of the architectural and cultural landscape in a nation searching for a place to anchor its grief.

In 1919 Prime Minister Lloyd George commissioned the renowned architect Edwin Lutyens, one of the principal architects of British war cemeteries in France and Belgium, to design a catafalque for London's Whitehall. The temporary structure was intended as a saluting point for the Peace Day Parade through London, but would be dismantled afterwards and replaced by a permanent memorial elsewhere in the city. A similar structure had been built for the Peace Parade in Paris and promptly removed afterward. Lutyens accepted the project, but wrote to Lloyd George that he would design "not a catafalque but a cenotaph,"[20] an empty tomb, in response to the fact that repatriation of the dead had been banned shortly after the start of World War I, and consequently the British war dead had not been buried at home. The project was completed in a matter of weeks, and the timber-and-plaster Cenotaph was ready in time for the London Peace Procession on July 19, 1919.

What happened next, however, was entirely unexpected. The public embraced the monument so wholly, laying wreaths at its base in such large numbers, that authorities had to delay taking it down. In spite of this response, however, officials still planned to erect a different monument in another part of London. Whitehall, the city's largest thoroughfare, was no place for an edifice of such large and impractical proportions; traffic would have to be directed around it, and it would break up the flow of the city street. But the public did not seem to mind the inconvenience, objecting virulently to the proposal for another memorial and demanding that the Cenotaph be left where it was (Figure 1). Something had happened that no British official had anticipated: people came to associate

FIGURE 1   The Cenotaph, London (Postcard)

the memorial not with ceremony, but with habit; residents of the city incorporated its presence into their daily lives. They expected to see it as they made their way through the city and could no longer imagine London without it. The writer J. M. Barrie wrote to Lutyens on August 6, 1919, "The cenotaph grows in beauty as one strolls alone o'nights to look at it, *which becomes my habit.*"[21] Over the years, it became such a natural part of the city that, as one observer noted in 1928, "It is the only monument in London which passers-by naturally and of their own accord salute."[22] And the *Times* commented in 1923, "There is nothing artificial in the annual observance at the Cenotaph. It has become part of the *expected order of things.*"[23]

So uncompromising was the devotion to the memorial that when the government decided to relocate the Armistice Day Service in 1923, the suggestion produced such widespread outrage that newspapers were overwhelmed with letters of protest. "It is all very well for Lord Curzon to fix on [Westminster] Abbey," one man wrote to the *Daily Chronicle,* "but that is not good enough for the people. If the Government want to go to the Abbey let them go. We, the people, want the Cenotaph, which to us is far more sacred than any church."[24] Indeed, the monument acquired unofficial religious proportions in the public mind, becoming "a shrine at which the whole Empire tenders its tributes to the heroes whose blood has cemented the imperishable fabric of national unity."[25] Its capacity to represent England's fallen soldiers was felt perhaps most powerfully in Sir Fabian Ware's description of the memorial as a way to imagine the staggering numbers of war fatalities. Ware, who was responsible for the formation of the Imperial War Graves Commission in 1917, stated that if the Empire's dead were to march four abreast down the streets of London, it would take them three and a half days to wind their way past the Cenotaph.[26] His image attests to the memorial's status as a literal measure of the nation's losses, an edifice that enabled people to conceptualize the inconceivable. Lutyens himself wanted the memorial to remain in Whitehall, not as a static sculpture but as a dynamic monument that would continue to generate human response. In a letter written shortly after the Peace Celebrations he reflected, "Many have suggested to me to place bronze figures, representing sentries, round it. This I would greatly regret: it would prevent living sentries being posted on days of ceremony."[27] Thus, even as the monument was marked indelibly by its prominence in the Peace Procession, it was through its dynamic relationship to the city, and through the spontaneous responses and the fierce devotion it generated not in Parliament but in the city streets, that the Cenotaph was "inherited," quite unofficially, by its country.

In the deliberations that followed the Peace Procession, one of the main arguments in favor of keeping the memorial in Whitehall was the fact that the public had become accustomed to seeing it there. These considerations eventually won out, and the temporary structure was rebuilt in Portland stone for the Armistice Day celebrations on November 11, 1920. It was never, however, officially inaugurated in a ceremony—a fact that meant that its ownership was never formally defined.[28] But of course, the question of who owned and was thus officially responsible for the Cenotaph was of no concern to those individuals who went out of their way to see it, or those who passed by it on their regular routes through London. For the monument had taken on a life of its own, whether the government willed it or not.[29] Through force of habit and expectation, a temporary structure became Britain's national war memorial.

The Cenotaph became an official memorial because it exceeded one set of expectations and became the source of other, unofficial expectations—those born of the habit of living with something in the most ordinary of ways. It became an organic part of people's existence, rather than a marker of ceremony and circumstance. And this, as I have suggested, is the very process that animates the habit-oriented inheritance in *To the Lighthouse*. Woolf, in fact, makes any prospect of inheriting the house officially entirely unavailable to the Ramsays: it is rented, not owned; like the Cenotaph, the question of official ownership makes no difference to those who turn (and return) to it in their memory and grief. Positing an inheritance that, like the Cenotaph's, bears no relation to traditional ownership, Woolf suggests that inheriting the spaces and possessions of the dead is a matter of coming back to these things and living with them. The house that had stood empty for a decade—a domestic version of the Cenotaph, the empty tomb—is inherited because it is returned to, inhabited; it becomes a place to take up old habits and to establish new ones. Only by returning to the house and picking up where they left off can the Ramsays reach the lighthouse; only by pitching her easel in the same spot can Lily complete the painting she had begun ten years before. It is through these habits, this return, that one can realize "the sure though distant hope of harvest" that Bentham attached to the legal sense of property—a process that suggests that Bentham's goal can nonetheless be realized outside the law.

To the Lighthouse thus responds to Betty Flanders's exclamation at the end of *Jacob's Room*—"Such confusion everywhere!"—with the assurance of the material world. "In the midst of chaos there was shape" (161), Lily Briscoe reflects. And that shape, I am proposing, is the shape of property, which functions not only privately but also publicly. The story of the Cenotaph, and by extension of

To the Lighthouse, offers an alternative, extralegal model for property and inheritance. At the very moment when expectations are undone, when one comes into property that one never expected or wanted to possess through circumstances one never anticipated, property calls upon us to inherit by inhabiting. It is this habitation that enables those who grieve both to remember and to carry on.

To inherit without law, without a will; to inherit traumatically, against one's will: it is to these acts that property after World War I speaks—and in speaking to this inheritance, these unexpected possessions announce the possibility of imagining a future by living, ironically enough, with those things which call the past to mind. For if the material world of possessions in *To the Lighthouse* speaks to private grief, it does so in the wider context of a nation struggling with those things left behind by its war dead. Property, both public and private, undid and exceeded the expectations of both nation and individual and, in its excessiveness, lent shape to the memory and the grief of those who would carry on.

It is in this practical sense that we can think of Vera Brittain's *Testament of Youth* as a kind of literary memorial—and not simply because it is a memoir. Immediately after Roland's clothes are taken away, Brittain reflects:

> What actually happened to the clothes I never knew, but, incongruously enough, it was amid this heap of horror and decay that we found, surrounded by torn bills and letters, the black manuscript note-book containing his poems.[30]

"In the midst of chaos there was shape" (161), Lily Briscoe thinks in *To the Lighthouse*—a shape that, "incongruously enough" indeed, became for Vera Brittain the shape of poetry. She subsequently threads Roland's poems throughout *Testament of Youth,* offering them as textual memorials to his life and to her own grief. Property and poetry—property *as* poetry—unexpectedly come together for her in the heap of Roland's possessions. More than fifteen years after his death, she makes his verse the stuff of the present, the fibers of a volume that—itself a piece of property—outlived them both.

Traumatic Inheritance

If law makes it possible to transfer property to the future by willing it, Woolf suggests that habit makes inheritance without wills possible by labor, by working ordinary possessions into the present after an unanticipated death. But while the habit that allows for unofficial inheritance may work similarly in both a memorial and an ordinary object, these instances of property also offer very different accounts of how property contributes to memory. A monument is built as a deliberate attempt to remember; it is erected for a purpose. Even when this reason is subject to debate—does it remember the dead or honor the living; mourn the war's devastation or celebrate its victory?—a monument is nonetheless recognized as a bearer of some meaning, contested though this meaning may be.

Put differently, a memorial like the Cenotaph, in its architectural grandeur and in the ceremonies associated with it, is extraordinary and imposing; it impresses itself in a way that an ordinary, inconsequential piece of property like a shoe cannot. The shoe, the soldier's kit, the objects left behind in an abandoned house—all of these seem to stand outside the system of meaning making. They render those who inherit them temporarily helpless because they cannot be assimilated readily into any process of signification. "I wondered, and I wonder still, why it was thought necessary to return such relics,"[31] Vera Brittain reflects, recalling the return of Roland's kit. These objects appear, in other words, to mean nothing at all. Other than referring metonymically to the dead who once possessed them, they do not offer themselves as anything significant or commemorative; it is not clear, practically speaking, what one should do with them.

This silence and nonreferentiality explains how these objects become instances of traumatic inheritance. For while a memorial may refer to a trauma, the ordinary objects inherited unexpectedly, without a will and against one's will, are *part of the very experience of trauma itself*; they break down a system of meaningful memory, upending our sense of what is precious and what now, by virtue of its being left to the living, becomes valuable simply because it endures. Thus, when Mrs. Leighton demands that Roland's soiled clothes be burned or buried, her words suggest that these belongings, rather than contributing to memory, in fact corrode it: "they even seem to detract from his memory and spoil his glamour." In other words, the trauma one experiences in receiving these personal effects issues not only from the reminder of a child's death; it is the trauma, too, of having a dignified memory dissolve before one's eyes, to be replaced by unseemly, ordinary, dirty things.

At the center of *To the Lighthouse*, however, is an image that is neither a willed possession nor a personal effect acquired after an unexpected death—an object that cannot be inherited because it is never completed: Mrs. Ramsay's reddish-brown stocking. The stocking appears alongside Mrs. Ramsay at the beginning of the novel, and then again in Lily's memory of Mrs. Ramsay at the end of it.

Readers are introduced to Mrs. Ramsay not only through her reassuring, hopeful words about the trip to the lighthouse, but also through the work that will occupy her throughout the novel's first section: "'But it may be fine—I expect it will be fine,' said Mrs. Ramsay, making some little twist of the reddish-brown stocking she was knitting, impatiently" (4). As the subject of Erich Auerbach's final chapter in *Mimesis,* the reddish-brown stocking has become something of a modernist figure par excellence. Its importance, for Auerbach, turns on the way the stocking's inconsequential appearance triggers an array of unfolding perspectives: it introduces a shift in narrative voice away from Mrs. Ramsay's free indirect discourse and to a more omniscient narrator, a slippage that Auerbach claims as part of modernism's legacy. "The important point," he writes, "is that an insignificant exterior occurrence releases ideas and chains of ideas which cut loose from the present of the exterior occurrence and range freely through the depths of time."[32]

But while this image is central to an explanation of modernist form, the question of its content is a more perplexing matter. For even as Auerbach rightly points out that the continuity of that particular section (the fifth of the novel's first part) "is established through an exterior occurrence involving Mrs. Ramsay and James: the measuring of the stocking,"[33] this emphasis on form cannot account fully for the image's persistence throughout the novel, for its appearance as part of the last memory Lily has of Mrs. Ramsay: "Mrs. Ramsay—it was part of her perfect goodness—sat there quite simply, in the chair, flicked her needles to and fro, knitted her reddish-brown stocking, cast her shadow on the step. There she sat" (202).

In keeping with Auerbach's claim, one might see the stocking's reappearance at the conclusion of the novel as yet another instance of narrative continuity, in which this random image knits together the work's disparate individuals and events. This understanding, however, would still leave open the question of its content. For if the stocking is indeed a random image, and its knitting an accidental, inconsequential occurrence, why is it part of Lily's memory at all? But if it is so important as to persist until the novel's last moments, why does Woolf leave it incomplete—why, ten years after Mrs. Ramsay's death, does Lily still remember her knitting the stocking? In a novel that continually returns to the question of what endures—"Who could tell what would last—in literature or in anything else?" (107), a guest at the Ramsays' dinner party asks—the reddish-brown stocking seems to function as an instance of that thing which does not survive.

Unlike the house with its drawers of ribbons and brushes, its closets full of clothing and shoes, it does not make its way—other than through Lily's memory—into the world after Mrs. Ramsay's death.

But Woolf uses the stocking to make a different, more ambitious claim about traumatic inheritance and carrying on. This claim, moreover, depends upon precisely the *unfinished* nature of the stocking, on the fact that it seems to die with the person who was making it. It cannot, therefore, be inherited—even in the unconventional, unofficial sense that Woolf offers in "Time Passes"—because its work has been interrupted, its progress frozen in time. "She stopped knitting; she held the long reddish-brown stocking dangling in her hands a moment" (3). The dangling stocking, which trails from Mrs. Ramsay's hand even as the novel closes, becomes an unreconciled object, an incomplete act around which Woolf formulates one of the novel's most haunting questions. What, she asks, becomes of this stocking? What, in other words, becomes of the unfinished work of the dead?

In bringing this image to the foreground, however, I do not intend to imply that Woolf meant it to have one particular meaning. Indeed, she refused to assign any concrete meaning even to the novel's central image: "I meant *nothing* by The Lighthouse," Woolf insisted in a letter to Roger Fry in 1927. "I saw that all sorts of feelings would accrue to this, but I refused to think them out, and trusted that people would make it the deposit for their own emotions—which they have done, one thinking it means one thing another another . . . directly I'm told what a thing means it becomes hateful to me."[34] What is crucial in this symbol is its role as a source of human action and agency; it is something to which "all sorts of feelings . . . accrue"—a lightning rod against a charged emotional background. The fact that its meaning changes with every reader suggests that Woolf is not interested in any finite value, but rather in what it means for something to have *sentimental* value. It is in this sense of sentimental value that we can begin to understand how the reddish-brown stocking functions in the novel. Its appearance as an extension of Mrs. Ramsay recalls the lighthouse's extension of the shore and, like the lighthouse, it does not seem to acquire any set meaning. It represents an unanchored image to which "all sorts of feelings would accrue," a figure of relation around which an entire emotional world is built.

Indeed, the brown stocking enters the narrative precisely as the *interruption* of meaning, as the point of rupture in a web of signification. For Woolf, this interruption and the confusion and incomprehension it precipitates enters as a necessary moment in the process of facing a world distorted by death and mourning.

She sets out the conditions of this changed world in "Time Passes," in a passage that suggests something of the brown stocking's and the lighthouse's resistance to meaning. Shortly after reporting Mrs. Ramsay's death in the novel's middle section, along with those of her son Andrew in the war and her daughter Prue in childbirth, Woolf's unmoored narrative voice offers a brief reflection that speaks at once to painting and writing, vision and imagination, symbol and meaning:

> At that season those who had gone down to pace the beach and ask of the sea and sky what message they reported or what vision they affirmed had to consider among the usual tokens of divine bounty—the sunset on the sea, the pallor of dawn, the moon rising, fishing-boats against the moon, and children making mud pies or pelting each other with handfuls of grass, something out of harmony with this jocundity and this serenity. There was the silent apparition of an ashen-coloured ship for instance, come, gone; *there was a purplish stain upon the bland surface of the sea as if something had boiled and bled, invisibly, beneath.* This intrusion into a scene calculated to stir the most sublime reflections and lead to the most comfortable conclusions stayed their pacing. It was difficult to blandly overlook them; to abolish their significance in the landscape; to continue, as one walked by the sea, to marvel how beauty outside mirrored beauty within. (133, emphasis added)

Woolf, however, is not just describing this disturbance of form and meaning but actively creating it—and creating it, I will suggest, specifically in the opaque figure of the reddish-brown stocking. The image is itself part of this disharmony; it is a stain, an intrusion and simultaneously an occasion to register a world whose surface looks unaltered but whose depths give evidence of something—most obviously, a devastating war—gone horribly wrong. This new reality, one marked in the novel by the sudden deaths of Mrs. Ramsay and her children, Andrew and Prue, enters without the solace of conventional wisdom or the comfort of traditional symbols. In this revised context, what can we make of the stocking's persistence? How can we account for the fact that this seemingly inconsequential object becomes one of the most memorable images in *To the Lighthouse*? And what might its haunting reappearance suggest about what the living inherit from the dead?

Unfinished Business

In a narrative that focuses on completing those acts left unfinished—the journey to the lighthouse, Lily's painting—Mrs. Ramsay's reddish-brown stocking becomes a concrete reminder of those things that cannot be completed. It is the only act left unfinished because Mrs. Ramsay dies while it is still in progress—or at least, so the narrative implies. But there is a sense in the novel that perhaps Mrs. Ramsay's knitting, or the spirit in which it was undertaken, is completed symbolically after all, embedded as it is in the journey to the lighthouse and related, in its role as a work of creation or art, to Lily's painting. As the novel opens, we find Mrs. Ramsay knitting in order to include the stocking in a package she intends to send to the lighthouse:

> "But it may be fine—I expect it will be fine," said Mrs. Ramsay, making some little twist of the reddish-brown stocking she was knitting, impatiently. If she finished it tonight, if they did go to the Lighthouse after all, it was to be given to the Lighthouse keeper for his little boy, who was threatened with a tuberculous hip; together with a pile of old magazines, and some tobacco, indeed, whatever she could find lying about, not really wanted, but only littering the room, to give those poor fellows, who must be bored to death sitting all day with nothing to do but polish the lamp and trim the wick and rake about on their scrap of garden, something to amuse them. (4–5)

The completion of the stocking, it turns out, is framed by an uncertain future ("it may be fine") and by anticipation ("I expect it will be fine"). This expectation, ungrounded in any verifiable fact, explains Mrs. Ramsay's impatience, as well as her tentative assurance to James, motivated not by certainty but rather by the wish to see her son's hopes realized, the protective desire to preserve his pure excitement about the trip. The task of making the stocking, moreover, is set in a series of conditionals—"*if* she finished it tonight, *if* they did go to the Lighthouse after all"—that confound the relationship between cause and effect: if the trip does not take place, then the stocking would not be given to the lighthouse keeper's boy. Similarly, if she does not finish her work, it would not be given either. By qualifying both acts as conditional and contingent, Woolf seems to suggest that Mrs. Ramsay's mind has conflated them. Certainly there is a sense that the two events, both factors in whether the lighthouse keeper's son will receive his gift, have become somehow—impossibly—causally connected for her: if she continues to knit, the trip might occur after all, in spite of the grim weather forecast. But her intention, of course, is more psychological than meteorological: if she does not stop knitting, she might protect her son's hopes for the trip. The longer she works, the longer James can look forward to the excursion. Yet even if Mrs. Ramsay may only be keeping up appearances for her son's sake, her husband sees her refusal to stop knitting as unreasonable, even dishonest. And so when he tells his wife, "You won't finish that stocking tonight" (122) and she accedes, "No,

I shan't finish it" (123) it seems as though she has finally come around to his view of things and relinquished her illusion that the trip will happen.

Ultimately, however, her hope is not so far-fetched: ten years after her death, Mr. Ramsay finds himself making the trip after all, even as he tells Lily, "Such expeditions . . . are very painful" (151–52). The trip's intention is rather unclear: no one seems to know what to take to the lighthouse, and James, no longer a young boy, has lost his childish enthusiasm for the outing. If the trip has any purpose, its unstated aim seems bound to Mrs. Ramsay—to what she used to send to the lighthouse, and by extension, what she did not send. Mr. Ramsay thus tells Lily, "he had a particular reason for wanting to go to the lighthouse. His wife used to send the men things. There was a poor boy with a tuberculous hip, the lightkeeper's son" (151). Mr. Ramsay's need to reach the lighthouse, however haltingly articulated, recalls his wife's gestures, her acts of compassion. For what he remembers is not simply those things she used to send to the lighthouse, but the spirit of sympathy in which they were proffered. The philosophically minded man, who writes books on "subject and object and the nature of reality," turns his thoughts from subjects and objects to consider the condition of people, of the lighthouse keeper's ailing boy and of the men who live in the lighthouse's less-than-ideal conditions. Mr. Ramsay's act thus reprises something of his wife's sympathetic imagination, of the questions meant to think herself into the position of the men across the water: "For how would you like to be shut up for a whole month at a time, and possibly more in stormy weather, upon a rock the size of a tennis lawn?" (5).

Lily, too, takes up something of Mrs. Ramsay's project in finishing the painting she began a decade before. But although both women are engaged in creative work, the connections between their efforts seem to end there. Mrs. Ramsay's creation, after all, is practical and homely; it demands no artistic deliberation on her part, but rather seems to be something she does almost instinctively, while talking to someone or thinking of something else. But Mrs. Ramsay's and Lily's projects are intimately related in one crucial way: both are contingent on the presence, literal or imagined, of another. For Mrs. Ramsay, this presence is her young son's, whose body she needs to measure the stocking. For Lily, the necessary presence is Mrs. Ramsay: she cannot complete her picture without imagining her at the scene of painting. "It must have altered the design a good deal when she was sitting on the step with James. There must have been a shadow" (160), Lily muses. Reconstructing her surroundings to recreate the original conditions of her painting, Lily remembers Mrs. Ramsay as a necessary condition of her own work: "When she thought of herself and Charles throwing ducks and drakes and of the whole scene on the beach, it seemed to depend somehow upon Mrs. Ramsay sitting under the rock, with a pad on her knee, writing letters" (160). In requiring the presence of another, the painting and the stocking reject the world of artistic isolation, investing their creations with an element of collaboration that resists the conditions of a "pure" work of art, one born of a solitary, remarkable mind working beyond the reaches of outside influences. The tasks that occupy Lily and Mrs. Ramsay resist this retreat from the world, refusing to relinquish the connection to an ordinary, shared existence.

But even as the two final acts in *To the Lighthouse*—the completed journey and the finished painting—extend and symbolically complete Mrs. Ramsay's unfinished stocking, the novel's conclusion suggests that this completion is not a product of two independent, unrelated acts. For Woolf intimates, in these final moments, that the events on shore and at sea are interdependent; one could not occur without the other. I would suggest, moreover, that these acts complete Mrs. Ramsay's work not only because they occur simultaneously—after all, two events could take place across vast distances, with those involved knowing nothing of each others' existence. What brings these events together, rather, is a powerful *recognition* of each other: of the boat from Lily's perspective and the shore as seen by Mr. Ramsay, James, and Cam. The connection between them, moreover, emerges not through a flight of the mind—this is no longer Mr. Ramsay's philosophy of imagining "a kitchen table . . . when you're not there"—but through a literal act of seeing. Prompted by her "instinctive need of distance and blue" (182), Lily looks up from her painting at the water, only to find her vision compromised: "again she was roused as usual by something incongruous. There was a brown spot in the middle of the bay. It was a boat. Yes, she realised that after a second. But whose boat? Mr. Ramsay's boat, she replied" (182).

This brown spot, I would suggest, is Woolf's gesture toward the brown stocking; as the stain or residue of this image, it is integrated into the simultaneous acts that end the novel. In a brief flash of color, the brownness of this lost object intervenes to link Mr. Ramsay and his children in the boat to Lily on the shore. Significantly, moreover, the vision does not appear with sudden clarity but is experienced first as an intrusion, blighting the sea's sparkling expanse and confounding Lily's ability to see. In this moment of not seeing clearly, when Lily refocuses her vision to identify Mr. Ramsay's boat, we begin to understand the brown stocking's function as a figure of *relation* rather than a symbol or meta-phor. For Lily's vision suggests that there is something about this brownness that cannot be looked through, something that resists the possibility of metaphor.

The account of ruptured meaning in "Time Passes," which called attention to "a purplish stain upon the bland surface of the sea as if something had boiled and bled, invisibly, beneath," thus becomes not only an admonition or description but also a prediction. It anticipates this very moment, in which a spot of color inter-rupts the expectations of a vision that has never failed to reassure or to satisfy. "This intrusion into a scene calculated to stir the most sublime reflections and lead to the most comfortable conclusions stayed their pacing. It was difficult to blandly overlook them; to abolish their significance in the landscape; to continue, as one walked by the sea, to marvel how beauty outside mirrored beauty within" (133). It is in this moment of stopping short, furthermore, that the brown spot—by extension, the brown stocking—becomes not an object but a thing, a distinc-tion that Bill Brown suggests marks a transition from interpretation to relation:

> We look through objects because there are codes by which our interpretive atten-tion makes them meaningful, because there is a discourse of objectivity that allows us to use them as facts. A *thing*, by contrast, can hardly function as a window. We begin to confront the thingness of objects when they stop working for us: when the drill breaks, when the car stalls, when the windows get filthy, when their flow within the circuits of production and distribution, consumption and exhibition, has been arrested, however momentarily. The story of objects asserting themselves as things, then, is the story of a changed relation to the human subject and thus the story of how the thing really names less an object than a particular subject-object relation.[35]

It is significant, moreover, that this thing intrudes upon Lily's vision not as a flash of brilliance or a dazzling hue but as a drab brown. For if the brown stock-ing haunts the narrative, it does so precisely in its plainness, in a way that recalls how the most unremarkable personal effects become the source of traumatic in-heritance, rendering those who receive them mute or powerless.

The brown spot that calls Lily's attention to the boat, figuratively uniting the respective efforts of Mr. Ramsay and Lily to complete the novel's unfinished business, suggests that these acts, taken together, symbolically finish the work of knitting the stocking that Mrs. Ramsay had left unfinished at the time of her death. But it has not only been knit; it has also, in this process of symbolic com-pletion, been claimed and by extension, inherited. Mingling their efforts with

Mrs. Ramsay's, Lily and Mr. Ramsay undertake the kind of work that Locke, in his labor theory of property, saw as the claim to ownership: "Whatsoever, then, he removes out of the state that nature hath provided and left it in, he hath mixed his labour with, and joined to it something that is his own, and thereby makes it his property."[36] As if answering Locke aesthetically, inflecting his concept of property with impressionism or even surrealism, Woolf fixes on that quality of the stocking, the brownness she has insisted on throughout the novel, removes it from one state—Mrs. Ramsay's hands—and mixes it with Mr. Ramsay's and Lily's endeavors. The brown spot on the water does not just recall the brown stocking in the manner of a memory prompt; it actively possesses it, laying claim to it in a way that is symbolic, but also distinctly material and visual. Mrs. Ramsay's stocking, it turns out, has been knitted after all.

Still Life

Yet the process of carrying on Mrs. Ramsay's project, of symbolically completing what she began by integrating—and thus inheriting—something of her work in progress, cannot fully account for the stocking's persistence. For even as the novel's final acts symbolically complete Mrs. Ramsay's efforts, the stocking itself will remain literally unfinished. But it is precisely in its incompleteness, I submit, that it becomes a figure for a complex relationship to history, and particularly to the history of a sudden, unexpected death. As an object frozen in the past, one that consistently reappears not as a finished product but as an unending process, the stocking becomes a figure for one of the primary tensions in *To the Lighthouse*. This tension, I will argue, is also at work in the emotional connection to property, a connection rooted in the wish that life stand still, and in the knowledge that this wish can never be granted: a tension, in effect, between remembering and carrying on. *To the Lighthouse* is permeated by moments of stillness, a notion which proves so central that its pursuit becomes Mrs. Ramsay's most enduring quality in Lily's mind:

> Mrs. Ramsay saying "Life stand still here"; Mrs. Ramsay making of the moment something permanent . . .—this was the nature of revelation. In the midst of chaos there was shape; this eternal passing and flowing (she looked at the clouds going and the leaves shaking) was struck into stability. Life stand still here, Mrs. Ramsay said. "Mrs. Ramsay! Mrs. Ramsay!" she repeated. She owed it all to her. (161)

How are we to understand the nature of this stillness? What does Mrs. Ramsay's wish suggest about memory and the ordinary world? I would like to consider these questions by turning to the novel's complex depiction of stillness, which emerges first as a literal, bodily habit, but moves beyond it to address how the past becomes a concrete part of the present.

The stillness in *To the Lighthouse* is not initially associated with memory but with the creation of a work of art. As the novel opens, Mrs. Ramsay appears only to be knitting; we soon learn, however, that she is in fact posing for a painting: "she was supposed to be keeping her head as much in the same position as possible for Lily's picture" (17). This position is reenacted later when Mrs. Ramsay demands the same thing of James, this time in relation to her own work:

> "And now . . . and now stand up and let me measure your leg," for they might go to the Lighthouse after all, and she must see if the stocking did not need to be an inch or two longer in the leg.
>
> Smiling, for it was an admirable idea, that had flashed upon her this very second— William and Lily should marry—she took the heather-mixture stocking with its crisscross of steel needles at the mouth of it, and measured it against James's leg.
>
> "My dear, stand still," she said, for in his jealousy, not liking to serve as measuring block for the Lighthouse keeper's little boy, James fidgeted purposely; and if he did that, how could she see, was it too long, was it too short? she asked. (26)

Arising from this scene of measuring is perhaps one of the most surprising and complicated sequences of *To the Lighthouse,* so striking that it inspires Auerbach's meditation on Woolf's craft in *Mimesis.* What begins as a banal moment—Mrs. Ramsay's pronouncement that the stocking is "ever much too short"—precipitates an unexpected onset of melancholia.[37] "Never did anybody look so sad," an omniscient narrative voice interjects: "Bitter and black, half-way down, in the darkness, in the shaft which ran from the sunlight to the depths, perhaps a tear formed; a tear fell; the waters swayed this way and that, received it, and were at rest. Never did anybody look so sad" (28).

For Auerbach, the technique of using a "random occurrence" to break open "the wealth of reality and depth of life to which we surrender ourselves without prejudice"[38] is resolutely modern, laying bare the common elements of human experience. This move, however, is not quite as random as Woolf (or Auerbach) would have us believe. The measuring of the stocking is, to be sure, a subtle act rather than a sweeping gesture, but it is also bound intimately to the task at hand.

For Mrs. Ramsay's instruction to James—"My dear, stand still"—enacts literally her deeper, impossible wish that her children retain their innocence, that their childish purity might never be tarnished. It is only natural that this wish emerges from a typical childhood scene, in which Mrs. Ramsay reads a story to James:

> Oh, but she never wanted James to grow a day older! or Cam either. These two she would have liked to keep for ever just as they were, demons of wickedness, angels of delight, never to see them grow up into long-legged monsters. Nothing made up for the loss. When she read just now to James, "and there were numbers of soldiers with kettledrums and trumpets," and his eyes darkened, she thought, why should they grow up and lose all that? (58)

Mrs. Ramsay's desire is already undone, however, by her knowledge that she wants the unattainable: a permanence that life simply will not afford. Even as she notes this futile wish, Woolf already speaks to its impossibility through the story's military allusion. Less than a decade after World War I, the content of the book Mrs. Ramsay reads to James evokes one of the very experiences that would deprive the boy of this innocence: the experience of a war that Mrs. Ramsay will never know, but whose shadow Woolf's readers would have sensed. "When she read just now to James, 'and there were numbers of soldiers with kettledrums and trumpets,' and his eyes darkened, she thought, why should they grow up and lose all that?" Woolf's choice is a portentous reminder that this scene would be repeated with tragic force in the years following Mrs. Ramsay's death. One would hear stories of soldiers that were no longer fictional, though they may well be just as unbelievable. The reality of the war, and Andrew Ramsay's death in it, would become the very loss of innocence that Mrs. Ramsay so longs to keep from her children. James's darkening eyes, which compose the youthful picture of a child consumed by nothing save the pretend military drama in a book, would be replaced by eyes that darken at a fate far worse than any faced by the storybook characters, if only because it is real.

Yet even as Woolf casts this shadow over Mrs. Ramsay's wish that her children never grow up, *To the Lighthouse* nonetheless suggests that there is something productive or attainable about this wish—that the desire to preserve a moment in time is more than the product of a mother's protectiveness. For these moments of stillness offer a way to preserve the past by opening up a possibility for reflection—and ultimately, for judgment. We find this moment of judgment at the Ramsays' dinner party in the novel's first part, "The Window," in a scene that gathers all of the characters together for the first and last time. As Mrs. Ramsay leaves the room and casts a backward glance at her guests, the question of what remains—"who could tell what was going to last—in literature or indeed in anything else?"—seems to press upon her with particular urgency:

> Where, Lily wondered, was she going so quickly?
>
> Not that she did in fact run or hurry; she went indeed rather slowly. She felt rather inclined just for a moment *to stand still* after all that chatter and pick out one particular thing: the thing that mattered; to detach it; separate it off; clean it of all the emotions and odds and ends of things and so hold it before her, and bring it to the tribunal where, ranged about in conclave, sat the judges she had set up to decide these things. Is it good, is it bad, is it right or wrong? Where are we all going to? and so on. (112, emphasis added)

Those things that endure, Mrs. Ramsay seems to suggest, are not simply accidents, residues left behind by chance. Rather, one *makes* these experiences last, committing them to memory by actively distinguishing, selecting, and transferring them to the future through an act of will—and, as Mrs. Ramsay's final reflection suggests, through a moment of judgment.[39]

This judgment, however, is suspended, left dangling—like the stocking itself—as an open-ended series of questions: "Is it good, is it bad, is it right or wrong? Where are we all going to? and so on." The urgency of these questions, together with their open-endedness, suggests that Mrs. Ramsay herself already senses how little control she will have over the answers—how, as Lily will reflect after Mrs. Ramsey's death, the dead "are at our mercy" (174). The unpredictability of what endures recalls those unexpected things left behind in the abandoned house, the painful acquisition of the soldier's kit—all of which insert themselves into the present in ways that confound Mrs. Ramsay's sense of what lasts: no one, after all, would have expected to find *these* things. And yet their existence—and their endurance—resists the careful self-consciousness with which Mrs. Ramsay selects her moment and brings it before the jury.

The stillness necessary for this privileged moment is troubling in yet another way, one that speaks to the impulse to set art apart from life, to preserve it in museums or galleries. This stillness, Woolf's novel implies, can be looked upon, but not lived with. It is in this sense that the Ramsays' empty, abandoned house in "Time Passes" is described in terms of its "loveliness" and "stillness"—qualities that together create a deadening effect:

> So loveliness reigned and stillness, and together made the shape of loveliness itself, a
> form from which life had parted; solitary like a pool at evening, far distant, seen from
> a train window, vanishing so quickly that the pool, pale in the evening, is scarcely
> robbed of its solitude, though once seen. (129)

Like the detached voice that narrates the passage, very little is human in either
loveliness or stillness, which together take on the shape of death, "a form from
which life had parted." The stillness so precious and memorable to Mrs. Ramsay
here corrupts the possibility of memory, making it impossible to grasp a moment as anything other than a frozen snapshot; nothing kinetic, nothing life-
like, remains. This lovely stillness creates, at most, a fleeting impression: one can
glimpse it from afar, in a rush that suggests the unrelenting passage of time, but
the impression quickly vanishes from consciousness. A still life has no permanence; its appearance affords a flicker of aesthetic pleasure but little more. These
moments ultimately become the "kitchen table when you're not there"—that
thing left behind to decay, a form without human contact or relation; a form, in
effect, without function.[40]

This is precisely why those moments of stillness—Mrs. Ramsay's "life stand
still here"—cannot survive without an additional, excessive, disturbing element,
one that shatters the lovely but stagnant "solitary pool." In breaking through this
stillness, the unexpected form creates a less beautiful but more memorable image. Thus Lily and William Bankes, remembering Mrs. Ramsay toward the end
of the novel, picture not her beauty but those moments that disturbed it:

> She was astonishingly beautiful, as William said. But beauty was not everything.
> Beauty had this penalty—it came too readily, came too completely. *It stilled life—froze
> it.* One forgot the little agitations; the flush, the pallor, some queer distortion, some
> light or shadow, which made the face unrecognizable for a moment and yet added a
> quality one saw for ever after. It was simpler to smooth that all out under the cover of
> beauty. (177, emphasis added)

The "queer distortion" in Mrs. Ramsay's beauty is bound to her perpetual connection to the crudely knit, homely brown stocking. Like the brown spot that
mars Lily's view of the sea, the stocking intrudes as that "little agitation" in what
otherwise might have been a flawless picture of a striking woman. It thus works
like Roland Barthes's *punctum* in *Camera Lucida,* which he describes as the element in a photograph that is not actively sought but which "rises from the scene,
shoots out of it like an arrow, and pierces me." It is not the intended result of

artistic composition but rather "that accident which pricks me (but also bruises me, is poignant to me)."[41]

Barthes's bruise, and the poignancy that follows from it, suggests why the things left behind in *To the Lighthouse* are precisely those unlovely things—old shoes, combs, personal effects—that seem to have no value at all, least of all artistic or aesthetic value. The reddish-brown stocking complicates this "worthless" economy further still, becoming in the process the novel's most enduring image, a companion piece to the lighthouse itself. Its unremarkable simplicity is made even less remarkable by the fact that it remains unfinished, that Mrs. Ramsay will always be knitting it in the memories of those who outlive her. And yet these very conditions make it possible to occupy a position that is at once dynamic and still: Mrs. Ramsay's work is a still life in its incompleteness, but is also remembered as a project that is still—perpetually—in progress. And it is through this progress, I would argue, that the stocking extends across time, compelling those who encounter its likeness to complete or extend it symbolically, without acquiring it literally.[42]

The novel's struggle with the idea of stillness—"is it good, is it bad, is it right or wrong?"—speaks to the tension between the desires both to remember and to carry on, evoking a process rather than a concrete meaning. And it is thus that it figures our expectations of property: the expectations that through property, one can preserve and pass along an enduring, pristine piece of the past and give that past a reassuring continuity. Seen in this light, the brown stocking is not just a signal of narrative continuity as Auerbach saw it; it imparts, too, an *emotional* continuity, not unlike the kind Bentham found in the interdependence of property and expectation. But in its incompleteness, it also punctures this continuity, resisting the very prospect of "life standing still" that it dangles before us.

Object Relations

If the reddish-brown stocking is not a piece of inherited property but rather a figure for the process of traumatic inheritance, what does it say about this process? What, in other words, does this kind of inheritance do to its heirs? I would like to approach these questions by looking at what becomes of the stocking after Mrs. Ramsay's death and to consider how its residue transforms the relationships of those who outlive her. We find this persistence most vividly at the end of the novel, when Mr. Ramsay reaches the lighthouse at the very moment Lily completes her painting. As she looks up and sees the brown spot on the bay, its opaqueness gives rise to a *moment of recognition,* suggesting that the novel's climactic ending is not merely the result of simultaneity, of two unfinished acts being completed at once. Instead, what matters is the mutual recognition of the actors, which issues from the stocking's residual, aesthetic afterlife and positions it as an object of relation.

Its position as a relational object, however, extends something of the place it occupied even while Mrs. Ramsay was alive, in a moment that occurs just after the dinner party in the first section. The scene finds Mr. and Mrs. Ramsay sitting silently in a room, she knitting and he reading. Their silence, however, is strained by each one's desire to hear the other speak: Mrs. Ramsay wants her husband "to say something . . . Anything" (122) while Mr. Ramsay "wanted the thing she always found it so difficult to give him; wanted her to tell him that she loved him. And that, no, she could not do" (123). When he finally breaks the silence, Mr. Ramsay speaks not to his desires but to the trivial fact of his wife's knitting. "You won't finish that stocking tonight," he tells her—and she, at last, capitulates. "'No,' she said, flattening the stocking out upon her knee, 'I shan't finish it.'" And then, as though giving in to an impulse she has been staving off throughout "The Window," Mrs. Ramsay offers a mundane substitute for the words her husband wants to hear: "'Yes, you were right. It's going to be wet tomorrow. You won't be able to go.' And she looked at him smiling. For she had triumphed again. She had not said it: yet he knew" (124).

This moment of resolution, Hermione Lee suggests, becomes a climax of the novel in that "both minds are simultaneously revealed to each other in silence" through the narrative's "lyrical fluidity."[43] Yet in taking shape through silence and lyricism, the exchange also draws our attention to the image through which this language must pass: their thoughts are "revealed to each other *in* silence," but they also pass *through* the brown stocking, are mediated and translated by it. In thus casting the stocking as an object of relation, Woolf draws together not only visions—as when Lily sees the brown spot on the ocean—but also voices. And in doing so, she posits this object as the thing that not only compels people to recognize each other, but also makes it possible for them to speak to each other in a way that reinforces and deepens their bond.

This resolution is extended in transmuted form to another encounter toward the end of the novel, one that forges a surprising connection between Lily and Mr. Ramsay. The encounter is surprising not only because both were, until then, unable to relate to each other in any meaningful way; it surprises, too, because of the banal object through which their reconciliation emerges. Both have returned to the Ramsay home to find themselves in respective states of alienation: Lily retreats into her painting and Mr. Ramsay into his self-pity. As he prepares to set off for the lighthouse, however, Mr. Ramsay approaches Lily in an attempt to elicit her sympathy—a sympathy that, echoing Mrs. Ramsay's earlier impassiveness, she cannot give him. As they face each other across what appears to be an unbridgeable silence, Lily turns her attention to the unlikeliest of objects—an extension of or metonym for the brown stocking:

> "What beautiful boots!" she exclaimed. She was ashamed of herself. To praise his boots when he asked her to solace his soul; when he had shown her his bleeding hands, his lacerated heart, and asked her to pity them, then to say, cheerfully, 'Ah, but what beautiful boots you wear!' deserved, she knew, and she looked up expecting to get it, in one of his sudden roars of ill-temper, complete annihilation. (153)

But Mr. Ramsay surprises her: instead of disparaging her triviality, he seems to delight in it. "Mr. Ramsay smiled. His pall, his draperies, his infirmities fell from him. Ah, yes, he said, holding his foot up for her to look at, they were first-rate boots. There was only one man in England who could make boots like that. Boots are among the chief curses of mankind, he said" (153). Rather than deflecting a connection to the man who has always been something of her emotional adversary, Lily feels overcome with emotion, warming to him in a way that she cannot fully comprehend. "Why, at this completely inappropriate moment, when he was stooping over her shoe, should she be so tormented with sympathy for him that, as she stooped too, the blood rushed to her face, and, thinking of her callousness . . . she felt her eyes swell and tingle with tears?" (154).

Why, indeed, does such an inconsequential object become the point of convergence for these seemingly irreconcilable personalities, for the artist's inchoate sensibility and the philosopher's uncompromising severity? The answer, I believe, has to do with the powerful—and practical—hold of ordinary objects in Woolf's novels, from the perplexing appearance of the shoes at the end of *Jacob's Room* to the clutter of belongings left behind in the Ramsay home, to the brown stocking that becomes the brown spot in Lily's vision and the boot on Mr. Ramsay's foot. In her unrelenting return to these things, Woolf attempts an act of recuperation: the restoration of value to an ordinary world, a world set aside by the lofty concerns of philosophers and overlooked by official acts of law and inheritance. In reclaiming the potential of these banal things, Woolf casts them as forceful objects of relation, igniting for Lily "that sudden flare (when she praised his boots), that sudden recovery of vitality and interest in ordinary human things, which too passed and changed into that other final phase which was new to her" (156).

Ironically, it is precisely as mediating figures that these "ordinary human things" make possible a more direct, less diluted emotional experience. "One wanted, [Lily] thought, dipping her brush deliberately, to be on a level with ordinary experience, to feel simply that's a chair, that's a table, and yet at the same time, It's a miracle, it's an ecstasy" (202). What Lily yearns for is an ordinary world that distills relationships into their purest form, creating the most direct connections rather than unmoored speculations on "subject and object and the nature of reality." "One wanted . . . to feel simply"—to find emotional intensity and clarity without conceptual clutter, to harness the ordinary world and allow it to shape the social world in a way that produces feeling rather than thought. And this is why the most ordinary memory Lily has of Mrs. Ramsay is the one that brings forth the flood of emotion that had eluded her, overwhelming her in a powerful wave of longing, sorrow, and nostalgia: "to want and want and not to have" (202). As if in response to this feeling—the novel's most intense emotional moment—Lily sees Mrs. Ramsay's image in its most ordinary guise: "Mrs. Ramsay—it was part of her perfect goodness—sat there *quite simply,* in the chair, flicked her needles to and fro, knitted her reddish-brown stocking, cast her shadow on the step. There she sat" (202, emphasis added). This moment, in which Mrs. Ramsay's simple image seems both to answer and precipitate Lily's emotional outpouring, is bound, not surprisingly, to the brown stocking. As the novel's ordinary object of relation, it makes possible not only relations among the living but also the most potent instances of connection between the living and the dead.

These relational experiences, characterized by their fundamental simplicity, ultimately recast what is typically read as Woolf's privileged moment of revelation as a moment of *relation*. It is in this sense that we can understand how Lily is able, after ten years, to complete her painting. For it turns out that the work of art itself is born not from an instance of revelation or epiphany, which we might reasonably expect given the novel's famous last line, "Yes, I have had my vision." Instead, Lily's painting emerges from the tangle of lines and shapes that, in spite of their visual confusion, all relate to each other:

> There was something . . . something she remembered in the relations of those lines cutting across, slicing down, and in the mass of the hedge with its green cave of blues and browns, which had stayed in her mind, which had tied a knot in her mind so that

at odds and ends of time, involuntarily, as she walked along the Brompton Road, as she brushed her hair, she found herself painting that picture, passing her eye over it, and untying the knot in imagination. (157)

It is in untying this knot—or tying it differently—that one attains a productive stillness: A moment of suspension that calls for active engagement, attention and thoughtfulness. "Now let me see if you can tie a knot" (154), Mr. Ramsay instructs Lily as they contemplate his shoe. These knots, I would suggest, become instances of the reddish-brown stocking by joining together perspectives, brush strokes, and emotions, forcing those who create or undo them to stand still and, in this brief stillness, to recognize the existence and experience of the other. And as the stocking and, by extension, Mr. Ramsay's boot both suggest, they also shatter a silence, break a kind of paralysis—the paralysis that arises in the face of those unexpected things one inherits by chance or accident, the silence precipitated by traumatic inheritance.

It may come as no surprise that many legal scholars see property not as the relationship between people and objects, but rather as the relationships among people with respect to an object. "We must recognize," one scholar notes, "that a property right is a relation not between an owner and a thing, but between the owner and other individuals in reference to things."[44] *To the Lighthouse* contains something of this relationship, but conceptualizes it well beyond the bounds of property rights, of "real" property that can be written into a will or even transferred without a will. The reddish-brown stocking's persistence suggests that those things that can never be inherited—the unfinished work of the dead—speak to this idea of mediation most of all. These incomplete acts not only underscore existing relationships, as a piece of property might do. As works in progress, they also call upon the living to relate to each other in new ways, to inherit something of the sensibility behind these incomplete acts, and to inherit this sensibility continually in different, dynamic ways.

"We perished each alone," Mr. Ramsay recites throughout the novel's last section, repeating it with an almost religious, incantational gravity. Yet in spite of this aloneness, *To the Lighthouse* suggests, we are bound to each other in things— in those things that people leave behind for each other, objects that demand attention and care precisely because it is not immediately clear what should be done with them. They may be ordinary, valueless, inconveniently located, decaying, unfinished. But Woolf suggests that it is through no premeditated act of will, but rather by way of intrusions and compromised visions, that the present pays its unofficial, but inherited, debt to the past.

Focused as they are on a writer who pays no notice to the judicial process, the preceding chapters have raised the issue of legal modernism by deliberately turning away from a thematic treatment of law. In doing so, they resist making a causal argument: to propose that literary modernism plumbs the depths of law's affective life is not to suggest that Woolf's fiction changed the law any more than it implies that novels should be agents of legal change. The claim, rather, is one of necessity rather than causality: modernist experimentation did not shape legal concepts or procedures that would develop in later decades, like the legal categories that guided the Nuremberg and Eichmann trials. But literary modernism, I submit, necessarily preceded these changes in law. Literature *had* to change before law did—simply because it could. That no international criminal trial took place after World War I should not surprise us. In addition to the vastly different nature of Nazi crimes from anything that transpired during World War I, language was still too static and the juridical imagination too restrained to bring about radical legal innovation.[45] When this legal innovation did occur, moreover, it was not enough to capture the international imagination of its own accord: the unprecedented trials of the post-Holocaust era could not be engaged exclusively as courtroom spectacles. As the following chapters will show, writers like Rebecca West and Hannah Arendt did more than present the public with the legal stakes of the trials they covered. They translated those trials from courtroom events back into literary language—and in making them literary, created a cultural experience of law rather than just a knowledge of legal procedure. The shaping of this experience would bring legal modernism into the later decades of the twentieth century.

PART II

Law's Modern Literariness

CHAPTER FOUR

Committed to Memory

Rebecca West's Nuremberg

For the law, like art, is always vainly racing to catch up with experience.
—Rebecca West, The Meaning of Treason[1]

The banality of evil is arguable, the banality of boredom is manifest.
—Patricia Meyer Spacks, *Boredom*[2]

To imagine law's encounter with the trauma of war is to tell a story of expectations—particularly, the expectation that law will make sense of catastrophe, generating an understanding of its vicissitudes and a judgment of its horrors. But this *story* of expectations suggests, too, the demands we bring to law: the story of our desire for a captivating encounter, one that makes sense because it brings us to the edge of our courtroom seats or at the very least, satisfies our desire for plot. Yet the experience of law is often quite another matter. Frequently, law's attempt to cope with historical disaster yields anything but an exciting narrative. Often, it is simply dull. What does one do when the story of law falls short of expectations—or worse, leaves us bored stiff?

The unprecedented experience of the Nuremberg Trial posed this question in monumental fashion, and it is from the perspective of this legal event that I propose to answer it. If World War I was experienced as an unprecedented military trauma, World War II extended this trauma into the juridical realm. With the establishment of the Nuremberg Laws in 1935, Nazi Germany created a legal basis for what has been called an "administrative massacre"[3]: a legal system that would pave the way for the horrors of the Final Solution. After the war, the Nuremberg War Crimes Tribunal[4] sought to reassert a world where law could once more align itself with justice.[5] From November 1945 until October 1946 in

Nuremberg's restored Palace of Justice, twenty-two defendants, all high-ranking Nazi officials representing a range of organizations—among them the SS, the Gestapo, the Reichsbank, and the German Armed Forces High Command—were prosecuted for committing Crimes Against Humanity. The Nuremberg Trial's 403 open sessions were conducted in four languages and presided over by eight judges: a high-stakes international affair of immense proportions.

While the lawyers and judges labored to make legal sense of the past and to leave a record for the future, the 250 journalists assembled in the Palace of Justice worked to convey this unprecedented legal event to the outside world. Trials, journalist Laurel Leff reminds us, hold a particular appeal for journalists, in that they contain "a satisfying narrative arc: they open, they close, with moments of drama (and tedium) in between. Most important, they give resolution in the form of a verdict. The Nuremberg trials had the additional allure of offering an explanation for the cataclysm the world had just endured."[6]

However, not all journalists relished the easily digestible format of the Nuremberg Trial's narrative arc. As a writer with no legal training, Rebecca West's reports from Nuremberg for *The Daily Telegraph* proved some of the most memorable and surprising—and it is in both senses that I would like to explore them as conveying an experience, rather than an explication, of law.[7] These essays are, I believe, instances of legal writing that transform the trial from the unlikeliest of vantage points, offering a sense of what it felt like to bear witness to a moment of historic justice. Despite their innovativeness, they have been almost entirely overlooked by critics, who instead focus on West's epic, genre-defying work *Black Lamb and Grey Falcon* (1941).[8] I propose to restore to these pieces their remarkable potency, and in doing so to explore the ways in which they shed light on Nuremberg in particular and on the relationship between law and culture in general. Engaging Nuremberg as an event that needs to be *experienced* rather than simply reported (or recorded), West suggests that it is the specific responsibility of the writer to take seriously the task of creating a legal event worth remembering.

Born in 1892, West lived through both world wars and wrote about each of them in a range of genres. In *The Return of the Soldier,* her first novel, West confronted World War I through a fictional world; by the end of World War II, however, she would no longer imagine this world in fiction, but would witness it as a spectator and correspondent for *The Daily Telegraph* at the Nuremberg Trial.

I want to think about the divergence of these approaches to war and history not merely as generic differences, but in terms of West's evolving sense of responsibility to history—a transformation that we find in her interwar prose, and one that dramatically alters her approach to remembering and recording the past.[9]

In *The Return of the Soldier* (1918), West embeds the experience of shell shock in a familiar romantic plot: the story of a man torn between two women. The novel centers on Chris Baldry, a soldier who returns from the front to a world he no longer recognizes. He cannot remember his wife, Kitty, and has forgotten everything about the life he led at the lush Baldry Court before the war, a place that now strikes him as sterile and foreign. Instead of this past, Chris's memory retreats fifteen years to the brief but intense love affair he had at age twenty with a woman named Margaret, who has since married and now lives with her husband in a nearby working-class town. When his wife Kitty and his cousin Jenny, the story's narrator, meet Margaret, they find themselves in the presence of a drab, lower-class woman whose homeliness makes it hard to imagine that she ever ignited passion in a man as worldly as Chris. The question of whether Chris will eventually recognize his present life, which he ultimately does, provides West with a suspenseful and modern narrative twist on the traditional love triangle.

But if World War I set the tone for the dramatic trajectory of West's first novel, her writing after World War II was decidedly less riveting: instead of finding drama in Nuremberg—or creating it herself in her dispatches—she insisted on telling the story of its incredible dullness. The trial felt like "water torture, boredom falling drop by drop on the same spot of the soul,"[10] and no amount of literary ambition could prevail upon West to recount it differently, according it gripping proportions to spark her readers' interest. Given the high stakes of the trial, it may have been wiser to sidestep this boredom and to focus instead, as most newspaper articles did, on Nuremberg's sporadic moments of courtroom drama. Instead, West chose to convey the atmosphere of the court in all of its unbearable dullness. Why does she deliberately flatten an event of such magnitude? What compelled West to write about World War I in a dramatic, fictional narrative but to record the trial of the Nazi criminals—presumably no less dramatic—with unparalleled matter-of-factness?

I would like to suggest an answer to these questions by examining West's sense of history and memory in her reports on Nuremberg, which effectively established her as a legal journalist. Despite having no formal training in law, she became the most renowned legal correspondent of her day after Nuremberg, covering trials at home and abroad. Yet she was ambivalent, even somewhat resentful, of this role. In an untitled and incomplete autobiographical sketch, written presumably toward the end of her life—she died in 1983 at age ninety—West looked back at her work as a legal reporter with a generous measure of irony:

> After the war I went out and looked at the world for the New Yorker. I did this because I realised that the world had wholly changed—and I still think it is under-reported. The first thing I did was the trial of William Joyce [who was tried and convicted for treason during World War II], and then I went to the Nuremberg trials. Unfortunately I did a number of trials connected with treachery . . . because they threw light on why people become totalitarians, and the result was that ever since every body has tried to make me go and report trials. When a serious crime has committed [sic] people telephone for the police and the doctor and then the newspaper syndicates get on to me. This is unfortunate because there is nothing I loathe like trials and law-courts. I sit and weep in court, which looks mad, and get a headache—and I have such contempt for people who go to trials for fun that I hate to be present when they are. The misery behind any trial is so great that one would have to be a monster not to be appalled.
>
> Now I have settled down to writing great long novels and I intend to do nothing else until I die, whenever that may be.[11]

West's description of her own apparent madness during a trial, "I sit and weep in court," seems startling from a writer who, by sheer virtue of her frequent exposure to courtrooms, should have been accustomed to her share of legal drama. Yet her disavowal of law and her desire to return to literature suggest a complicated emotional relationship to public justice, one that differs sharply from the sensational swell of collective emotion that ordinarily accompanies a high-profile trial. What can we make of West's determination to leave the courtroom? What does her loathing of the law tell us about her experience of it? How can West's account of, and ambivalence about, law shed light on the expectations one brings to public manifestations of justice?

The Banality of Judgment

Rebecca West's *Daily Telegraph* pieces on the Nuremberg Trial and postwar Germany, a three-part series innocuously titled "Greenhouse with Cyclamens," are anything but stories of suspense. Indeed, West begins her report by undoing immediately any illusion that the story of Nuremberg will offer the same engaging appeal as a novel, recounting her arrival at the Palace of Justice in a tone bound to surprise her readers:

> It took not many minutes to get to the courtroom where the world's enemy was being tried for his sins; but immediately those sins were forgotten in wonder at a conflict which was going on in that court, though it had nothing to do with the indictments considered by it. The trial was then in its eleventh month, and the courtroom was a citadel of boredom. Every person within its walk was in the grip of extreme tedium.[12]

West lampoons the penchant for drama in these opening lines, building anticipation and deflating it just as quickly and absurdly. Rather than approaching the trial as a watershed moment in international justice, she describes it as one of the dullest events in world history—boredom "on a huge historic scale" (11). The trial had become excruciating for everyone: the judges, lawyers and secretaries, translators and guards—all, that is, save the defendants—wanted nothing more than to put the entire affair behind them:

> All these people wanted to leave Nuremberg as urgently as a dental patient enduring the drill wants to up and leave the chair; and they would have had as much difficulty as the dental patient in explaining the cause of that urgency. Modern drills do not inflict real pain, only discomfort. But all the same the patients on whom they are used feel that they will go mad if the grinding does not stop. (7–8)

"The symbol of Nuremberg," West concludes pointedly, "was a yawn" (9).

Of the possible reactions to the Nuremberg Trial, West's was not what readers might have expected, and she likely suspected as much. For in spite of the seemingly bottomless quantities of evidence presented before the Tribunal, the event itself promised a terse drama before a rapt international audience. It would become "the greatest trial in history," declared Norman Birkett, one of the British judges. "The historian of the future will look back to it with fascinated eyes. It will have a glamour, an intensity, an ever-present sense of tragedy that will enthrall the mind engaged upon its consideration."[13] Robert Jackson, the chief American prosecutor at the trial, reinforced this promise of rapture in his powerful opening address. "That four great nations, flushed with victory and stung with injury stay the hand of vengeance and voluntarily submit their captive enemies to the judgment of the law is one of the most significant tributes that Power has ever paid to Reason,"[14] Jackson stated.

Yet by drawing out Nuremberg's boredom in a manner unsurpassed by her contemporaries—not to mention the historians, legal scholars, political theorists, or philosophers who would write about it years later—West reminds us of a critical feature of the trial that turned out to be neither glamorous nor intense. Her observations in the Palace of Justice point toward a fundamental feature of law's encounter with trauma: that the legal process makes catastrophe available through ritualized but ultimately boring discourse. Rather than a flat-footed reflection, however, West's protracted meditation—her homage—to boredom raises vital questions about the relationship between being bored and doing justice. What can one make of an event that had promised to seize the world's attention but instead lulled it into a bored, indifferent numbness? What does this boredom do to, and for, West's analysis of the trial? More broadly, what does it do to law and to the experience of justice at Nuremberg? I examine West's insistence on boredom not merely as a rhetorical attempt at irony, humor, common sense, or a gambit for shock value. Instead, I explore it as a strategic and psychological process that gives rise to an experience worth remembering in the first place.

"Greenhouse with Cyclamens" subtly but forcefully suggests that boredom constitutes not only a necessary feature of the law; it ultimately forms a critical dimension of the legal process by leaving room for the active creation of memory. West's response to Nuremberg thus offers a twofold argument: First, that trials will most likely be boring—that their structural features, from the recitation of evidence to their adherence to rules and strictures, are bound to underwhelm. Beyond this fact of boredom, however, is West's second, and underlying, suggestion: That this tedium is productive, creating a space for memory that law, as a procedural rather than a social practice, threatens to shut down. This memory, in other words, becomes possible both because *and* in spite of the judicial process.

In his classic essay on the subject "On the Psychology of Boredom," Otto Fenichel offers a valuable, commonsensical understanding of boredom as a state of mind that arises when *"something expected does not occur."*[15] And indeed, the heightened expectations surrounding the Nuremberg Trial posed one of the most difficult challenges to those journalists charged with conveying its proceedings to a watchful world. How does one explain—and more crucially, make interesting— the fact that "something expected does not occur"? How, furthermore, does one remain faithful to these unmet expectations and still make the trial's experience meaningful beyond them? This was a task facing the many reporters sent to distil courtroom events into tidy summaries for readers at home. Laurel Leff has noted that the *New York Times* reporters typically took the position of the prosecution, following the story from its vantage point with little attempt at objectivity.[16]

West observed something else in the dominant newspaper accounts: that reporters tended to focus on instances when the defendants were impudent or uncooperative—that is, on the trial's rare moments of drama. She was deeply skeptical of these narratives, which she saw as privileging the exceptions that had little to do with the rule of boredom that presided over the courtroom.

The trial, it should be noted, was not the first time that West had criticized her contemporaries for dissociating from the present. In her interwar essay, "The Dead Hand," she explores the vicissitudes of memory instantiated in London's architecture. In this piece, West insists that works of art—buildings, monuments, novels—should be integrated into everyday life, rather than standing apart from it. Her point is not merely an aesthetic one, but is rather a historical argument about the ills of turning away from the present. Along these lines, West criticizes London's architecture as being old, safe, unrelated to the life around it. Walking through Picadilly, she is struck by the city's indifference to the present; "[n]ot one single architect," she observes, "has found it possible to erect anywhere in those two miles a façade that has any reference to modern life." London, the quintessentially modern city, turns out to be an escapist's haven, where one "can disregard, and dislike for their invasions on my reverie, the people in the streets who happen to compose the age in which I live."[17] And the same disavowal of modernity, West contends, extends to literature as well. She moves from the "comfortable revisiting of the past" in architecture to an analogous impulse in fiction, lambasting the novels being published (and much to her dismay, praised) in England at the time. "Now, why did these books enjoy the passionate favour of the English critics?" she asks. "The answer," she continues, "is simply that they contain nothing that is relevant to our age. They are blankly not contemporary. They might quite well have been written in 1899."[18]

Her explanation is contrary by design: discerning critics, after all, would be expected to prize contemporary, relevant works over old-fashioned novels. West clarifies her point by framing this reactionary critical practice in the context of the war and as a symptom of the postwar era. In the current literary climate, the excessive praise heaped on second-rate novels issues not from personal whim or solipsistic taste but from the generational divide after 1918:

> There is now, due to the very slowly emergent consequences of the war, a very clean-cut division between young and old minds. The books which are liked by people under forty are, as a general rule, not the same as the books which are liked by people over forty; and this means that some of the older writers find themselves diminishing

in importance far more rapidly than men who have arrived at such eminence have done during their lifetimes in any other age. They frequently try to arrest the landslide by tampering with our critical standards. They overpraise work done in the old manner (which is naturally followed by second-rate and timid minds) and underpraise work done in the new manner (which is naturally followed by first-rate and audacious minds).[19]

The questions of relevance and contemporariness, West implies, would not have become pressing had the war not precipitated a generational rift that would see the old guard of critics attempting to stem the tide of new writing, and thus unduly praising old-fashioned novels. Nor is this impulse just a product of nepotism or protectionism; it stems from the tendency to avoid a painful present by turning back to a more reassuring past. It is not, in other words, merely a generational tug-of-war that produces over-praise of bad novels. It is rather, as West sees it, "this English habit of wandering into the past as a refuge from the distressful present."[20] Yet however ardently one wishes for the restoration of prewar life, this return only reinforces, with renewed vigor, the division between past and present, old and young. In spite of the consolation it affords, West suggests that such a retreat into the past comes at great social cost. The outdated relation to postwar reality does more than shape bad taste in interwar novels: it prevents genuine engagement with the people who share one's present. "I can disregard, and dislike for their invasions on my reverie, the people in the streets who happen to compose the age in which I live." This fundamental disregard for people, and the irresponsibility produced by this indifference, creates the conditions out of which West's reflections on the Nuremberg Trial arise.

Instead of representing Nuremberg solely as a monumental instance of justice, West felt compelled to offer readers a way to wander back into the past of the trial without the reassurance of a predictable, self-fulfilling, and ultimately reassuring plot. Most newspaper reports, however, did precisely that, writing of the trial in a way that fulfilled the expectations of readers at home—that is, as an epic drama of good versus evil. Along these lines, the court itself was often symbolized as an enclave of hope and possibility in contrast to its bombed-out, desolate surroundings. Janet Flanner, who reported on the trial for the *New Yorker*, saw precisely this contrast in the proceedings. As another highly regarded female journalist, her observations present us with a telling contrast to West's:

> The reason for the presence of us all here—an exotic, shut-off, quadripartite community, about two thousand strong—is the Tribunal, which seems a small island of hope,

sanity, and justice surrounded by the sullen, Vallhalla-minded Germans and their ruined town. There are a hundred and sixty journalists in Nuremberg—momentarily the world's largest news group in one place covering one event . . . We ourselves have only one daily newspaper to read . . . Phone calls to London are difficult, since they must go through a military switchboard to Frankfurt, be transferred there, through another military switchboard, to England, and then through another military switchboard to the London civilian circuit, while snowstorms have broken down the line in France . . . In Nuremberg, all we know is what we see and hear.[21]

Flanner's "Letters from Nuremberg" privilege the court as a kind of consecrated space, even as they hint at the claustrophobia of its ad hoc community—a small price to pay for hope, sanity, and justice. There is a sense in her description, moreover, that Nuremberg's insularity oddly bolstered the trial's drama, setting the stage for a struggle of hope in the face of destitution. It is perhaps in view of this tension that Flanner, even as she documented the trial's atmosphere, devoted her reflections primarily to judicial issues in various courtroom scenes. Her reports on the trial never veer far from the law, staying close to its proceedings and probing their implications with acumen and focus.

The juxtaposition of courtroom and town in "Letters from Nuremberg" extends the moral position adopted by the prosecution at Nuremberg, which invoked this contrast in framing the Tribunal's aim to restore civilization after barbarism.[22] For West, however, the trial's contrasts—whether between court and town or humanity and barbarism—conveyed very little of what actually went on there. Unlike Flanner's "Letters from Nuremberg," "Greenhouse with Cyclamens" rarely delves into the legal substance of the case, straying far beyond the juridical to depict people and places in the town. Where Flanner found "an exotic, shut-off, quadripartite community" in Nuremberg's enclave of journalists and "a small island of hope, sanity, and justice," West identified a situation that shared an uneasy resemblance to the imprisonment of the men in the dock:

> What irked was the isolation in a small area, *cut off from normal life* by the barbed wire of army regulations; the perpetual confrontation with the dreary details of an ugly chapter in history which the surrounding rubble seems to prove to have been torn out of the book and to require no further discussion; the continued enslavement to the war machine. To live in Nuremberg was in itself physical captivity, even for the conquerors. (9, emphasis added)

West's "cut off" community is vastly different from the "shut off" one that Flanner described. Where Flanner saw hope burdened with the inconvenience of seclusion,

West detected a troubling state of solitary confinement. The trial's isolation from its environs created a situation in which history was confronted in a vacuum, becoming the purview of the Tribunal but bearing little relevance, and consequently generating little discussion, for those not directly charged with carrying out justice. Like the buildings that towered over London as monuments to the past, the trial threatened to become an event that one could revisit—if one were even awake to do so—only in the past tense, without consideration for its relevance to one's own time.

Between Content and Form

Instead of approaching the Tribunal as a study in contrasts, noting rifts between the judges' dignity and the city's destitution, and seeing them as personifications of virtue and evil, West figures trial and town as parts of a larger whole. In advancing this claim, "Greenhouse with Cyclamens," as the mundane reference in the title suggests, sets the trial side by side with the strange, if quotidian life surrounding it: rather than intruding upon everyday life, it seems to blend, surprisingly and disconcertingly, with its contours. "The trouble with Nuremberg," West writes, "was that it was so manifestly a part of life as it is lived. The trial was of a piece with the odd things that happened on its periphery, and these were odd enough" (55).

West is drawn to this periphery because it helps to explain a great deal about the strange encounters one experienced not only in Nuremberg but also in Berlin, and presumably throughout much of postwar Germany. For just as the Nuremberg Trial surprised in its dullness, Berlin in 1946 caught one off guard by presenting all manner of seemingly "normal" encounters that, were one to scratch the surface, would reveal themselves as nothing more than façades. Thus a bookstore that holds out the promise of a leisurely read turns out to contain little save Allied propaganda; and a bustling café, when one enters it, is full of people perched gloomily over cups of watery coffee. The irreconcilability of appearance and reality meant that "one was always being disconcerted by coming on a familiar form without its familiar content" (35).

This discrepancy between form and content turned out to be one of the most perplexing aspects of Nuremberg, precisely because the form one had expected—the unfolding of an absorbing legal drama—buckled under the weight of the trial's "citadel of boredom." And if the drama did not unfold as expected,

West suggests, this was partly because the narrative so often accorded it had little to do with the actual relationship between courtroom and town.[23] The task of amplifying this relationship beyond the usual binaries took West outside the court and into the town surrounding it. In her wanderings, she found not Janet Flanner's "sullen, Vallhalla-minded Germans" but an assortment of strange and curious individuals who flouted expectation, and who consequently could not be summed up handily—and certainly not in legal terms.

West's juxtaposition implies, moreover, that the form-content opposition exists as part of the trappings of law itself—that the law takes complex, unique events and people and concisely sums them up. By describing simple individuals who defy simple explanation, her narrative adds force to the idea that Nuremberg was not idiosyncratically boring, but that there was something structural and essential about its boredom. Put simply, this "flattening out" is the way trials operate; to do justice *in* law is not, in other words, to do justice *to* life. And this is as it should be: for in filling in the picture of Nuremberg's surroundings, emphasizing those extralegal encounters that contribute to the overall experience of the trial, "Greenhouse with Cyclamens" illustrates the importance of creating memory independently from but simultaneously with law. It is not enough to assume that law, strictly conceived, will do the work of memory, or even set the terms by which the past is remembered. To assume as much would be to relieve those uninvolved with the trial of the burden of remembering it, or the harm it sought to address. Something else—some other narrative—needed to be embedded in the legal story so as to make the trial memorable. West's writing, I propose, fashions this other narrative, and with it, the terms of memory set by the peculiar encounters in Nuremberg's periphery. If, as Otto Fenichel noted, boredom arises when "something expected does not occur," Rebecca West comes at this formulation differently, shifting the focus to the unexpected and inviting the question: *if the expected does not occur, what does?*

Her answer unfolds as a series of encounters in Nuremberg's environs, the first of which involves an old woman whom West and her companions met in a village just outside Nuremberg on the evening before the trial's last day. The woman popped her "frizzled and grizzled head" (55) over a fence and proudly announced to the group that she "shot their King Edward." When they finally understood her to mean that she had gone shooting with King Edward, the woman launched into a tirade about the men on trial, inquiring whether Sauckel had been convicted. She sincerely hoped he had been, because she held him personally responsible for "bringing these wretched foreign labourers into our Germany." When someone murmured that these workers would rather have stayed home, the woman heartily agreed: "Yes, yes, of course they should have been left at home, the place for a pig is in the stye. Oh, hanging will be too good for Sauckel, I could kill him with my own hands" (56). In her eagerness to speak with the English visitors, she then asked why, although "of course it was terrible what Hitler did to the Jews," the British nonetheless saw fit to appoint a Jew as their chief prosecutor. When someone meekly informed her that Sir David Maxwell-Fyfe was not a Jew, she laughingly admonished, "Oh, you English are so simple; it is because you are aristocrats. A man who calls his son David might tell you that he was English or Scotch or Welsh, because he would know that you would believe him. But we Germans understand a little better about such things, and he would not dare to pretend to us that he was not a Jew" (57).

Soon after this absurd exchange, West describes a woman who was employed as a servant in the villa that housed the trial's guests. Passing West's group on the road to town, she stopped to ask whether Streicher had been sentenced. When she learned that a sentence had not yet been passed, the woman grew silent, then declared that she hoped he would be hanged. She had been hoping for his punishment even before the war, when Streicher had visited the village and she and her husband had taken their children to the Town Hall to hear him speak. The speech, she recalled, began innocuously enough by addressing politics. But Streicher then shifted into "filth, gibbering filth about the Jews, describing the sexual offences he pretended they committed and the shameful diseases he pretended they spread, using dreadful words" (59). When she and her husband tried to usher their children out of the hall, several SS men forced them back to their seats. West recreates the moment, invoking the woman's shock and indignation: "Yes, quite young boys had forced her and her husband to stay with their children in this bath of mud. Again she fell silent, and her face was a solid white circle in the dusk. Then she burst into a rage of weeping, and went away" (59).

These profoundly human, disturbing, or odd vignettes—of which I have described but two—are embedded in West's portrait of Nuremberg without accompanying explanation. For how does one respond when the sentiments—like those that Sauckel and Streicher should be convicted—make sense, but when the reasons behind them seem to miss the larger picture? None of these people seemed to strike West as particularly evil, and yet there is something deeply unsettling, even insidious, about their skewed, myopic vision of the horrors of the recent past. It is as though the lens through which the trial is viewed had lost its focus, leading one into conversations with individuals who believed that, indeed, the Nazis should be punished, who were outraged at what happened to the Jews—and yet who had come to these convictions from the unlikeliest of vantages, through racism or narcissism rather than, say, a commitment to international human rights. Something expected, indeed, did not occur, but that something had nothing to do with what was happening inside the Palace of Justice.

In her refusal to speculate about the meaning of these episodes, West seems to undercut the Tribunal's pedagogical aim. While the prosecution worked to make a sea of documents intelligible, and thus to make catastrophe understandable, her depictions of life outside the Palace of Justice upset this clarity, conveying the experience of Nuremberg as a series of muddled encounters that resisted tidy explanations. Yet this muddle, West implies, was part of daily life for those who sat in the Palace of Justice and waited for the defendants to be sentenced. The trial's importance as a landmark of international justice—a status with which West certainly agreed—ultimately had no bearing on the feelings of ordinary people, who continued, in ways both jarring and ludicrous, to applaud the Tribunal's convictions for their own solipsistic reasons. Rather than serving as glosses on the trial, these strange encounters extended its quotidian dimensions, and particularly what West saw as the ordinariness of the men in the dock. For what she means in claiming that "the trial was of a piece with the odd things that happened on its periphery" is that the strange, noteworthy, or downright startling was perpetually enmeshed with the most banal of details. And so it was that the accused looked nothing like the terrifying criminals one had expected. These expectations might be surmised from Janet Flanner's description of Hermann Goering on the stand: "There were not more than a few hundred people in the courtroom. They had the awful privilege of listening to the personal recital of a man who helped tear apart millions of lives, as if with those large, white hands that gestured as he sat on the Nuremberg witness stand."[24]

For West, such moments of "awful privilege" were scarce indeed. Instead, those who witnessed the trial found themselves straining to discover traces of evil in the defendants' resounding ordinariness: "Not the slightest trace of their power and their glory remained," West writes; "none of them looked as if he could ever have exercised any valid authority" (4). The trial made it difficult to distinguish the defendants as personifications of evil: "So diminished were their personalities that it was hard to keep in mind which was which, even after one had sat and looked at them for days; and those who stood out defined themselves by oddity rather than character" (4–5). Goering and his large hands did not produce terror in the hearts of spectators; according to West, he struck a far more risible pose: "Goering still used imperial gestures, but they were so vulgar that they did not suggest that he had really filled any great position, it merely seemed probable that in certain bars the frequenters had called him by some such nickname as 'The Emperor'" (4).

Similarly, other defendants were far from memorable or even, for that matter, noticeable. Even those who "were still individuals" (5) looked strikingly like people one might find in the streets of Nuremberg, or anywhere else for that matter. Streicher, West muses:

> was a dirty old man of the sort that gives trouble in parks, and a sane Germany would have sent him to an asylum long before. Baldur von Schirach, the Youth Leader, startled because he was like a woman in a way not common among men who looked like women. It was as if a neat and mousy governess sat there, not pretty, but never with a hair out of place, and always to be trusted never to intrude when there were visitors: as it might be Jane Eyre. And though one had read surprising news of Goering for years, he still surprised. He was so very soft. Sometimes he wore a German air-force uniform, and sometimes a light beach suit in the worst of playful taste, and both hung loosely on him, giving him an air of pregnancy. (5–6)

Nor did this flatness of character change once the defendants had been convicted. Thus when Goering made his final appearance in court, "it was not evident that he was among the most evil of human beings that have ever been born" (63). If this claim sounds at all familiar, perhaps this is because it would be made nearly two decades later in Hannah Arendt's *Eichmann in Jerusalem* (1963), which I discuss in the next chapter. Indeed, the connection between Arendt's famous (and famously controversial) argument, suggested in the enduring phrase in its subtitle, *A Report on the Banality of Evil,* and West's "Greenhouse with Cyclamens" has yet to be fully acknowledged or addressed, but I would suggest that Arendt's position owes much to the one set out in "Greenhouse with Cyclamens." West, however, offers more than a reflection of banal evil: she actively fashions this banality herself, giving us some of our most unlikely descriptions of the men in the dock. And in doing so, she emphasizes the importance of the trial as a first-order experience rather than a basis for a wider philosophical claim about evil—a focus that may go a long way toward explaining why her reflections have been eclipsed by Arendt's.

In concentrating on the banality of Nuremberg, West suggests that the difference between what is remembered or forgotten, what keeps us in suspense or causes our attention to slacken, hinges on the difference between what is distinct and what is not. This is implied in West's own turn of phrase: an issue of whether something is "*a part* of life as it is lived"—integrated with it, indistinguishable from it—or whether it stands *apart* from it, differentiating itself in a way that lops off past from present, good from evil. These distinctions, West insists, were manifestly unavailable in the Nuremberg Trial. What distinguished the trial was, ironically, a *refusal* to distinguish, in certain crucial instances, between those who were being judged and those who sat in judgment. West thus notes the Tribunal's acquittal of German naval Admirals on the grounds that Allied forces had also engaged in unrestricted submarine warfare. "This *nostra culpa* of the conquerors," she reflects, "might well be considered the most important thing that happened at Nuremberg. But it evoked little response at the time, and it has been forgotten" (53). It has been forgotten, West implies, in part because it is plainly unpalatable. But it has also been forgotten because it did not make the accused stand out, instead eroding the distinction between prosecution and defense, a blurring of categories that conveys something fundamental about the difficulty of sitting, day after day, in a trial whose beginning had become a distant memory and whose end was nowhere in sight.

If there was a distinction worth making in Nuremberg for West, it was between those who were there to witness the trial and those who were not. For if "the trouble with Nuremberg is that it was so manifestly a part of life as it is lived," this difficulty was not limited to those people who attended or participated in the proceedings. Above all, it troubled those who read about it from a distance, turning to the newspapers to get a sense of the events in Germany. And it is to these people that West addressed her account of the trial, not simply as a reporter, but above all as a witness:

> It was necessary, and really necessary, that a large number of persons, including the heads of the armed and civil services, should go to Nuremberg and hear the reading of the judgment, because in no other conceivable way could they gather what the trial had been about. Long, long ago, the minds of all busy people outside the enclave of Nuremberg had lost touch with the proceedings. The newspaper reports inevitably concentrated on the sensational moments when the defendants cheeked back authority, and to follow the faint obtrusions of the serious legal issues which made their way into the more serious journals would have taken the kind of mind which reads its

daily Scripture portion and never misses; and that kind of persistence carries one ir-
resistibly to the top of the grocery store, and no further. (32–33)[25]

The necessity of witnessing the trial, and the blindness of those who did not witness it, drives West's report. For "the trouble with Nuremberg," it turned out,
was that those who heard about it from afar received a false sense of what went
on there, and thus would remember the trial only through its dramatic representations in the public press.[26] But these exceptional moments, like the legal procedure set out by the Tribunal, did not convey "what the trial had been about." For
those who sat through its eleven months, the trial's states of exception—those
moments that would be showcased in the newspapers and preserved in historical
records—only underscored the experience of being "cut off from normal life."
Reaching beyond this isolated enclave and blurring the distinctions between life
inside and outside the courtroom, West bore witness to Nuremberg as "a place of
sacrifice, of boredom, of headache, of homesickness" (18).

The Possibility of Memory

In framing her essays not just as journalistic accounts but above all as eyewitness testimonies, Rebecca West gave the trial a component it sorely lacked. The
prosecution had made the calculated decision to downplay human eyewitnesses
in favor of documentary evidence, responding to the fear that individuals on the
stand would be far less reliable and far more impeachable than captured Nazi
documents. "We must establish incredible events by credible evidence," Robert
Jackson wrote in a report to President Truman the summer before the trial.[27]
West might thus be seen as supplying a human voice—not from the witness
stand as in the Eichmann trial, but from the press gallery.

Nuremberg's architects were well aware of the limitations of their design: the
trial was convened quickly and bore visible traces of its hasty construction. But
the prosecution found consolation in the future, linking their fate with the promise of history and the labor of the historian. From Norman Birkett's pronouncement that "The historian of the future will look back to it with fascinated eyes"
to Robert Jackson's conviction that "its full development we shall be obliged to
leave to historians,"[28] there is a sense of hope, conviction, and confidence that the
trial would (and should) be left to history. For West, however, such confidence
gave way to an unsettling worry: that in being subject to history, the trial will

no longer be available to living memory. Like London's distinguished architecture that West described in the interwar years, the trial would acquire historical grandeur that would make it "blankly not contemporary," setting it apart from everyday concerns, much like the trial itself. The prospect of forgetting clearly troubled West, accounting for her refusal to lapse into terse drama or legalese in her report of the trial. Before long, she reasoned, everyone would return home and Nuremberg would become a distant memory. "The trial had begun to retreat into the past. Soon none of us, we believed, would ever think of it, save when we dreamed about it or read about it in books" (70). These dreams, however, would never quite pierce the fabric of daily life; instead, they threatened to relegate the trial and the crimes it prosecuted to the realm of the unreal.

West's approach to the trial goes beyond what her first biographer describes as a combination of "hard investigative reportage with theatrical scene-setting"[29]— a view that sets her work in line with countless other examples of colorful journalism, as well as with the intellectual view of law as a public drama or "theater of justice." In defiance of these positions, West's reports do more than provide a sketch of the trial: they fashion a complex map of memory and with it, a future for Nuremberg that exceeds the pages of history books through stories that bear *repeating* rather than recording. In supplying the trial with a context, giving it a sense of place, West's report suggests that memory demands a location, a *lieu de mémoire*. This phrase, borrowed from historian Pierre Nora,[30] calls to mind the cultural and national phenomenon of "housing" collective memory. "Greenhouse with Cyclamens," however, recasts this sense of memory: rather than anchoring it in one particular location—most obviously the Palace of Justice—West details a seemingly unconnected series of places, a collection of sites that bear no resemblance to monuments, memorials or other consecrated "spaces of memory." In carving out a landscape of people and places, West's peripatetic approach to the trial reaches beyond Nora's notion of collective memory. Her sense that place is vital to the act of remembering takes root in the ancient and medieval elaboration of the architectural mnemonic, whereby an individual maps the details to be remembered onto the backdrop of a physical location. "The structure of memory, like a wax tablet, employs places [loci] and in these gathers together images and letters,"[31] argued Cicero. But it is not enough, in West's account of Nuremberg, to think of places in order to remember the legal or historical import of the trial. One needs to encounter these places and people fully—that is, chaotically—

engaging with rather than employing them. The act of remembering thus becomes, at this unprecedented historical juncture, a lived *experience* rather than an instance of recall.

In keeping with this notion, "Greenhouse with Cyclamens" lays out a mnemonic technique not unlike that used by individuals with remarkable memories. Drawing upon the technique of using places as memory prompts, West's wanderings through Nuremberg resemble those in one of the most famous case histories of such memory, which was recorded by the Soviet psychologist A. R. Luria in his book *The Mind of a Mnemonist*. I would like to draw upon the extraordinary memory of Luria's patient in order to articulate more concretely how West shapes her reflections on the trial, and to consider what implications this shape has for the future of legal memory.

In the mid-1920s, Luria began treating a patient, Sherashevsky ("S." in Luria's narrative), who appeared to have an inexhaustible memory. Luria followed his subject over a period of thirty years, regularly testing him with series of words, numbers, or letters, which S. could reproduce in any order and which, even after the passage of several years, he did not forget. But rather than putting his subject to the test, the study called scientific method into question, compromising Luria's ability to measure the object of his study and forcing him to describe it qualitatively rather than quantitatively:

> When S. read through a long series of words, each word would elicit a graphic image. And since the series was fairly long, he had to find some way of distributing these images of his in a mental row or sequence. Most often . . . he would "distribute" them along some roadway or street he visualized in his mind. Sometimes this was a street in his home town, which would also include the yard attached to the house he had lived in as a child and which he recalled vividly. On the other hand, he might also select a street in Moscow. Frequently he would take a mental walk along that street—Gorky Street in Moscow—beginning at Mayakovsky Square, and slowly make his way down, "distributing" his images at houses, gates, and store windows. At times, without realizing how it had happened, he would suddenly find himself back in his home town (Torzhok), where he would wind up his trip in the house he had lived in as a child.[32]

S.'s strategy for remembering integrates the strange with the familiar, embedding an unrelated series of words within a topography that he can imagine, and revisit, in his mind's eye.[33] S. described his infallible memory not as the result of focus, of the sort that one might summon by staring intently at an object so as to recall it later. Instead, he explained, "I recognize a word not only by the images it evokes but by a whole complex of feelings that image arouses. It's hard to express . . . it's not a matter of vision or hearing but some over-all sense I get."[34] The images that S. sees, moreover, do not figure as symbols, each serving as a lightning rod to which he can then "append" the words he needs to recall. Instead, they function as a kind of map that, once animated in his mind, he can follow by intuition rather than rote.

It is this "over-all sense," I propose, that West pursues in narrating the Nuremberg Trial through its ordinariness. The episodes she depicts chart avenues of experience through which one can trace one's way not to the Tribunal's juridical signposts but to the broader, more unwieldy "complex of feelings" of "what the trial had been about." Rather than pinning down Nuremberg as a legal turning point or summarizing it with the resounding voice of judgment, she gently coaxes an entire world out of the courtroom—a world as perplexing as it is real.

The infinite capacity of S.'s memory, however, turned out to be both blessing and curse. For his ability to remember everything was accompanied by the burden of forgetting nothing—by an incapacity, in other words, to draw distinctions, to separate out the things that matter from his vast chain of memories. In his forward to Luria's case history, Jerome Bruner writes that the nonselectivity of S.'s memory means that "what remains behind is a kind of junk heap of impressions."[35] Reading a simple passage in a book becomes a painfully complicated procedure, since every word calls up an image that prevents S. from grasping the overall meaning of a sentence:

> I'm slowed down, my attention is distracted, and I can't get the important ideas in a passage. Even when I read about circumstances that are entirely new to me, if there happens to be a description, say, of a staircase, it turns out to be one in a house I once lived in. I start to follow it and lose the gist of what I'm reading.[36]

If his description feels very much like West's digressions in "Greenhouse with Cyclamens," perhaps this should not surprise us. For her, however, this inability to distinguish, to have one image dissolve into the next, was an intrinsic part of what it felt like to be at Nuremberg. It was the feeling of being confronted with an event that threatened to collapse into just such a "junk heap of impressions": a confusing, overwhelming accumulation of evidence spread over a seemingly interminable progression of days. Yet this muddle of one moment shading into the next conveys what it felt like to be at the trial, without history books or hindsight to confer meaning and perspective. And whether one sees this junk heap as sensory overload or sensory deprivation, one can readily acknowledge the urgency of finding meaning in the excess created by the trial. For what the observer remembers from Nuremberg will lay the foundation for what future generations recall, determining whether this past matters to ordinary individuals for whom neither law nor history is a vocation.

The pressure that West felt to commit the trial to memory, and the mnemonic wanderings that emerged from this commitment, illuminate a critical difference between the particular demands of memory after each world war. Memory after World War I was seen in light of its widespread instances of shell shock; the duty to remember was accompanied by the need to *recover* memory. But if such recovery was the focus of West's narrative tension in *The Return of the Soldier,* it was eclipsed by her determination to *build up* memory at Nuremberg, fashioning it out of the trial's bottomless tedium. There was, in short, nothing to recover: faced with the burden of forgetting, West creates the memorable experience denied her at Nuremberg by other means.

From Event to Experience

Despite its slow pace, which bore the weight of deliberation and a juridical steady hand, the Nuremberg Trial would never be able to fully absorb the scope of the catastrophe it was designed to address. Perhaps this is the nature of law generally, just as it was part of Nuremberg particularly. As West observed one year earlier at the 1945 trial of William Joyce, who was tried and convicted in London for broadcasting Nazi propaganda in England during the war:

> For the law, like art, is always vainly racing to catch up with experience . . . By a gross inappropriateness judges and legislators are described always as sitting, the one in the bench, the other in the House of Commons or the House of Lords; for in fact they run, they run fast as the hands of the clock, reaching out to the present with one hand, that they may knot it to the past which they carry in their other hand.[37]

It is in this race towards an ungraspable experience that Nuremberg faltered as well. For all of its staggering reams of documents, matched by its staggering dullness, the trial sought an experience—and sought to *become* an experience—that was never attained. The trial, West reflected, was "an unshapely event, a defective composition, stamping no clear image on the mind of the people it had been designed to impress. It was one of the events which do not become an experience" (262–63).[38]

West's conception of law pits the trial's tediousness against the law's break-neck speed, a tension that epitomized Nuremberg at its deepest level. "Here was a paradox," she writes. "In the courtroom these lawyers had to think day after day at the speed of whirling dervishes, yet were living slowly as snails, because of the boredom that pervaded all Nuremberg, and was at its thickest in the Palace of Justice" (18). Caught between this swiftness and its contrapuntal tedium, it became impossible to grasp, and thus to absorb, the encounter with justice in any lasting way. Drawing out the trial's boredom, West's essays clear a temporal space, slowing down the pace of justice and making discovery—and the experience in its wake—possible.[39] Nuremberg's tedium became not simply a description of the trial, but an essential part of West's effort to make it available to memory as an experience in its own right. For in creating a mnemonic map which brought Nuremberg into the cultural imagination, West needed more than creative license: she needed license to wander, literally and figuratively, beyond the court's confines, discovering the people and places that made the trial "a part of life as it is lived."

For West, telling the story of how the law functions may explain how a legal mind works, but it tells very little about how a bored mind works—and it is *this* mind that ultimately shaped and was shaped by the experience of the trial. Consequently, West was untroubled by the lack of focus that so plagued Luria's S. For if her experience resembles that of the mnemonist—"I'm slowed down, my attention is distracted, and I can't get the important ideas in a passage"—this slowness was precisely what she needed to get at the experience that no strictly legal account of the trial could express. The important ideas that elude S. are, in her mind, the purview of lawyers and historians, whose job it is to condense the trial into its pivotal moments and key concepts; their analysis, however, will leave little to remember about what the confusing, dull experience of justice felt like.

To remember the trial, moreover, is also to withhold interpretation of the strange encounters that happened there. It is thus that the unexplained encounters in Nuremberg continue to perplex, creating an unanalyzed core that makes memory possible. As Walter Benjamin explains in "The Storyteller":

> There is nothing that commends a story to memory more effectively than that chaste compactness which precludes psychological analysis. And the more natural the process by which the storyteller forgoes psychological shading, the greater becomes the story's claim to a place in the memory of the listener, the more completely is it integrated into his own experience, the greater will be his inclination to repeat it to someone else

someday, sooner or later. This process of assimilation, which takes place in depth, requires a state of relaxation which is becoming rarer and rarer. If sleep is the apogee of physical relaxation, boredom is the apogee of mental relaxation. Boredom is the dream bird that hatches the egg of experience. A rustling in the leaves drives him away.[40]

A story is compelling, in Benjamin's understanding, because its meaning has not been exhausted; the moment it reaches its interpretive limit, it ceases to be told or repeated: there is nothing left to say, nothing worth (or in need of) remembering.

Faced with an experience of overwhelming proportions, West offers no interpretation of Nuremberg, no clear-cut legal analysis. Instead, she embarks on a series of associations and encounters that describe rather than explain, refusing to restrict the trial to a particular legal moment or to the unequivocal pronouncement of a verdict. When explanations fell short, when the trial confused more than it clarified, she relaxed her mind to take in the stories that never made it into the courtroom, resisting the impulse to evaluate or footnote them and instead, committing them to memory.

Judgment's Context

The sense of distraction that characterizes West's coverage of Nuremberg led her to what arguably became the unlikeliest discovery of all, the centerpiece of her writing on the trial: the greenhouse with cyclamens. For if "the symbol of Nuremberg was a yawn," West supplants this yawn with a resolutely ordinary image, yet one so compelling for her that she took it as the title for all three of her Nuremberg essays. In a trial that offered more than its share of potential symbols, from the Palace of Justice to the prisoners in the dock to the horrific images in the film screened in the courtroom, "Nazi Concentration Camps," West chose instead to present the trial through an image that seems ill-fitting in its banality. "Often people said, 'You must have seen some very interesting sights when you went to the Nuremberg Trial.' Yes, indeed. There had been a man with one leg and a child of twelve, growing enormous cyclamens in a greenhouse" (127). What is the significance of West's use of these cyclamens? In a report devoted to relating the experience of judgment and justice after the war, why not rely on symbols that would call up the trial directly, signaling explicitly Nuremberg's unique place in history and law?

The answers to these questions come to us, unsurprisingly, through storytelling rather than explanation. And the story, naturally, begins with West's bored, distracted state of mind, which leads her to notice the greenhouse from the

converted castle where the journalists were staying. Intrigued, she sets out to
"see how the Germans had kept that form of luxury going" (29), anticipating
little more than one would find in an English greenhouse after the war, "a desert
place of shabby and unpainted staging, meagerly set out with a diminished store
of seed boxes" (29). What she finds, however, undoes her expectations:

> But the door was open; and it admitted to a scene far distant in time and space. This
> might have been a greenhouse in one of the great English or Scottish nursery gar-
> dens before 1939; or one might push the date back further, to a time when labour was
> still cheap. There was perfect cleanliness and perfect neatness here, and it was full of
> plants . . . There was a row of canna lilies, scarlet and orange and crimson, bright with
> health; there were many obconica primulas, which perfectly exhibited their paradoxi-
> cal character of being open-faced and brilliant yet recognisably members of a shy and
> cool family; and there were rows upon rows of beautifully grown cyclamen which
> would have done credit to a specialist firm. (29)

This flourishing greenhouse, only a short distance from West's temporary resi-
dence in the converted *Schloss,* surprises her because it looks as though it belongs
in another time, before the war had decimated any prospect of abundance and
made luxuries like flowers things of the past. In an odd, unexpected aside, West
stumbles upon a symbol of nostalgia, a scene that seems as impossible in the
present as it was comforting in the past.

But this was not the first time West had come across this image and taken it as
emblematic of the experience of Nuremberg and postwar Germany. For flora had
already established itself in many minds as of a piece with so many of the chill-
ing ironies about the Holocaust—chief among them the irony that a nation of
such refined culture could descend to unspeakable depths of barbarism. Shortly
before her description of the greenhouse, West notices flowers elsewhere, while
speaking with the French doctor who maintained the exhibits of Nazi atrocities
at the Palace of Justice. Turning in his hand a lampshade made of tattooed human skin, he reflected, "These people where I live send me in my breakfast tray
strewn with pansies, arranged with exquisite taste. I have to remind myself that
they belong to the same race that supplied me with my exhibits, the same race
that tortured me month after month, year after year, at Malthausen [sic]" (23).
The contrast between the gruesome object in his care and the delicate flowers he
received each morning prompts West to contemplate not irony but mystery:

> And indeed flowers were the visible sign of that mystery, flowers that were not only
> lovely but beloved. In the window-boxes of the high-gabled houses the pink and purple
> petunias were bright like lamps. In the gardens of the cottages that bordered a road

which was no longer there, which was a torn trench, the phloxes shone white and clear pink and mauve as, under harsh heat, they will not do, unless they are well watered. It is tedious work, training clematis over low posts, so that its beauty does not stravaig up the walls but lies open under the eye; but on the edge of the town many gardeners grew it thus. The countryside beyond continued this protestation of innocence. A path might mount the hillside . . . [but] it would not lead to any place where it was not plain that Germany was a beautiful country, inhabited by a people who loved all pleasant things and seemed to mean no harm. (23)

As the German countryside spreads out before her in bright bursts of flowers, West is deeply conscious of the darkness rent by their radiance. For it was not simply that these flowers made the postwar desolation a little more bearable, lining the bombed-out road with bright colors or restoring to the hillsides some of the loveliness they once possessed. Nor was the "mystery" of these flowers only a matter of irony born of resilience amid destruction, or more tragically, the irony of a nation of people whose "lovely and beloved" flora inspired an abiding affection that did not extend to human beings.

To be sure, West was attuned to these ironies, but did not limit the flowers to this symbolism alone—almost as though she were resisting the temptation to make use of an all-too-convenient cliché. Instead, she immediately complicates this image of life amid death: picking up on the lampshade in the French doctor's hands, she superimposes the artifact onto her reflections on the resurgence of plant life, carefully noting how "the pink and purple petunias were bright like lamps." In yoking the image of blooming life to the doctor's material reminder of atrocity, West casts aspersions on the "mystery" of these bright spots of rebirth among the ruins. In linking these two lamps—one a stark, all-too-literal reminder of death, the other a vestige of nostalgia or hope—West subtly suggests that one invariably begets the other. The light given off by the pink and purple petunias is brighter for having cast its beams through the thick darkness of the doctor's lampshade—and the very fact that one looks toward this light serves as a bleak reminder of the past that so many in 1946 were anxious to forget.

In dwelling on the "visible sign of that mystery" of civilization and destruction, West veers briefly toward the sentimental or at least the existential. By making the floral lamp and human lampshade contingent images, drawing one out of the other, she backs away from any potential sentiment or philosophy. But her interest ultimately lies in more practical matters: in the intricacies of the life surrounding Nuremberg and of what and who made this existence possible. And so she observes moments later how remarkable this spread of flora truly was given the postwar circumstances: "It might seem that it would never be very interesting that somebody had started a brisk business on potted plants. But this was Germany, this was 1946; and it was as if one were in a lock, and saw the little trickle of water between the gates which meant that the lock was opening. The war had burned trade off Germany as flame burns skin off a body" (29). And yet this trade, unlike the lampshade of human skin she described moments earlier, is capable of being revived—even, strangely enough, of resisting political restrictions. For it was likely that the greenhouse near the *Schloss* had been active even during the war, flouting Hitler's regulations; it was just as likely, West speculates, that it was now defying Allied restrictions, which would be unlikely to approve of using German fuel and labor to grow flowers.

The greenhouse's existence is of a piece with West's broader interest in things set off from the life around them. In this sense, her story of the greenhouse invites comparison with another, equally isolated and artificially constructed space—but one that emitted none of the life in which she now found herself: the concentration camp barrack. The contrast between the two places could not be starker: one a moist, warm, life-giving space, the other a bleak vision of death and inhumanity at its most brutal. Her depiction of the greenhouse invokes its ghostly counterpart without explicitly comparing it, becoming another instance of the associative quality of West's memory.

This focus on the practical matters of the greenhouse's existence prompts West to consider the individual responsible for its upkeep. Contrary to her expectations, the greenhouse was not tended by several gardeners: "[T]here was only one man to be seen, who was closing a light at the other end of the greenhouse with a clumsiness which was explained when he stumped off to another light on two crutches. He had lost a leg" (30). West's observation initially seems a pathos-imbued description of an amputee who, despite his suffering, had found a means of livelihood in the bleak Nuremberg landscape—a testament to survival and determination. But her point is altogether different:

> The twitch and roll, twitch and roll of his walk, recalled another difference between the British and the German lot. The Nazi Government had shown a monstrous cruelty to its own people in two respects. They did not dig out their dead from the ruins after air-raids ... Neither did they make the proper effort to furnish artificial limbs for their war casualties, and an appalling number of one-armed and one-legged men were to be seen in the German streets. (30)

The cyclamen grower, whose only assistant was a twelve-year-old child, thus becomes not just a testament to postwar resilience nor an invitation to ponder the pity of war, extending such pity even to the citizens of the nation being judged at Nuremberg. Instead, he represents a more general tendency of his own government, which treated with brutality not just those it deemed "outsiders" but also its "exemplary" citizens. As a casualty of war, this man instantiates a wider phenomenon: a reminder of a crucial difference between England and Germany that invites not only revulsion but above all, judgment. It is thus that West's complex description, which seems to have little to do with idioms of law or justice, steers its readers towards judgment nonetheless. The mind distracted by the proceedings inside the Palace of Justice seeks refuge in the steady revival of life outside its purview. And these extralegal experiences, West suggests, were also part of the experience of law, allowing one to pass judgment by other means, refusing to confine it solely to the official work of the Tribunal.

In creating a landscape of seepages—of justice leaking slowly and unpredictably beyond the framework created to contain it—West did not suggest the existence of two independent realms of judgment, one official and "artificial," the other organic and accessible in the ordinary world outside the court. For the cyclamen grower—the human image that invites curiosity, pity, and judgment—would not exist without the trial and the influx of potential customers it brought to Nuremberg. Indeed, his business began at the start of the trial, when he realized just how many foreigners would descend upon Nuremberg. Now he had come to depend on the steady stream of buyers and so, like the defendants themselves, he was not terribly anxious to see the Tribunal close its doors:

> He wanted to know how many trials were likely to be held in Nuremberg now that this one was finished, and whether as many Americans and British and French officials would be here to conduct these others; and it was plain that though he was aware that he would be told that the number would be less, he longed to hear that it would be not much less. He enquired whether any of the English people now here would be likely to stop off in Holland on the way home and would be able to send him Dutch seeds. He would have more to say, but the greenhouse was getting dark. (32)

West's story of the cyclamen grower is a narrative of contingencies: of a business brought to life with the onset of the trial, of a man she would not have encountered had the journalists' quarters not been sufficiently close to his greenhouse. Folded into this context, the cyclamens, in their surprising dependence on the trial, become aesthetic reminders of the life quietly unfolding around the site of judgment. For the Nuremberg Trial not only restored justice after the war; it also brought to life a world around it—a life that could only be glimpsed when one left the Palace of Justice to explore its bombed-out surroundings. From this perspective, the trial set the tone for a future that its own architects and participants, as temporary visitors, would never see. Justice, West implies, has consequences that far exceed verdict, sentence, or for that matter, law.

West's symbolism unfolds as a web of associations: it is always relational, alerting us to the complexity of symbolizing justice and history. The cyclamens, which appear initially as hackneyed symbols of beauty and civilization in an era of barbarism or survival in the wake of destruction, become emblems that demand a *context,* stubbornly reminding us that justice is not a solitary pursuit. Rather than offering the cyclamens as self-contained images, she embeds one symbol in another: the greenhouse *with* cyclamens, attended *by* a one-legged man—all of which are situated in the shadow of the *Schloss,* itself in the shadow of the Palace of Justice.

By summoning the cyclamens in her effort to describe and subsequently to remember Nuremberg, West's complex symbolism recalls another image from World War I: the Flanders poppy. As a figure for postwar memory, the poppy was claimed for the poetic imagination in one of World War I's most famous poems, John McCrae's "In Flanders Fields" and its Romantic tribute to heroism:

In Flanders fields the poppies blow
Between the crosses, row on row,
That mark our place; and in the sky
The larks, still bravely singing, fly
Scarce heard amid the guns below.[41]

Introduced in 1921 by the British Legion to recall Britain's war dead, the poppies were distributed each year in time for Armistice Day, and continue to be manufactured today for the annual Remembrance Sunday commemorations. As Geoff Dyer reflects upon visiting the battlefields of World War I: "So strong are these feelings that I wonder if there is not some compensatory quality in nature, some equilibrium—of which the poppy is a manifestation and a symbol—which means that where terrible violence has taken place the earth will sometimes generate an equal and opposite sense of peace."[42] The eternal sleep that these poppies both induce and symbolize speaks to nature's ability to restore a sublime sense of peace after the war. They grow over the battlefields naturally: no one plants them or nurtures their growth. They are ironic, organic, and—in their brightness and solitariness—seem to speak for themselves, requiring no additional narrative or context. In other words, they serve memory in a way that is fundamentally opposed to the remembrance West outlines in "Greenhouse with Cyclamens."

The cyclamens that flourish in Nuremberg do not call up images of a natural world gradually healing itself in the war's wake—though West, as I have suggested, certainly played with this traditional sense of irony. Absent their caretaker and his customers, there would be no such images to speak of: Nuremberg would be another war-torn city without signs of the life that, literally and metaphorically, would grow over the scars of the past. Instead of using a discrete symbol, West complicates the vicissitudes of memory, and her complex web of connected experiences and images suggest that no symbol on its own will suffice to call to mind a disastrous era where grief was tended by law, where remembrance became entangled with justice—and where this justice, as West reminds her readers time and again, was meted out in the dullest of ways.

"There is not so much banality of evil," writes philosopher Avishai Margalit, "as banality of indifference."[43] In wending her way out of Nuremberg's boredom, Rebecca West writes precisely against this indifference. She identifies in Nuremberg a fundamental problem of sensibility: a sense that the trial's dullness eroded one's capacity to feel. Those who sat in the courtroom were rendered senseless or, to put it bluntly, were bored out of their minds—and as West feared, out of their memories as well. Because this indifference works against memory—how can one remember if one doesn't even care?—one must work around it as best one can. But "Greenhouse with Cyclamens" offers another approach: not working *around* but working *through* this boredom, harnessing it to shape an experience that mattered to memory.

I am not claiming this process of "working through" boredom allowed one to overcome it; in this sense, my use of the phrase parts ways with its usual sense of psychoanalytic *Durcharbeitung*. My emphasis, rather, is on boredom as a genre—and a pretext—to arrive at justice by other means. This does not imply, moreover, that what happens in the courtroom is not itself justice, but that it is vastly different from the justice that occurs in the outside world. Whether we cast these differences as legal or social, explicit or subtle, monumental or minor is of little importance here. More critical is that these modes of justice do not exist in opposition to each other: not legal *versus* social, but legal *and* social justice as part of a larger cultural, historical imaginary in which official and unofficial judgments happen simultaneously. While it may be tempting to identify these two forms of justice as indifferent to each other, doing so would overlook the ways in which they are in fact contingent: one form of justice bears on the other, exposing the other's capacities and failures.

Proponents and detractors of the Nuremberg Trial have vigorously debated whether it was a fair or merely a show trial. The aim of this chapter has not been to weigh in on this debate but to examine the trial in narrative terms, and in doing so to conceptualize its affective and cultural legacy. I have argued for a legacy that uses the trial's boredom as a means to justice on an ordinary, social scale. Even as this more homespun justice sheds light on the trial's limitations, injustices that the court could never recognize or rectify, it also needed this official justice in order for these encounters to be recognized as more than just economic or political asides. The legal process set the stage for these encounters—but it was ultimately not the same stage upon which they played out. In this process of judging outside the law, the memory of the Nuremberg Trial itself was made. And as West reminds us, what we make of it, we make ourselves.

In West's "making" of the trial, our ideas about justice are profoundly related to the way we experience an event *as it occurs*. Indeed, the tedium of Nuremberg extended some of West's private sentiments about World War II, which she and many others referred to as "The Great Bore War."[44] As her most recent biographer put it, "If the bombing of London terrified and saddened people, it also bored them, as they became accustomed to the underground shelters and awaited the bombers' arrival."[45] And as West herself wrote of those times, "The air . . . beats with a faint pulse which slows down one's own . . . The mind swings loose of the present."[46] These sentiments seemed to reassert themselves in Nuremberg, which contrary to expectations was neither gripping nor exhilarating. Perhaps this is part of the very reason it fell short: it was *experienced* rather than imagined. It was this experience, one marked by West's position as a witness at the trial, which also differentiates "Greenhouse with Cyclamens" from *The Return of the Soldier*. West, like her narrator Jenny, must imagine the war in fiction and can thus accord it dramatic but always somewhat unreal proportions. Yet no such fantasy could enter into her account of Nuremberg if she was to convey the trial faithfully. To do it justice, she implies, is to record it without embellishment, with unwavering directness.

West's account suggests, moreover, not only that boredom accounts for a substantial part of the Nuremberg experience and thus needs to be woven into the trial's story. She insists, above all, that this tedium itself became the *purveyor* of this experience. It was thus not against but through this boredom that one could take responsibility—which for West, amounted to making memory. Thus, even as she critiqued the trial for being "an unshapely event, a defective composition, stamping no clear image on the mind of the people it had been designed to impress," her work implies that this very unshapeliness, this nonexperience, calls upon us to actively remember the trial, to fashion mnemonic techniques that give it body, amplitude, and above all enough time to wend our way down the avenues of memory.

"Greenhouse with Cyclamens" reminds us that the most memorable moments are ironically not always those that stand out, that captivate us. Those events that fall short of our expectations and threaten to recede into obsolescence also, it turns out, call upon us to *work* in order to commit them to memory. The Nuremberg Trial may have been tedious and uninspiring. Yet the consequences of forgetting even the dullest trial, of leaving its details solely to the historian or the novelist, would be grim indeed. It is in this spirit that West concludes "Greenhouse with Cyclamens I" with a tribute to bravery: "Brave [were] the men who, in making the Nuremberg trial, tried to force a huge and sprawling historical event to become comprehensible. It is only by making such efforts that we survive" (267). In spite of all there was to lose—foremost, perhaps, the captive audience that had gathered in the courtroom—those responsible for the trial did an invaluable service to justice.

In committing the Nuremberg Trial to memory through the ordinary if odd world around it, West makes an ethical and normative point. If memory is ethical, it is so because of the commitments we bring to it. And if it is normative, it is because we insist on those commitments, fashioning ways to ensure that they continue to be meaningful in the present rather than being enshrined as a still life, a closed chapter of the past. This insistence, moreover, means more for West than simply articulating one's commitments. Rather than announcing the imperative to remember, she subtly and carefully crafts a landscape that steers one toward remembrance. Hers is a dynamic world full of strange encounters, surprising experiences, and unlikely symbols. And yet the more one passes through it, the more memory is set in motion—a movement made possible because memory is given a context and a *sense* rather than a verdict.

By making the Nuremberg Trial dull, ordinary and, above all, relevant, West puts forth a new sense of responsibility for history: The trial may well be legally exemplary, but it is also, in its tedium, emphatically contemporary. As such, it cannot be dismissed as an isolated experience whose uniqueness borders on irrelevance or obsolescence. It is worth remembering because, like the people in the streets of London, it may be disregarded and forgotten all too easily. But as West pointed out in her interwar essay "The Dead Hand," it also "happen[s] to compose the age in which I live;" it is intimately bound with the concerns of everyday life and thus demands our due care. In this light, Nuremberg's postwar sense of justice continues to be meaningful long after the court has adjourned. What emerges from West's understanding of contemporariness, ordinariness and relevance is thus a new relationship to the past, which no longer offers a refuge from the ills of the present. Instead, the present demands our total engagement, forcing a break with the past and compelling us to face reality without the distinguished, but never quite relevant, shelter of monumental precedent.

It seems more than coincidence that our cultural memories of the two most famous post-Holocaust trials have been shaped by women writers who were neither lawyers nor historians. Rebecca West's journalism on Nuremberg gave us the best-known report of that trial; Hannah Arendt's *Eichmann in Jerusalem* would do the same for the Eichmann trial. Each of these narratives contains an account of how and why law should matter after World War II—a nomos that yokes ethical obligation to legal subjectivity. Like Virginia Woolf before them, West and Arendt share a steadfast commitment to ordinariness: the unremarkability that West saw in Nuremberg's former Nazis would be raised to the level of social and political theory in Arendt's phrase "the banality of evil." But as the next chapter proposes, we owe more to Arendt than this shift in the nature of criminality admits. Her response to the trial—the story of a witness rather than a legal specialist—suggests that the cultural life of law has perhaps less to do with judicial expertise than with a social sensibility at once communal, story-driven, and unrehearsed.

CHAPTER FIVE

From Witness to Neighbor

Arendt's Eichmann

This Court is forever adding new stories to the temples of constitutional
law, and the temples have a way of collapsing when one too many story
is added.

—Robert H. Jackson[1]

Not one of us will leave here as he was before.

—Haim Gouri[2]

[I]t is as a neighbor that man is accessible: as a face.

—Emmanuel Levinas[3]

Competing Accounts of Justice

In May 1960, Israeli secret service agents kidnapped Adolf Eichmann from
his home in Buenos Aires and brought him to Israel to stand trial for crimes
against the Jewish people. Prime Minister David Ben-Gurion viewed the trial
as a unique opportunity to educate Israelis about the atrocities perpetrated by
the Nazi regime on Europe's Jewish population. The nation's youth were of particular interest to Ben-Gurion: the 1950s were characterized in Israel as a decade
of silence, during which the Holocaust existed as an unspoken taboo; the trial
presented a means of breaking this silence and giving the Holocaust both speak-
ability and existence for those who had not experienced it directly. For both Ben-
Gurion and Attorney General Gideon Hausner, the trial marked an unparalleled
moment in which a Jewish nation could bring to justice one of its most prominent victimizers. The Eichmann trial thus fell into line with a common observation: that trials serve a purpose beyond justice alone, functioning as pedagogical
tools to instruct a wider public about a nation's past and to establish a trove of

documentation for future historians and researchers. An admirable mission, to be sure, but far more complicated than it would seem.

Looking back at the trial that he prosecuted, Gideon Hausner's reflections in his memoir demonstrate his belief that the trial succeeded particularly in this first objective:

> The reaction of the youth, who followed the trial with great interest, was summed up in a phrase that recurred in many letters and school essays: "Our eyes have been opened." The trial thus proved to be a strong educational factor in strengthening Jewish consciousness. The interest of the younger people in the events of the Nazi holocaust continues unabated.[4]

But Hannah Arendt, who observed the trial as a correspondent for the *New Yorker*, sounded an unequivocally different note. Writing from Jerusalem to her friend and former teacher Karl Jaspers, she recounted:

> The country's interest in the trial has been artificially whetted. An oriental mob that would hang around anyplace where something is going on is hanging around in front of the courthouse. A surprising number of children between 3 and 10. What I hear from the real youth is quite a different story. This is their parents' business, they say. It doesn't concern them. But if it interests their parents, then it is legitimate. What goes unexpressed: We have more important things to do.[5]

Arendt's condescension—phrases like "oriental mob" were of a piece with her disdain for Polish Jews (*Ostjuden*) like Hausner, and her admiration for German Jews (*Yekkes*) like the presiding Judge Moshe Landau—did not go unnoticed in her own time, and her supercilious tone still remains one of the more problematic elements of *Eichmann in Jerusalem*. Still, her account of an indifferent youth points to a fundamental tension between Arendt's and Hausner's evaluations of the trial. Arendt's narrative tells of a public that simply wants to carry on with the business of daily life; for her, the trial reinforced rather than bridged the differences between generations.

Even more important than this failure to educate the youth, for Arendt, was that the trial's extraneous pedagogical aim promoted a misunderstanding of law's purpose, and thus a misappropriation of legal means. In *Eichmann in Jerusalem*, she laid out a strictly legalist ideal of law, in opposition to those who turn to jurisprudence with ulterior motives:

> The purpose of a trial is to render justice, and nothing else; even the noblest of ulterior purposes—"the making of a record of the Hitler regime which could withstand the

test of history," as Robert G. Storey, executive trial counsel at Nuremberg, formulated the supposed higher aims of the Nuremberg Trials—can only detract from the law's main business: to weigh the charges brought against the accused, to render judgment, and to mete out due punishment.[6]

This chapter takes the tension between Arendt and Hausner in particular, and between proponents and detractors of the Eichmann trial in general, as its point of departure. I am interested, however, in looking past the debate over the trial's success or failure to focus instead on its wider effect: the transition it precipitated from a specifically legal to more broadly social obligation. Specifically, I argue that the trial's social and historical legacy was to make listening a duty of care—a responsibility, in other words, that comes from tort law rather than criminal law. To chart this movement into torts involves mapping a series of tensions in the trial: tensions between private and public realms, between the individual and the community, and between tort law and criminal law.

The Israeli journalist and writer Tom Segev credits Arendt's thesis, whether one agrees with it or not, with establishing an intellectual legacy for the trial through its notion of the banality of evil: "The book created a worldwide debate, and that was the Eichmann trial's contribution, albeit indirect, to the century's political thought."[7] In contrast to this view, my reading of Arendt maintains that her report's most significant contribution extends beyond her insistence on the defendant's ordinariness as an inherent feature of his relationship to radical evil. The banality of evil is Arendt's analytical term, and an incisive criticism of why the prosecution in Jerusalem pursued something akin to a historical red herring. But her ethical claim, I would argue, lies elsewhere, and demands that we read beyond the banality of evil. In doing so, I approach Arendt from two perspectives: first, the aesthetic and formal implications of her account, and second, the connection she adumbrates between the Eichmann trial and tort law. First, this chapter examines how Arendt uses narrative form to challenge the story of the trial. I propose that the form she uses—the report—has a latent content underlying its manifest one, and that this underlying claim is ethical in nature. I then look at the question of ethics from a different vantage, that of tort law, from which I argue that the value of Arendt's work lies in its subtle expression of a sense of obligation, one that resembles, counterintuitively, Anglo-American tort law rather than international criminal law.

Reading Arendt for affective resonance rather than purely political or historical argument, we begin to grasp how the Eichmann trial produced an effect that neither the Israeli prosecution nor Hannah Arendt fully expressed, an outcome at once social and juridical. The process of hearing witnesses tell their stories—as distinct from the Nuremberg Trial's strictly documentary evidence—gave new political and social life to a legal principle: the neighbor principle, with roots in the law of torts rather than criminal law. Arendt, unwittingly and in spite of herself, gave voice to a new version of the neighbor principle, as did Gideon Hausner in his memoir *Justice in Jerusalem*. In proposing that the Eichmann trial animated this legal principle anew, I also suggest that the expansion of responsibilities it entailed evoked feelings of duty and negligence that persist to this day. The ethical stance that insists on listening as an act of responsibility, and silence as an act of omission or negligence, informs a range of contemporary responses to trauma, from the creation of Holocaust testimony archives to the slogan that arose at the height of the AIDS crisis, Silence = Death.[8] This sense of ethics is present in Arendt's work, with one crucial difference: In her assessment, one of the chief problems in the Eichmann trial was not silence, but an overabundance of speech. The chorus of voices in the prosecution's case made it difficult to listen to the individual and to be moved by that person's suffering. There are, to be sure, other models for such "ethical listening"—most obviously, of course, the practices of psychoanalysis and religious confession. These contexts, however, do not connect ethics directly with justice. I believe that Arendt's response to the Eichmann trial provides us with precisely such a model. Reading Arendt for her emotional subtleties as a witness to the trial, we find something beyond the claims of political theory or social commentary. We find, particularly in some of the text's less explicitly philosophical moments, the seeds of an ethics—and a justice—of listening.

This chapter seeks to illuminate how Arendt's reaction to one of the trial's humbler witnesses in particular, and the trial's legacy in Israel in general, animated this ethical position by drawing on the neighbor principle, which defined negligence by outlining the individuals for whom one was responsible. Reading this principle into the legacy of the Eichmann trial suggests how the event invoked the doctrine of duty of care in a much broader sense than the law intends. No longer limited to a legal framework, due care emerged as a social ethic, encouraging a sense of the nation that was not limited to victims, survivors, or litigants—a sense of community that transcended the collective. In this community, the key figures became neighbors rather than witnesses, and responsibility became a matter of listening to the stories—rather than the official testimonies—that would never be told in a court of law.

To expand obligation beyond the legal sphere does not mean, however, to disavow the good that can come of historic trials. Rather, it is to ask how the practice of law can imbue the ordinary with the juridical and the profane with the ethical. By way of an answer, I look at Arendt's text from several perspectives: First, as a counternarrative to the story put forward by the prosecution; second, as an attempt to set the trial within the context of a particular kind of genre—the genre of the report; third, as an expression of the underlying desire for justice beyond the law. I contend that what we learn from Arendt is not a mistrust of the legal process or a cynic's view of the Jerusalem court as a show trial. More trenchant than this, Arendt's account inadvertently implies that the conception of injury and reparation at stake in the Eichmann trial resembles tort law—inadvertently because Arendt objected to the trial as a means to the end of reparation or compensation. My aim is not to determine whether she is right, but to read her against herself, taking her observations as an index of the social reaches of law and thus accounting for its nonlegal effects. The category of the social was a notoriously vexed one for Arendt, but in its very complexity—in the fact that of all of her concepts, it was perhaps the least worked out[9]—it offers a way to imagine the normative and ethical community created by the trial.

Justice Beyond the Nation

In looking to torts to understand the Eichmann trial, this reading marks a turn away from viewing it as an exercise in nation building. Certainly from the perspective of nationalism and political identity, Arendt's critique of the trial anticipates Wendy Brown's claims about the relationship between injury and politicized identity, which Brown locates in Nietzsche's concept of *ressentiment*. The politics of *ressentiment,* she explains, "produces an affect (rage, righteousness) that overwhelms the hurt; it produces a culprit responsible for the hurt; and it produces a site of revenge to displace the hurt (a place to inflict hurt as the sufferer has been hurt). Together these operations both ameliorate (in Nietzsche's terms, 'anaesthetize') and externalize what is otherwise 'unendurable.'"[10] Indeed, accounts of the Eichmann trial frequently describe a Nietzschean dynamic in which "the moralizing revenge of the powerless"[11] gave rise to public suggestions of how best to torture and kill Eichmann and to newspaper statements declaring "Eichmann is not a human being."[12]

This chapter proposes, however, that the Eichmann trial generated a feeling beyond *ressentiment* and that its force emerged through the creation of an affective, ethical bond beyond national identity and nation building. To understand the nature of this bond, it is important to grasp the way in which Arendt positions herself as a guardian of law, a neutralizing presence to Hausner's unfortunate melodrama. Arendt saw a pressing need to provide a corrective measure for what promised to be a troubling thicket of historical facts, particularly the dark reality of the Jewish councils (*Judenräte*), the municipal administrations charged with implementing Nazi orders. She wrote to Jaspers before the trial of her fear that Eichmann's testimony would establish "to what a huge degree the Jews helped organize their own destruction. That is, of course, the naked truth, but this truth, if it is not really explained, could stir up more anti-Semitism than ten kidnappings."[13]

Addressing this concern herself, Arendt supplemented the court's account of history with her own narrative, which has been widely criticized for serious errors and oversights. Yet her tone of conviction masks an uncertainty that is easily glossed over. As Seyla Benhabib has noted, *Eichmann in Jerusalem* is marked by inconsistencies that point to Arendt's ambivalence on a number of controversial issues. "The Eichmann trial was a watershed of sorts," writes Benhabib, "because it brought to the fore the contradictions with which Hannah Arendt had struggled existentially and conceptually all her life."[14] Benhabib pinpoints the tension in Arendt's thought between the universal and the particular, conveyed in statements like the following from the Epilogue of *Eichmann in Jerusalem:* "Insofar as the victims were Jews, it was right and proper that a Jewish court should sit in judgment; but insofar as the crime was a crime against humanity, it needed an international tribunal to do justice to it" (269). While declarative in tone, Arendt's suggestion of two distinct and competing legal possibilities conveys a position rife with ambivalence and unresolved deliberation. The importance of Arendt's report, it seems, lies in these contradictions, which point to the trial's complexities and to the tensions inherent in jurisprudence. Yet these tensions are not Arendt's alone: nowhere is the conflict between the universal and the particular more evident than in the trial itself, particularly in the prosecution's attempt to bring private stories—the testimonies of over one hundred witnesses—into a public account, which it portrayed as the final chapter of a longer history of persecution. Eichmann himself often presented a private foil to the public narrative that the prosecution sought to tell about him. While the Israeli attorneys worked feverishly to show how his story converged with the larger tragedy of Jewish history, Eichmann remembered events not in their broader historical context but in their relationship to his career and personal ambitions. The profile that took shape over the course of the trial seemed more petty bureaucrat than brutal killer, an individual bent on advancing his position rather than furthering Nazi ideology. The trial's main antagonist turned out to be incapable of filling his role's larger-than-life dimensions.

Years before her assignment in Jerusalem, Arendt had already drawn a character sketch of personalities like Eichmann's in her 1945 essay "German Guilt," in which she argued that the recourse to the private world, and the retreat from public and political life, constituted the hallmark of the quintessential bourgeois individual. "What we have called the 'bourgeois' is the modern man of the masses," she wrote, "not in his exalted moments of collective excitement, but in the security (today one should rather say the insecurity) of his own private domain."[15] Arendt here foregrounds a crucial element of her criticism of the Eichmann trial, namely that while the prosecution dwelled entirely on these "moments of collective excitement"—on evidence of murderousness and avowed hatred born of a fervent allegiance to National Socialism—Hausner repeatedly found himself facing a defendant who spoke exclusively from the confines of his private experience. "Eichmann remembered the turning points of his own career rather well," Arendt notes with characteristic sarcasm, "but . . . they did not necessarily coincide with the turning points in the story of Jewish extermination or, as a matter of fact, with the turning points in history" (53).

The irony of what Arendt would come to think of as this comically empty individual—comic because he concealed no substantive thoughts to speak of—is that his solipsistic, private perspective was expressed in utterly impersonal language. His was a language of idioms, a string of clichés which his judges would angrily call "empty talk" (2); he himself apologized for being unable to think of a word at one point with the admission that "Officialese [*Amtssprache*] is my only language" (48). In contrast to his bland, myopic mode of expression, the prosecution presented witnesses who spoke to the devastating reality of forced deportations and the mass murder of Europe's Jews. Arendt took issue with the procession of witnesses not only because many of their accounts had nothing to do with Eichmann directly, but also because their language came dangerously close to its own variety of officialese. There was little that was unique or personal about their language: it trafficked in well-worn narrative devices and dramaturgical techniques. The recourse to public language was no accident in light of Hausner's conscious choice to put prominent individuals on the stand, people "with a talent for expressing themselves,"[16] as he put it, many whom had already published their stories. Arendt found these polished performances objectionable, prompting her to treat skeptically the one hundred witnesses for the prosecution "who, country after country, told their tales of horror" (223)—a phrase suggesting that these "horror stories" constituted a genre of sorts, which grew increasingly stale and transparent with each repetition.

Describing these witnesses as job candidates, she depicted them as competing for a place in Jewish and Israeli history: "all but a mere handful of witnesses were Israeli citizens, and they had been picked from hundreds and hundreds of applicants" (223). But the trope that Arendt saw as most fitting to the trial's witnesses was that of actors: the opening pages of *Eichmann in Jerusalem* present the court as theater, where "the proceedings happen on a stage before an audience, with the usher's marvelous shout at the beginning of each session producing the effect of a rising curtain" (4). The prosecution's witnesses, as she saw it, were chosen for their roles like actors auditioning for a play, delivering performances of which Arendt was deeply skeptical. It was a display that smacked contrived, with witnesses as actors, Hausner as director, and Ben-Gurion as stage manager. In the inappropriate fusion of theater and courtroom, it came as no surprise to her when the trial's excesses gave way to courtroom fiascos, as they did when the writer K-Zetnik fainted on the stand.[17] In such a well-rehearsed and carefully staged production, perhaps it was inevitable that the occasional minor character would miss his mark.

The trial's theatricality, together with its commingling of public and private stories, produced a deep discomfort in Arendt: "As witness followed witness and horror was piled upon horror," she wrote, "they sat there and listened in public to stories they would hardly have been able to endure in private, when they would have had to face the storyteller" (8). Her comment acquires literal shape in the courtroom, where witnesses did not face the audience but were positioned directly across from Eichmann—a set that Arendt described in detail at the beginning of *Eichmann in Jerusalem*: "One tier below the translators, facing each other and hence with their profiles turned to the audience, we see the glass booth of the accused and the witness box" (3). Arendt's story of the trial, besides the more explicit one about its theatricality, is also that of a missed encounter between witness and audience. It proved impossible to stage this encounter in the courtroom, since it required that one face the storyteller, listening in private rather than at a public hearing. The act of facing the storyteller, in other words, required an effort beyond the courtroom—an expansion of legal acts into the social world.

If Arendt felt that the prosecution's case established nothing beyond "the right of witnesses to be irrelevant" (225), Gideon Hausner saw the matter quite differently. The sheer volume of testimonies, he reflected, constituted a form of collective redress, allowing individual witnesses to stand in for those who had not lived to testify:

> The narratives were so overwhelming, so shocking, that we almost stopped observing the witnesses and their individual mannerisms. What impressed itself on the mind was an anonymous cry; it could have been voiced by any one of the millions who had passed through the Gehenna. The survivors who appeared before us were almost closer to the dead than to the living, for each had only the merest chance to thank for his survival.[18]

While Hausner found it painful to listen to one terrible story after another, he appeared curiously untroubled by the process through which individuals faded into anonymity as their stories became those of "anyone" and "everyone." The transformation from the particular to the anonymous can be seen as a means by which to avoid the full glare of individual suffering. Faced with stories that beggared the imagination, it was easier—and perhaps, some believed, nobler—to project the narrative into abstraction and to posit the witness as a symbol of Jewish tragedy.

Witness Versus Symbol

In contrast to this collective voice, I would like to examine the testimony of a witness who stands out for Arendt in his unalloyed singularity, garnering her esteem and approval. His testimony gives voice, quite unexpectedly for Arendt, to the unreasonable expectations of justice, the deepest hopes one has of law— a sensibility that affords a portal into the emotional undercurrent that impels individuals and nations alike to litigate their most profound sorrows. Arendt's account of the trial seems in this moment to relinquish its critical tenor, adopting a tone of pathos and admiration, however briefly.

The witness, Zindel Grynszpan, was the father of Herschel Grynszpan, whose assassination of a German diplomat in Paris sparked the *Kristallnacht* pogroms in 1938. "Mr. Hausner's first background witness did not look as though he had volunteered. He was an old man, wearing the traditional Jewish skullcap, small, very frail, with sparse white hair and beard, holding himself quite erect" (227). In contrast to Hausner's account of individual voices fusing into "an anonymous cry," Arendt is moved by the particularity of Grynszpan's testimony, so struck by his simplicity and humility that she is willing to overlook the bald fact that neither his story nor his son's had any direct relation to Eichmann.

What initially affected Arendt was Grynszpan's reluctance: a witness who "did not look as though he had volunteered," Grynszpan testified without ulterior motive, presenting himself neither as a spokesperson nor an authority. In exacting detail, Arendt tells the story of his arrival in Germany and the political circumstances that left him stateless:

> He had come to Germany in 1911, a young man of twenty-five, to open a grocery store in Hanover, where, in due time, eight children were born to him. In 1938, when catastrophe overcame him, he had been living in Germany for twenty-seven years, and, like many such people, he had never bothered to change his papers and to ask for naturalization. Now he had come to tell his story, carefully answering questions put to him by the prosecutor; he spoke clearly and firmly, without embroidery, using a minimum of words. (228)

Sensing the force of the man's unadorned language, Arendt allows his testimony to speak for itself, quoting him at length as he recounts his forced deportation from Germany to Poland in 1938:

> "The rain was driving hard, people were fainting—on all sides one saw old men and women. Our suffering was great. There was no food, since Thursday we had not eaten..." They were taken to a military camp and put into "stables, as there was no room elsewhere... I think it was our second day [in Poland]. On the first day, a lorry with bread came from Poznan, that was on Sunday. And then I wrote a letter to France... to my son: 'Don't write any more letters to Germany. We are now in Zbaszyn.'"

Arendt breaks off Grynszpan's testimony with her own words, underlining the surprising power of one quiet voice:

> This story took no more than perhaps ten minutes to tell, and when it was over—the senseless, needless destruction of twenty-seven years in less than twenty-four hours—one thought foolishly: Everyone, everyone should have his day in court. Only to find out, in the endless sessions that followed, how difficult it was to tell the story, that—at least outside the transforming realm of poetry—it needed a purity of soul, an unmirrored, unreflected innocence of heart and mind that only the righteous possess. No one either before or after was equal to the shining honesty of Zindel Grynszpan. (229–30)

The testimony, notes Deborah Nelson, "produces a moment of both engagement and resistance" for Arendt, signaling "perhaps the only eruption of sympathy in the prose of *Eichmann in Jerusalem.*"[19] But what, precisely, moved her to such a profound degree? What was it about Grynszpan's story, in addition to its "shining honesty," that produced this uncharacteristic moment in Arendt's narrative? I would like to suggest that what sparks this shift in tone is the clash between knowledge and feeling—more specifically, the manner in which general, historical fact is rendered meaningless in the face of individual, felt experience. "Don't write any more letters to Germany," Zindel Grynszpan instructs his son. "We are now in Zbaszyn."

Arendt understood perfectly what this laconic statement meant, having mentioned the city of Zbaszyn nearly 200 pages earlier in her factual description of Nazi Germany's progression toward the Final Solution. She wrote near the beginning of her historical account of "the wholesale expulsion of some fifteen thousand Jews, who from one day to the next were shoved across the Polish border at Zbaszyn, where they were promptly put into camps" (43). Grynszpan's testimony, then, told her nothing that she did not already know; by her own admission, she was one of the many spectators at the trial who did not need a history lesson. The courtroom, she commented, "was filled with 'survivors,' with middle-aged and elderly people, immigrants from Europe, like myself, who knew by heart all there was to know, and who were in no mood to learn any lessons and certainly did not need this trial to draw their own conclusions" (8). This knowledge, as Arendt noted, was already well established by the time of the Eichmann trial; Raul Hilberg's seminal work *The Destruction of the European Jews* was published in 1961, and the Nuremberg Trials had left a solid historical record of Nazi atrocities fifteen years earlier. But Grynszpan's statement of fact gestured toward a devastating experience, the fullness of which could not be accounted for by any archive. And it was *this* story, "the senseless, needless destruction of twenty-seven years in less than twenty-four hours," that overwhelmed Arendt, prompting the uncharacteristic aside, "One thought foolishly: Everyone, everyone should have his day in court."

For although many people, as Arendt insisted, already "knew by heart all there was to know," their awareness existed as a public narrative of history and national identity—an "officialese" that everyone understood to be a matter of historical record. But in the testimony of this reluctant witness, she encountered neither an Israeli citizen nor a writer who had taken it upon himself to speak for others. Here was a witness who, in his "shining honesty," did not symbolize anything other than his own experience, representing no one but himself. He stood out, in other words, as a counterexample of the role typically accorded the prosecution's witnesses, who were summoned to speak on behalf of both the living survivors and dead victims, as well as to signify the transformation of the Jewish people from statelessness to nationhood. Hausner observed, "Some of the witnesses at the trial were symbolic of this transformation. Rivka Yoselewska, the woman miraculously saved from the dead, had lost everything in a mass grave at Zagorodskie, yet she survived, remarried, and, in spite of a heart condition, gave birth to two other children. Here was a Jewish rebirth reflected in the destiny of an individual."[20] Hausner's impassioned characterization aside, it is less clear what, precisely, this rebirth means. Nearly four decades later, the historian Hanna Yablonka visited the elderly Yoselewska and remarked, "I am no longer sure today if this is what the trial's architects had in mind by way of a revival. Yoselawska did rehabilitate herself and did establish a new family, but at the time I spoke to her, neither of her sons was living in Israel. Which makes it a rather bittersweet sort of revival."[21]

Yet even Arendt recognized a symbolic dimension to the trial in Israel's right to represent the victims of Nazism. She wrote to Jaspers in 1960, "Israel has the right to speak for the victims, because the large majority of them (300,000) are living in Israel as citizens. The trial will take place in the country in which the injured parties and those who happened to survive are."[22] The categories Arendt invokes—victims, citizens, injured parties—figure here in the symbolic order of a legal system, in which individuals are counted (and spoken for) on the basis of whether, and how, they fit into these classifications. For the most part, however, Arendt found the trial's insistence on symbolism troubling, and we might thus read her text as an effort to resist it, presenting itself in the form of an unclassifiable report: neither legal scholarship nor objective journalism; difficult to pin down politically, and literary in tenor without adhering to any particular literary convention. To understand the force of her counternarrative, it is important to address these formal questions separately and to take up the question, in Hayden White's sense, of the content of Arendt's form.[23]

The Report as Genre

Given Arendt's approval of Grynszpan and her aversion to the prosecution's melodramatic witnesses, it is tempting to identify her with modernists like Hemingway or Cather and their legacy of laconic, hard-boiled, precise language.

Certainly if Arendt champions an aesthetic in *Eichmann in Jerusalem*, it consists of simplicity, directness, and an avoidance of metaphor or hyperbole—a minimalist modernism. The testimonies of "professional" witnesses thus "did not prove the rule of simplicity or of ability to tell a story" (224); they were too ensnared in the prosecution's objective of teaching the world a history lesson.

Yet in privileging economy above theatricality, this "rule of simplicity" suggests more than an avoidance of histrionic, excessive or self-conscious speech; it also makes a claim about the relationship between genre and justice, between a trial and the story one tells about it. Arendt's discussion calls attention to how generic conventions (and the ethical connotations they imply) went unheeded in practice, falling far short of the ideal of law. She is quick to take up the formal issue by calling attention to it in the report of the book's title. I want to consider what it means to think about the report as a genre, and to ask what Arendt gains—what the stakes are—in using it. The question of form ultimately concerns the relationship between storyteller and audience and as such, it speaks to the ethical relationship that takes hold in any kind of aesthetic—in this case, the aesthetic of responsibility.

Echoing her description of Gryszpan's testimony—"without embroidery, using a minimum of words"—Arendt wrote to Mary McCarthy following the book's publication: "What a risky business to tell the truth on a factual level without theoretical and scholarly embroidery."[24] In identifying her own work with his testimony, she places them under the same rubric of minimalism and the resistance to grand historical theories. We might thus read *Eichmann in Jerusalem* as itself a kind of testimony, an account that does not submit to historical or philosophical explanations, confining itself instead to unadorned facts. The embroidery Arendt refers to implies something more than overblown rhetoric; it suggests a broader fabric of scholarship, stitched together through the academic's impulse to explain or hypothesize, citing facts in order to advance a certain theory or brand of scholarship. Most of the prosecution's witnesses seemed to uphold this position all too well, seldom displaying "the rare capacity for distinguishing between things that had happened to the storyteller . . . and what he had heard and read and imagined in the meantime" (224). The trial, in other words, revealed just how hard it was to tell one's own story, and how much easier to relate personal experiences to existing, general ones. In the process, an individual's uniqueness deteriorated, since people mattered only insofar as they corroborated the narrative put forward by Ben-Gurion and Hausner. As Arendt explained it, judgment comes more easily when one bases it on general theories or groups, "the larger the better," with the result that "distinctions can no longer be made, names no longer named." (296). Working against this broad-based, "official" version, Arendt commits herself to facts rather than theories, particularly those details left out of the prosecution's account. By presenting her book as a report, she positions it, inasmuch as possible, outside existing historical theories, endorsing only the plainspoken truth. The absence of theory, moreover, also means an absence of genre; as such the "report" of her book's title appears as the closest approximation of an account free from genre—in effect, a genreless genre.

To cast her work in this light implies not only adherence to certain ethical principles but also a rejection of those elements typically associated with genre. A report—ideally—resists the sanctimonious or vengeful judgments that might accompany melodrama or tragedy. But beyond this, it also avoids one of the more glaring pitfalls of generic conventions: the use of stock characters or symbolic figures. In spite of every attempt by the prosecution to paint the portrait of a quintessential villain, Arendt remained firm in her conviction that "Eichmann was not Iago and not Macbeth, and nothing would have been farther from his mind than to determine with Richard III 'to prove a villain.' Except for an extraordinary diligence in looking out for his personal advancement, he had no motives at all" (287). Dana Villa suggests that the determination to find this prototype—and if he cannot be found, to invent him—says more about the "deeply rooted need for a picture of the 'representative perpetrator'"[25] than it does about the ready-to-hand truth of such symbolism. It also says a great deal about how difficult it is to think of criminal law in terms other than motive.[26] Thus, even as the phrase Crimes Against the Jewish People, like Crimes Against Humanity before it, established a new legal category, this rubric alone could not account for the complex new criminal upon which the Nazi regime depended. And it is *this* criminal, the person Arendt described as someone who "*never realized what he was doing*" (287), who needed to be recognized at the Eichmann trial. Changing the terms of the crime and the criminal required more than a new legal form; it demanded a new narrative content, a story to accommodate the criminal who acts without thinking, whose banality is sufficiently evil to hold him morally and legally culpable.

Consistent with Arendt's resistance to symbolism, moreover, is her refusal to view her ideas in *Eichmann in Jerusalem* in symbolic terms. She objected vehemently to those who would interpret the work as positing a "little Eichmann" in all of us. "Oh no!" she countered at a conference held in her honor, "There is none in you and none in me." Such gross generalizations mar the capacity to see Eichmann as an individual and to deal with his actions in individual terms. "This doesn't mean that there are not quite a number of Eichmanns," Arendt continued. "But they look really quite different. I always hated this notion of 'Eichmann in each one of us.' This is simply not true. This would be as untrue as the opposite, that Eichmann is in nobody. In the way I look at things, this is much more abstract than the most abstract things I indulge in so frequently—if we mean by abstract: really not thinking through experience."[27]

The significance of experience, which for Arendt is always something concrete rather than general or abstract, cannot be underestimated. Arendt was concerned, like Walter Benjamin before her, with what she saw as a widening gap between experience and the ability to communicate it, a troubling inability to talk across differences. "Experience has fallen in value,"[28] Benjamin wrote in the storyteller, addressing the silence after World War I and the deluge of information that overwhelmed the individual voice. In Arendt's post–World War II corollary to Benjamin, "not thinking through experience" amounts to not thinking in terms of the particular—and it is particularity that mattered to Arendt above all. As Dana Villa reminds us, "the desire to turn Eichmann into a symbol of the 'authoritarian personality' destroys the dimension of particularity which is the book's raison d'être. Arendt's focus on *this* man and his deeds is forgotten, the better to narcissistically worry about 'the Eichmann in each one of us.'"[29] The particular emerges as the very basis of responsibility, which is obscured by the reliance on all-encompassing explanations. Arendt goes so far as to suggest that theories bolster denial, offering a refuge from the less vaunted work of facing the truth and providing instead an "escape from the area of ascertainable facts and personal responsibility" (297).[30]

In her account, questions of motive are irrelevant: psychological depth is not what Arendt is after, and not only because she believed that people like Eichmann had no depth to speak of. Her approach, in keeping with the genre-free form of the report or the chronicle, sets out to describe individuals' surfaces rather than their depths in order to arrive at a more sweeping analytical and aesthetic position. If the past is an outline or chronicle, then the person—in outline form—is a silhouette. Walter Benjamin begins "The Storyteller" with this very image, invoking it to underscore the importance of distance over proximity. To understand the nature of the storyteller, Benjamin claims, "does not mean bringing him closer to us but, rather, increasing our distance from him. Viewed from a certain distance, the great, simple outlines which define the storyteller stand out in him, or rather, they become visible in him."[31] It is the silhouette rather than the intimate portrait that allows for perspective, setting a person against the background of his or her times. Like a report, a silhouette takes the form of an outline, tracing a person in broad strokes, attending to form rather than substance. In our post-psychoanalytic era, this certainly strikes a counterintuitive note in trading surface for depth and distance for intimacy. But this wider berth, for both Benjamin and Arendt, constitutes the very position of ethics. Suggestive rather than exhaustive, declarative rather than dogmatic, it imposes no interpretation or judgment and resists filling in details unnecessarily. As the visual manifestation of the report or chronicle, the silhouette resists both generalization and an overreliance on detail: it cannot be general because it belongs to a specific individual, but neither does it depend on psychological theories or descriptions of a person's inner life.[32]

Seeing individuals in outline form, against the dark background of a tragic period, helps us to recognize them as exceptions in their times. It suggests that even in a historical era characterized by intolerance and suffering, moral choices were possible—or as Arendt put it in the introduction to *Men in Dark Times,* "even in the darkest of times, we have the right to expect some illumination." The importance of this exceptionality lies in its specificity: in contrast to the situation in which "distinctions can no longer be made, names no longer named," it offers a name, a distinction—and the possibility of judgment rather than speculation. Zindel Grynszpan presented just such a face and a name: he reflected no destiny, fit no classification. Dressed in old-world garb, speaking without metaphors, he told his story as a narrative of baseless destruction rather than emblematic resurrection. What people, among them Arendt herself, encountered in his testimony was the existence of a private individual, an injured person whom one could imagine encountering outside the courtroom. The particularity of his account suggested that his was a story that could be told—with as much damning specificity— by any number of survivors who had not been selected to bear witness.

From Witness to Neighbor

I would like now to come at this issue of the trial's narrative from a different direction, in order to think about how the formal dimension of Arendt's work relates to tort law. I look to tort law because, like genre, it is similarly tied to questions of responsibility and acknowledgment that are always at play in the concern for the proper form of telling a story. But in addition to this, tort law also tells the story of compensation—and it is this particular issue that proves so vexing to Arendt in the Eichmann trial. The confusion between torts and criminal law, indeed, represented one of her central disagreements with Ben-Gurion and Hausner. The kind of redress they sought, to her mind, had no place in a trial of this nature, which addresses injury to a community rather than an individual:

> The wrongdoer is brought to justice because his act has disturbed and gravely endangered the community as a whole, and not because, as in civil suits, damage has been done to individuals who are entitled to reparation. The reparation effected in criminal cases is of an altogether different nature; it is the body politic itself that stands in need of being "repaired," and it is the general public order that has been thrown out of gear and must be restored, as it were. It is, in other words, the law, not the plaintiff, that must prevail. (261)

Arendt's point that the emotions driving the trial stem from civil rather than criminal law should be taken seriously. For she seems, quite presciently, to anticipate the structure of so much of post-Holocaust justice, most notably in the form of material claims against Nazi Germany. Yet even if Arendt is right, her objection points us toward tort law by denying its validity, a gesture that ultimately establishes it as a fact in the juridical imagination of the trial. What this ultimately speaks to is the nature of the connection between criminal and civil law, which is fundamentally affective: what we want, particularly in a case of such staggering harm, is reparation for each and every victim who comprises a wider community. What we can have, in the context of criminal law, is the symbolic reparation—the criminal's punishment—that figuratively heals the corporate body. Yet what Arendt construes as a misapprehension of law may be less misunderstanding than outright resistance: a refusal to accept symbolic justice when only individual reparation—itself symbolic, but at least personal—will do. It marks an unwillingness to conceive of justice without the individual, to grant that the body politic is anything but a collection of real bodies.

"One thought foolishly," Arendt felt after seeing Grynszpan on the stand, "Everyone, everyone should have his day in court." What would it mean to fulfill this "foolish" wish, and to grant every injured person a moment of justice, if not in the capacity of officially designated witnesses? Hausner's reflections offer one possibility for imagining these extralegal witnesses not as a collective, but as private individuals: "It came as a discovery to many that we are actually a nation of survivors," he wrote. "The editor of a leading newspaper told me, after listening to the shattering evidence of a woman witness in court: 'For years I have been living next to that woman, without so much as an inkling of who she was.' It now transpired that almost everyone in Israel had such a neighbor."[33] The "nation of survivors" becomes, by the end of Hausner's reflections, less a unified country than a collection of neighborhoods; the "discovery" of survivors amounted to seeing these individuals as part of a social fabric, rather than a historical record.

An evocative resonance runs through these statements—Arendt's "Everyone, everyone, should have his day in court," and Hausner's "Almost everyone in Israel had such a neighbor." Their remarks—one an unreasonable wish, the other a demographic fact—jointly point toward the forceful undercurrent of feeling that the trial set in motion: the sense that justice, and the responsibility it demands, is owed to everyone, but that practically speaking, everyone cannot have his day in court. The legacy of the trial was to ignite this foolish, impossible wish and to give it life beyond the law, in a nation built not of citizens and witnesses but of neighbors—and in which justice transpired in the responsibility these neighbors felt for each other. This responsibility, furthermore, was felt not in the letter of the law but in its spirit, in what Oliver Wendell Holmes saw as the very basis of jurisprudence itself: intuitions, felt necessities and, I would add, the unwieldy, unreasonable but undeniable emotions we bring to our visions of justice and our hopes for law.

I would like to think about this rare moment of "foolish thought" in Arendt and the neighbors who emerged as survivors—or in the legal sense, potential witnesses. Specifically, I want to consider the neighbor as a critical figure in the process of acknowledgment—indeed, as the *human figure of acknowledgment* in law and beyond it. The figure of the neighbor functions as a transitional, mediating, simple figure—simple because it is unclaimed by any particular discourse, mediating because it exists between the public and private realms. But whether public or private, the common law instructs its subjects that once someone qualifies as a neighbor, that individual is owed a measure of due care.

The relationship between negligence and neighbors, with roots in the biblical charge to love thy neighbor,[34] figures importantly in tort law with respect to duty of care, the standard of care required of an individual so as to avoid harming others. In the first half of the twentieth century, the neighbor's biblical roots were replanted in modernist soil through a basic legal question: "Who then, in law is my neighbour?" This was Lord Atkin's question in the British opinion *Donoghue v. Stevenson* (1932), in which the House of Lords famously ushered in

modern negligence law in the unlikely case of a woman who found a decompos-
ing snail in her bottle of ginger beer. The neighbor achieved a new public life
within law—and as I will argue, outside it as well—when this ostensibly private,
local figure is thus installed in the wider context of responsibility under conditions of alienation. With anonymity as a guiding principle, the *Donoghue* court
had to imagine—and to invite individual citizens to imagine—how one should
act to avoid hurting the nameless, faceless people with whom one may (or may
never) come into contact.

In formulating the "neighbor principle," *Donoghue* set out the definition of
negligent behavior by placing limits on those people to whom one owed a duty
of care, emphasizing the general requirement to avoid harming one's neighbor,
rather than highlighting specific behaviors—duties—that one must avoid in order not to be negligent:

> The rule that you are to love your neighbour becomes in law, you must not injure your
> neighbor; and the lawyer's question, Who is my neighbour? receives a restricted reply.
> You must take reasonable care to avoid acts or omissions which you can reasonably
> foresee would be likely to injure your neighbour. Who then, in law is my neighbour?
> The answer seems to be persons who are so closely and directly affected by my act that
> I ought reasonably to have them in contemplation as being affected when I am direct-
> ing my mind to the acts or omissions which are called into question.[35]

The potential unwieldiness of this logic has been criticized by legal scholars, who
cite problems like the imprecision of phrases such as "reasonable care" and "reasonably foresee."[36] Yet the opinion's innovativeness as precedent transcended
this vagueness by shifting the focus of injury from *how* to *whom*. To shift to the
imagined person, as opposed to the imagined act, is to project a silhouette: the
human outline of responsibility. Rather than delineating the harmful act, Lord
Atkin called attention to the necessity of imagining the potentially injured party.
Thus *Donoghue v. Stevenson*, which articulated the change of obligation from
feeling to action or theology to jurisprudence—from "love thy neighbor" to "you
must not injure your neighbor"—precipitated an even more significant shift by
demanding that individuals consider who might be injured by their actions (or,
in the absence of due care, inaction).

Atkin's question, too, would prove crucial for modernists in their search for
new strategies to relate public and private experience: Who, indeed, is one's
neighbor? How might one write responsibility into being, with regard to people
one may never set eyes on—one's "neighbors" next door, on the other end of a

busy street, on the other side of a crowded city, or for that matter, in another country? In the context of the silence that preceded the Eichmann trial, the injurious action can be perceived as silence at best, and a crime of negligence or omission—*not* listening—at worst. The testimonies of the trial's humbler witnesses, Zindel Grynszpan among them, put forward the notion that to hear other such stories constituted a form of obligation and not to hear them, a form of negligence.

In reading *Donoghue v. Stevenson* alongside *Attorney General v. Adolf Eichmann,* I am not suggesting that the Eichmann trial amounted to a torts case of epic proportions, although I will be suggesting that its latent content consisted of a tort rather than just a crime. Rather, its social force—registered by Arendt, articulated by Hausner—harnessed and expanded the potential of Lord Atkin's neighbor principle by conceiving of witnesses not as legal actors but as neighbors deserving a duty of care. The trial provoked this sensibility where one expected it least, implying that in this case of a traumatic, unmastered past, duty of care amounted not simply to observing the events in the courtroom—or to hearing the stories of representative witnesses—but perhaps most importantly, to listening to the unofficial, undocumented stories of those individuals in one's vicinity.

Arendt herself understood the neighbor's significance as a potentially ethical individual, having devoted a substantial portion of her doctoral thesis, "Love and Saint Augustine," to the place of the neighbor in Augustine's thought. Her interest in this figure formed part of her preoccupation with the concept of neighborly love, which she saw as exhibiting a central tension in Augustine: If one is to love one's neighbor as oneself, yet also to deny oneself in loving God, then how can the neighbor be understood "in this love which is both God-given and self-denying"?[37] In answering this question, Arendt interpreted neighborly love as the foundation of both equality and social duty:

> Though freedom of choice recalls the individual from the world and severs his essential social ties with humankind, equality receives a new meaning—love of neighbor. Yet the new meaning denotes a change in the coexistence of people in their community, from being inevitable and a matter of course to being freely chosen and replete with obligations.[38]

In her analysis, the neighbor in Augustine's theology produced a sense of community predicated on obligation rather than fate, choice rather than chance. It is also, one might add, a relationship based not on intimacy—the intimacy inherent in love—but on proximity.

Indeed, the neighbor's potential begins in nearness (a nearness that appears throughout tort law, most obviously in the notion of proximate cause); the sense of responsibility in the neighbor principle has to do not with preexisting bonds among people—not blood ties or shared history—but with physical nearness. And it is this relationship, above all, that needed to be developed and enlivened in the emergent Israeli state. Where once the Jewish people imagined connections through blood ties, the formation of a Jewish state demanded that this relationship be made anew. Ethnicity had to give way to the more straightforward but no less complicated reality of living side by side. Reflecting on the necessity of such a shift and on the potentially disastrous relationship between blood and land—*Blut und Boden*—Slavoj Žižek remarks:

> The member of a state is defined not by his or her "blood" (ethnic identity) but by being fully acknowledged as residing in the state's territory. And the state's unity was historically established by the violent erasure of local blood links. In this sense, the modern state is the outcome of an "inner migration," of the transubstantiation of one's identity . . . And perhaps, as was made clear in Fascism, violence explodes when one tries to deny the gap and bring the two dimensions of blood and soil into a harmonious unity.[39]

More than half a century later, Žižek draws conclusions similar to Arendt's in her treatment of Augustine: to think in terms of proximity rather than ethnicity, coexistence rather than transcendence, means to bring into existence a new way of being responsible. In Arendt's reading of Augustine, the feeling of love remains intact; the challenge as she saw it was to interpret and reconcile love of the divine and love of persons. In a legal context, however, this obligation becomes something rather different: a responsibility not to love one's neighbor, but to treat her with due care—a transformation, as we saw in *Donoghue v. Stevenson,* from feeling to action.

This action, in the context of Israel's post-Holocaust silence, was for Arendt an uncompromising matter of fact: a duty to relate the most painful truths and to acknowledge their existence. In the essay "Truth and Politics," Arendt replied to critics of *Eichmann in Jerusalem* who accused her of betraying the Jewish people by calling attention to the *Judenräte*, charging her with incriminating the Jews in their own destruction. She defended her decision by pointing to facts that are "publicly known, and yet the same public that knows them can successfully, and often spontaneously, taboo their public discussion and treat them as though they were what they are not—namely, secrets."[40] The painful reality of the *Judenräte* was one such fact; the brutal past of Nazi atrocities was another. In describing a nation's open secrets, Arendt traces the transition from knowledge to acknowledgment. And she suggests, moreover, that these facts have the capacity to generate social relations, the very ties that the new State of Israel (and more widely, international Jewry) so urgently needed:

> Factual truth, [unlike the isolation of philosophical truth], is always related to other people; it concerns events and circumstances in which many are involved; it is established by witnesses and depends upon testimony; it exists only to the extent that it is spoken about, even if it occurs in the domain of privacy. It is political by nature.[41]

Public and private coincide in these statements of fact, together with the personal and political. At least two discursive scenarios emerge in her description: first, the witnesses' testimony and second, the ostensibly independent discussions that take place when factual truths are "spoken about." After a prolonged silence, and in the face of forbidding taboo, the courtroom testimony of a witness serves to ratify and vivify fact, but also to set in motion the discussions that continue long after the trial ends. This fact, no longer unspoken, begins to redefine the contours of social, extralegal life—to be "spoken about" and "related to other people." The process, in short, is that of the passage from the legal to the social world, from knowledge to acknowledgment—or in human terms, from witness to neighbor.[42]

If there is any justice to be had in this articulation of factual truths, it is social justice, broadly conceived. In its legal iteration, however, Arendt's sense of justice bears little resemblance to these fact-producing relationships, coming closer instead to her understanding of the isolation inherent in philosophical truth. Legal justice, Arendt insisted, "demands seclusion, it permits sorrow rather than anger, and it prescribes the most careful abstention from all the nice pleasures of putting oneself in the limelight" (6). Her assertion was of course intended as a criticism of the Eichmann trial's exceedingly public nature, a publicity promoted by Gideon Hausner, whose opening speech—lasting a total of eight hours—found a rapt audience throughout the country. But her depiction of justice strikes a sharp contrast with the far more social scenario she would sketch six years after the trial in "Truth and Politics," defending her account in *Eichmann in Jerusalem* not on the basis of legal justice but on that of factual truth.

Once again, these differences—more ambivalences, I suspect, than discrepancies —help to clarify the relationship between the exclusively legal domain and the wider social sphere, or put differently, the movement between law and culture. For if legal justice begins in abstemious seclusion, it ends—ideally—in broader social justice, in which the legal subject is transformed into a social one. A conversation is thus set in motion that legal procedure cannot (and should not) contain. But the witnesses on the stand, who for Hausner and others gradually lost their individuality to become an "anonymous cry," also implicated—rather than signified—a world beyond the courtroom. In this context, uniqueness was returned to the individuals who would tell their stories not as witnesses, but as neighbors. Factual truth, in the trial's postscript, brought justice out of its seclusion in the courtroom, turning legal knowledge into social acknowledgment.

An analogy, one drawn by Arendt herself, proves instructive here. It concerns Rolf Hochhuth's controversial 1963 play *The Deputy*, which centers on Pope Pius XII's role during the Holocaust. The connection between Hochhuth's representation of the Pope and Arendt's depiction of Eichmann was obvious to many: both focused on men in positions of power who might have saved countless lives had they diverged from their duties. Hochhuth's play sparked a heated controversy over the Catholic Church's complicity during the Holocaust and a debate over whether the play indicted all Catholics. Arendt identified with Hochhuth as a writer whose work, like her own, was wrongly understood to pass judgment rather than set out facts—the judgment that all Catholics are guilty, in Hochhuth's work, and that Europe's Jews share responsibility for their own annihilation, in Arendt's. But Arendt was not alone in sensing a resonance between the Eichmann trial and *The Deputy*. Susan Sontag, drawing the connection between Eichmann and Pius, went even further, relating the dramatic form itself to the trial, and calling the Eichmann trial "the most interesting and moving work of art in the past ten years."[43] Like many of her contemporaries, Arendt (and Sontag) found Hochhuth's drama compelling less as a work of art (which she saw as negligible at best) than as a historical document. "The play is almost a report, closely documented on all sides, using actual events and real people, reinforced by 65 pages of 'historical sidelights' written by Hochhuth and anticipating nearly all arguments that have been raised against it."[44]

Buttressed by unimpeachable facts, Hochhuth's play was more legal exhibit than theatrical production—in the words of one critic, "a German doctoral dissertation in verse."[45] Setting aside Arendt's affinity for German doctoral dissertations, it is easy to understand why she was drawn to *The Deputy,* seeing in it a version of the report presented in *Eichmann in Jerusalem:* rather than issuing a judgment or positing a theory, it documented the facts. Hochhuth's main character, like Eichmann, could and should not be raised to a mythical or symbolic level. Neither Pope Pius nor Adolf Eichmann is Iago or Macbeth, and the play is not a parable but a precise account of one individual's actions.

One is immediately struck by the irony of the comparison between these two "exhibits"—the play that, in its dull recitation of facts, felt more like a trial, and the trial whose auditioned witnesses and emotional performances turned the courtroom into a theater. In their specific contexts, each might be said to miss the mark: the play succeeded as a report or dissertation but failed as a theatrical production; the trial created drama but overstepped the letter of the law. In the failures of each, however, we grasp something vital about the problem of both theater and law. Theater, which needs larger-than-life actors, cannot possibly accommodate the realities of true-to-life individuals—humble, ordinary, inarticulate victims. And law in its strict sense, as we saw in Chapter Two's discussion of *Palsgraf v. Long Island Railroad,* does away with the qualities that make these victims individuals to begin with: the details that make them uniquely human and their stories uniquely *theirs.* The possibility of doing justice to these stories, it seems, lies somewhere between the recognition of these failures, between the austerity of the impersonal report and the melodrama that misses the legal point. And it is a possibility that can only be realized, I believe, when we commit to living with these unfulfilled promises, acknowledging them by drawing out social possibilities from legal regrets.

Moreover, there is a further, more political danger in theater that takes us back to Nietzsche's *ressentiment.* In the national outcry of the trial that sought to return to law the human voice excluded at Nuremberg, we might detect an alarming echo of another, earlier Nuremberg: the public displays of outrage in the Nuremberg rallies. The connection would seem inadmissible, even blasphemous, particularly given recent political debates surrounding Middle Eastern politics. My point is very different: not an analogy with Nazism, which would be politically suspect to begin with, but a sense that the *differences* between the vengeance of the Eichmann and that of the Nuremberg rallies tell us a great deal about the justice of the former and the injustice of the latter. Both, significantly, were expressions of collective outrage and demands for redress. Yet the Eichmann trial was of a vastly different order not only because neither persecutor nor victims were fantasmatic, that is, shaped by paranoia, propaganda, and postwar frustration. Well beyond this, and far more significantly, the trial redeems itself from the potential of *ressentiment* by opening up another level of justice, becoming an unofficial trial of postwar speechlessness. To think about the proceedings' effect in these terms is not to project psychological or other motives onto this inaction, determining whether it is a symptom of grief, trauma, denial or hope. It is, rather, the existence of this unofficial accusation on its own that matters, the idea that the law did not *have* to be the agent of breaking the country's silence. If the law condemns Eichmann, then the trial might be said to condemn the State of Israel—or more precisely, the citizens of the fledgling state—for negligent silence.

Here, then, is the crucial and discomfiting affinity with Hochhuth's play: that *The Deputy* in a direct way, like the Eichmann trial in an oblique way, put silence itself on trial. Two offenses, in other words, were prosecuted in Jerusalem, one explicit and the other implied: first, the *crime* of genocide, and second, the *tort* of silence—and that the party accused of this silence is Israel itself. But perhaps this is precisely what revolutionary trials do: not just fulfill our need for vengeance or redress, but call into question our acts, omissions, beliefs, and assumptions. Trials that cut to the heart of nations or communities must also, I submit, cut them to the quick, evincing pain and remorse not just on the part of the accused or the victims, and making clear the need for a far-reaching social reorganization beyond the court's decision. Seeing this trial-within-a-trial as a display of vengeance rather than as the tacit prosecution of a silent nation—a trial by fire, so to speak—Arendt was unable to recognize the laying out of the social and ethical terms that gave the trial its afterlife long after Eichmann's execution.

It is widely recognized among scholars and writers that the Eichmann trial precipitated a shift in Israel from blaming the victim to blaming the persecutor,[46] and from viewing the Holocaust as a public rather than a private trauma. This transformation, as Tom Segev explained in his study of Israel and the Holocaust, *The Seventh Million,* was catalyzed by the trial's radio broadcasts, which gave events in the courtroom a place in everyday life:

> The trial became, from this point onward, the central event in the lives of many Israelis. People waited in line for hours at Beit Haam's doors for entrance passes. A television camera in the courtroom relayed the proceedings to a hall in the nearby Ratisbonne convent, which was also generally full. In those days Israel still had no television broadcasts, but much of the trial was carried live on radio; everywhere,

people listened—in houses and offices, in cafés and stores and buses and factories. The stories of terror mixed in with the sounds of routine.[47]

For those carrying on with their daily business outside *Beit Haam,* the trial made listening a quotidian matter, an ordinary rather than an exclusively legal obligation: the "sound of routine" coincided with the sound of tragic stories. Hearing these stories—"everywhere, people listened"—became more than courtroom procedure (which, in any case, was heard rather than seen), embedding itself in the unofficial contours of individual lives. The force of the Eichmann trial was thus to bring people out of seclusion, awakening a nation to the existence of private individuals with stories to tell, experiences no less searing than those of Hausner's witnesses. Law opened the floodgates for these painful stories that could not be contained or exacted in any strict juridical sense.

Building on Segev's observations, Shoshana Felman has argued that the public and private realms were reorganized in Jerusalem in a revolutionary manner: the Eichmann trial, she claims, produced "a *legal process of translation* of thousands of private, secret traumas into one collective, public, and communally acknowledged one."[48] But the trial not only brought about the recognition of a public trauma through the testimonies of witnesses; it also translated this collective trauma *back into* the private world of individuals, creating obligation beyond the court by extending it to the less formalized (and less predictable) structure of social life.

Elsewhere Felman maintains that "the conceptual revolution in the victim" that emerged in the Eichmann trial "renders sacred our own obligation to listen to the victim, to strive to take cognizance of victimization wherever it might be and to help redeem it from its silence."[49] The trial thus marked a turning point not simply because it broke a protracted silence, but above all because it made listening an act of responsibility and acknowledgment, one that reinforced a duty of care and prevailed upon individuals—not as citizens, witnesses or judges, but as neighbors—to take upon themselves a duty *to* care for the fate of their neighbors' stories.

Arendt's striking response to Grynszpan's testimony elicited a sentiment derived from torts rather than criminal law—and this is precisely the Eichmann trial's enduring power. For what moved Arendt and others who experienced the trial firsthand were those moments that spoke to the most far-reaching implications of tort law: the feeling that law ought to account for everyone, to give everyone his day in court. But the knowledge that this wish is impossible—that countless potential witnesses will not be able to testify in an official capacity—creates a space within criminal and tort law. It produces a sweeping demand that insists on the negligence of silence, forgetting, and indifference to the private anguish of one's neighbors. In the humbler, less literary or representative stories of people like Zindel Grynszpan, the Eichmann trial ultimately revealed the singularity of each survivor, each neighbor, each potential witness. Their stories, it turned out, became opportunities to confer an unexpected social dimension upon the duty of care.

Epilogue

Justice Without Proportion

In her essay "How It Strikes a Contemporary" (1923), Virginia Woolf calls upon her generation to embrace its present without measure:

> Nor has any generation more need than ours to cherish its contemporaries. We are sharply cut off from our predecessors. *A shift in the scale*—the war, *the sudden slip of masses held in position for ages*—has shaken the fabric from top to bottom, alienated us from the past and made us perhaps too vividly conscious of the present. Every day we find ourselves doing, saying, or thinking things that would have been impossible to our fathers. And *we feel the differences which have not been noted far more keenly than the resemblances which have been very perfectly expressed.*[1]

Suggesting that the seismic shifts occasioned by catastrophic history had given rise to this new present, Woolf symbolizes the incalculable losses of her generation through the image of imbalance, "a shift in the scale." The brute force of the war, before which the old bulwarks of order and sense crumbled, could not be balanced against the mundane task of carrying on. No word or deed in the present could offset the weight of the calamity.

For Woolf, this imbalance is not only born of an experience whose enormity cannot be grasped; it issues as well from those immeasurable, imperceptible feelings that arise when we attempt to master what cannot be controlled. The reassurance of familiar patterns obscures those "differences which have not been noted" but which, as Woolf insists, are deeply felt.

To arrive at justice by way of intuition is to chart an alternative course away from earlier substantive notions in legal theory and philosophy. Whether in the natural law doctrine *lex iniusta non est lex*—an unjust law is not a law—from Cicero to Lon Fuller or in theories of positive law from Austin to H. L. A. Hart, one finds time and again a belief in the availability (or potential) of clear criteria for what justice is and how to attain it. The modernist commitment to feeling also shifts the focus away from John Rawls's path-breaking theory of justice as fairness, which invokes the scales-of-justice image through its notion of redistribution.[2] This is not to say, of course, that a modernist sense of justice is in any sense opposed to fairness, only that it casts its lot with intuition and inarticulateness rather than reason or intellect. The justice elaborated under modernism takes seriously the speechlessness of emotional states, finding in them the seeds of accountability—or rather, the pressing need for new forms of responsibility.

A modernist revision of justice, moreover, originates in a sense of loss—not only in terms of the grief and trauma here associated with the world wars, but also the loss that inevitably occurs when we turn to law to make sense of our bewilderments, injuries, and sorrows. In a legal world, James Boyd White reminds us:

> Something new is made . . . but something is lost as well. The law builds itself, over time, by discarding possibilities for speech and thought as well as by making them; and what it discards is for some person or people a living language, a living truth. Such losses cannot be avoided, but should be faced directly by the law, and by those who speak its language, as losses for which it, and we, are responsible.[3]

The task of facing these juridical losses, I have been arguing, begins in a profound sense that justice can no longer be deduced rationally or calibrated intellectually. Indeed, this was apparent to Freud at the very beginning of World War I, when he proposed that the reliance on traditional understandings of death in wartime only revealed with greater clarity that "we are once more living psychologically beyond our means."[4]

To discover new means, and to do so without knowing the ends in store, would require the patience and courage to step into this beyond, and to imagine what course would be possible after war's destruction. It is a task that modernists would take on in suggesting how ordinary feelings might dictate responses to extraordinary circumstances. In this sense, Jean-François Lyotard famously described the beginnings of postwar justice as arising from emotion rather than cognition:

> Suppose that an earthquake destroys not only lives, buildings, and objects but also the instruments used to measure earthquakes directly and indirectly . . . The scholar claims to know nothing about it, but the common person has a complex feeling, the one aroused by the negative presentation of the indeterminate.[5]

This "complex feeling" of the ordinary individual is useless to the lawyer or historian who operates under traditional "cognitive rules" of evidence and thus sets such impulses aside, insisting "that history is not made of feelings, and that it is necessary to establish the facts."[6] For Lyotard, however, this feeling marks the moment before the emergence of new language, "the unstable state and instant of language wherein something which must be able to be put into phrases cannot yet be"—a state he names the *differend*.[7]

Such a commitment to living with this inarticulate state—to listening to the silence of gut feeling—characterizes legal modernism in both literature and law. Its foundation is the temporary clearing away of knowledge to make way for the force of sensibility and to experience fully what Roberto Unger has called "the sense of being surrounded by injustice without knowing where justice lies."[8] To which Thomas Keenan would add: "It is when we do not know exactly what we should do, when the effects and conditions of our actions can no longer be calculated, and when we have nowhere else to turn, not even back onto our 'self,' that we encounter something like responsibility."[9] To cast justice in such subjective, affective terms is to recognize that the limits set out by law as to where responsibility begins and ends cannot possibly do justice to the sense that, as Levinas put it, "we are responsible beyond our intentions"[10]—and, I would add, beyond our institutions. As such, one might say that our responsibility *beyond* points to a responsibility within—a duty *to our intuitions*—thereby dictating an accountability that extends beyond the traditional outlines of law.

These very intuitions—Oliver Wendell Holmes's "felt necessities"—produce another imbalance: a gulf between what is and what ought to be. These surprising intuitions—imperceptible, inarticulate, and unarticulated though they may be—are the basis for changing or creating a normative world. Our sense of how things ought to be, guided by our unspoken feelings of how things are, does not generate a proportionate world; instead, it makes the prospect of a balanced order at once impossible and undesirable.

In her appeal to law's most enduring image—the scales of justice—Woolf reminds us of the traditional conception of balance as a form of redress. Setting the world aright, in this understanding, means restoring its equilibrium: putting our actions, thoughts, and feelings into their proper place so that none remain unchecked. Yet legal modernists like Woolf, West, and Arendt suggest that responsibility begins precisely in imbalance. Woolf strikes this imbalance in her novels, writing against the proportion meted out by the Dr. Bradshaws of the

world and positing in its stead a world of interruptions, aberrations, and accidental encounters. The proportional world is undone by the undistinguished dead
in *Jacob's Room* and by strangers who spoil our best-laid plans in *Mrs. Dalloway.*
It is undone further by those unassimilable, mundane objects that both elicit
and confound memory in *To the Lighthouse.* West commits herself to remembering the Nuremberg Trial by allowing the story of its boredom to overtake,
in a strangely disproportionate way, the story of law. And Arendt, even as she
understands the communal rather than the individual aim of criminal law, still
conjures the impossible scenario of giving each person his day in court. Nothing
in the normative claims of these writers calls for the remedy of proportion.

Set against Arendt's idea of "care for the world," which implies a fundamental commitment to institutions, we might understand legal modernism as
postinstitutional—not in the sense of postmodern but in its accounts of justice
in excess of what legal or official institutions can possibly achieve. Care for the
world becomes a way of retaining the impulses at the heart of law's institutional
framework but setting them in the fabric of a more sweeping social justice. This
is not visionary so much as practical. Woolf's preoccupation with the treatment
of shell-shocked soldiers, West's concern that Nuremberg will have no meaningful place in cultural memory, and Arendt's fear that the Eichmann prosecution
in Jerusalem was so caught up in making history that it did not do enough to
foster community, all speak to the complicated relationship between institutions
and *intuitions.* Their writing gives body to the belief that responsibility has a
sensibility that law responds to—indeed, helps us identify—but cannot possibly
contain.

Each of these writers directs us toward a normative world through the experience of feeling in a way that suggests a crucial difference between legal and
literary responsibility. This difference is not one between reflection and action
or feeling and thinking: it is, ultimately, a difference of scale. In its commitment
to a balanced world, the legal process, symbolized by the scales of justice, denies
the felt necessities and imperceptible upheavals that make our most meaningful,
unbridled responses possible. The revolutionary insights of legal modernists like
Woolf, West, and Arendt take root in this surrender to imbalance, preserving
rather than rectifying it. In the aftermath of historical catastrophe, they suggest,
justice must be disproportionate.

These moments of disproportion arise, moreover, precisely when one is no
longer focused on striking a balance or "getting it right." "We keep straight on,"

Woolf notes in *Jacob's Room*—and as a corollary, "our passions are uncharted." The cost of staying on course, Woolf implies, is feeling itself; the undiverted life, we might add, is the indifferent one. Writing against indifference, legal modernists restore a capacity to feel, returning us to the fullness of an unbalanced life through the precariousness of sensibility.

To lose balance: it is here, in the unanchored, unreasoned, and unreasonable experience that the loose material of feeling rises to the surface and that responsibility, in its purest, most inexpressible and most expansive form, can take hold.

Reference Matter

Notes

Introduction

1. Michael Walzer, *Just and Unjust Wars* (1977; New York: HarperCollins, 1992) xxxi.

2. For discussions of the relationship between World War I and modernism, see (in chronological order): Paul Fussell, *The Great War and Modern Memory* (London: Oxford UP, 1975); Samuel Hynes, *The Soldier's Tale: Bearing Witness to Modern War* (New York: Penguin Books, 1997); Margot Norris, *Writing War in the Twentieth Century* (Charlottesville and London: UP Virginia, 2000); Vincent Sherry, *The Great War and the Language of Modernism* (Oxford and New York: Oxford UP, 2003).

3. While my conception of legal modernism shares some attributes with David Luban's in his book *Legal Modernism* (Ann Arbor: U Michigan P, 1994), the arguments I advance here nonetheless construe it in very different terms. For Luban, legal modernism is ultimately a way of understanding the particular nature of the academic movement Critical Legal Studies and its formulation of new ways to address legal injustice through narrative in the twentieth century. Luban shows how this movement—or any movement that would fall under the category of legal modernism—shares essential features with the high modernism of the avant-garde. While I generally agree with Luban's claims, my own approach sees legal and literary modernism as far more integrated than his book allows, and as existing in a necessarily complementary relationship.

4. See Michael Levenson, *Modernism and the Fate of Individuality: Character and Novelistic Form from Conrad to Woolf* (Cambridge and New York: Cambridge UP, 1991); Tamar Katz, *Impressionist Subjects: Gender, Interiority, and Modernism Fiction in England* (Urbana and Chicago: U Illinois P, 2000); *Crowds,* eds. Jeffrey T. Schnapp and Matthew Tews (Palo Alto: Stanford UP, 2007).

5. For treatments of modernism explicitly concerned with its public dimensions, see (in chronological order): Michael Tratner, *Modernism and Mass Politics: Joyce, Woolf, Eliot, Yeats* (Stanford: Stanford UP, 1995); Michael North, *Reading 1922: A Return to the Scene of the Modern* (New York: Oxford UP, 1999); Pericles Lewis, *Modernism, Nationalism,*

and the Novel (Cambridge, UK: Cambridge UP, 2000); Mark S. Morrison, *The Public Face of Modernism: Little Magazines, Audiences, and Reception, 1905–1920* (Madison: U Wisconsin P, 2001); Marc Manganaro, *Culture, 1922: The Emergence of a Concept* (Princeton: Princeton UP, 2002); Jed Esty, *A Shrinking Island: Modernism and National Culture in England* (Princeton: Princeton UP, 2004); Mark Wollaeger, *Modernism, Media, and Propaganda: British Narrative from 1900–1945* (Princeton: Princeton UP, 2006); Patricia E. Chu, *Race, Nationalism and the State in British and American Modernism* (Cambridge: Cambridge UP, 2006).

6. Walter Benjamin, "The Storyteller," *Illuminations*, ed. Hannah Arendt, trans. Harry Zohn (New York: Schocken Books, 1968) 84. For a discussion of how Benjamin articulates a relationship between justice, injustice, and silence, see ch. 1 ("The Storyteller's Silence: Walter Benjamin's Dilemma of Justice") in Shoshana Felman, *The Juridical Unconscious: Trials and Traumas in the Twentieth Century* (Cambridge: Harvard UP, 2002).

7. Wendy Brown, *States of Injury: Power and Freedom in Late Modernity* (Princeton: Princeton UP, 1995) xii.

8. For just some of this breadth of methodologies, see (in chronological order): James Boyd White, *Heracles' Bow: Essays on the Rhetoric and Poetics of the Law* (Madison: U Wisconsin P, 1985) and *Justice as Translation: An Essay in Culture and Legal Criticism* (Chicago: U Chicago P, 1990); Peter Goodrich, *Oedipus Lex: Psychoanalysis, History, Law* (Berkeley: U California P, 1995); Judith Butler, *Excitable Speech: A Politics of the Performative* (New York: Routledge, 1997); Nan Goodman, *Shifting the Blame: Literature, Law, and the Theory of Accidents in Nineteenth-Century America* (Princeton: Princeton UP, 1998); Peter Brooks, *Troubling Confessions: Speaking Guilt in Law and Literature* (Chicago: U Chicago P, 2000); Austin Sarat, *When the State Kills: Capital Punishment and the American Condition* (Princeton: Princeton UP, 2001); Shoshana Felman, *The Juridical Unconscious: Trials and Traumas in the Twentieth Century* (Cambridge: Harvard UP, 2002); Nasser Hussein, *The Jurisprudence of Emergency: Colonialism and the Rule of Law* (Ann Arbor: U Michigan P, 2003); Piyel Haldar, *Law, Orientalism, and Postcolonialism: The Jurisdiction of the Lotus Eaters* (London: Routledge Cavendish, 2007); William P. MacNeil, *Lex Populi: The Jurisprudence of Popular Culture* (Stanford: Stanford UP, 2007).

9. Robert Cover, "Nomos and Narrative," *Narrative, Violence and the Law: The Essays of Robert Cover,* eds. Martha Minow, Michael Ryan, and Austin Sarat (Ann Arbor: U Michigan P, 1993).

10. In approaching law along these lines, I build on Martha Nussbaum's claims in *Upheavals of Thought,* which looks to literature to understand the relationship between emotions and judgment. Nussbaum maintains, "Emotions are not just the fuel that powers the psychological mechanism of a reasoning creature, they are parts, highly complex and messy parts, of this creature's reasoning itself" (3). Against the commonplace philosophical distinction between thinking and feeling, which posits emotions as irrational distractions from the headier business of reason, Nussbaum sees emotions as "intelligent

responses to the perception of value" (1). Similarly, legal scholar Robin West has argued against the incompatible opposition between justice and care, viewing them instead as necessary preconditions of each other. "[W]hile 'justice' is typically associated with universal rules, consistency, reason, rights, the public sphere, and masculine virtues, 'care' is typically associated with particularity, context, affect, relationship, the private sphere, and femininity" (23). Taking issue with this division, she maintains that "[t]he pursuit of justice, when successful, *must* also be caring, and the activity of caring, when successful, must be mindful of the demands of justice" (24). Martha Nussbaum, *Upheavals of Thought: The Intelligence of Emotions* (Cambridge, UK: Cambridge UP, 2001) and Robin West, *Caring for Justice* (New York: New York UP, 1997).

11. Oliver Wendell Holmes, Jr., *The Common Law* (1881; New York: Dover Publications, 1991) 1.

12. Holmes 1.

13. Patricia Ewick and Susan Silbey argue eloquently for such an understanding of law in *The Common Place of Law: Stories from Everyday Life* (Chicago: U Chicago P, 1998). See also Naomi Mezey, "Out of the Ordinary: Law, Power, Culture, and the Commonplace," *Law and Social Inquiry* 26:1, pp. 145–167 (2001).

14. See Alex Zwerdling, *Virginia Woolf and the Real World* (Berkeley: U California P, 1986); Brenda R. Silver, *Virginia Woolf Icon* (Chicago: U Chicago P, 1999); Melba Cuddy-Keene, *Virginia Woolf, the Intellectual, and the Public Sphere* (Cambridge: Cambridge UP, 2003); Christine Froula, *Virginia Woolf and the Bloomsbury Avant-Garde: War, Civilization, Modernity* (New York: Columbia UP, 2005).

15. Walter Benjamin, "The Storyteller" 89.

16. See Carol Gilligan, *In a Different Voice* (Cambridge: Harvard UP, 1982) and Robin West, *Caring for Justice, supra* note 10.

17. For an excavation and genealogy of the relationship between the detail and the feminine, see Naomi Schor, *Reading in Detail: Aesthetics and the Feminine* (New York: Methuen, 1987).

Chapter One

1. John G. Fleming, *An Introduction to the Law of Torts* (Oxford: Oxford UP, 1967) 47.

2. Jane Austen, *Northanger Abbey,* ed. Marilyn Butler (1818; London: Penguin Books, 1995) 33–34. My emphasis.

3. Virginia Woolf, *The Essays of Virginia Woolf,* Vol. 2, ed. Andrew MacNeillie (London: Hogarth Press, 1986) 60.

4. Walter Benjamin, "The Storyteller," *Illuminations,* ed. Hannah Arendt, trans. Harry Zohn (New York: Schocken Books, 1968) 87. My emphasis.

5. Ibid., 84.

6. On the history of torts, see G. Edward White, *Tort Law in America: An Intellectual History* (New York and Oxford: Oxford UP, 1985), Peter Bell and Jeffrey O'Connell,

Accidental Justice: The Dilemmas of Tort Law (New Haven: Yale UP, 1997), Saul Levmore, *Foundations of Tort Law* (New York: Oxford UP, 1994), Marshall Shapo, *The Duty to Act: Tort Law, Power, and Public Policy* (Austin: U Texas P, 1977), Robert Rabin, *Perspectives on Tort Law* (Boston: Little, Brown: 1995).

7. *Indiana Springs Co. v. Brown*, 74 Northeastern Reporter 615 (1905) at 616.

8. For a detailed history of the role of accident law in American law, history, and politics, see John Fabian Witt, *The Accidental Republic: Crippled Workingmen, Destitute Widows, and the Remaking of American Law* (Cambridge, MA: Harvard UP, 2004).

9. Guido Calabresi, *The Costs of Accidents: A Legal and Economic Analysis* (New Haven and London: Yale UP, 1970) 17.

10. *Holmes v. Mather* (1875) L.R. 10 Exch. 261 at 267.

11. *Holmes v. Mather* 267, 268.

12. I do not intend to suggest that misfortune and injustice are equivalent terms—rather that in seeking to rectify injustice, the law is willing to allow for a measure of misfortune. For a sustained account of the differences between these terms, see Judith N. Shklar, *The Faces of Injustice* (New Haven and London: Yale UP, 1990).

13. Oliver Wendell Holmes Jr., *The Common Law* (1881; New York: Dover Publications, 1991) 94–95. Emphasis in original.

14. *Lynch v. Knight* (1862), 9 H.L.C. 577 at 590.

15. *Dulieu v. White & Sons* (1901) 2 K.B. 669 at 685.

16. *Dulieu v. White & Sons* 675.

17. While *Dulieu* made some progress toward a legal recognition of emotional harm, it only partially convinced courts that these harms existed independently of physical damage. So strong was the hold of physical injury, and so tenuous that of psychological harm, that many judges continued to insist on some form of physical manifestation in awarding damages to victims of nervous shock. It was commonly argued, for instance, that "Where there is no substantial physical injury claimed and the relationship between the injury caused by the impact and the mental condition for which damages are sought is not shown, as here, the lack of consequence is a matter of law for the court. Lacking that relationship we do not believe that mere impact can act as a vehicle for the recovery of damages for nervous shock or emotional injury, it not being contended that the nervous shock of the plaintiff below was a physical injury." *Monteleone v. Co-Operative Transit Co.* (1945) 36 S.E. 2d. 475, 128 W. Va 340 at 348–49. For an earlier case, see also *Spade v. Lynn & Boston R.R. Co.*, 47 N.E. 88 at 89 (Mass. 1897): "[T]here can be no recovery for fright, terror, alarm, anxiety, or distress of mind, if these are unaccompanied by some physical injury; and, if this rule is to stand, we think it should also be held that there can be no recovery for such physical injuries as may be caused solely in such mental disturbance, where there is no injury to the person from without."

18. The extension of this principle is *stare decisis et non quieta movere*, "to adhere to precedents, and not to unsettle things which are established." *Black's Law Dictionary*, 5th Ed. (St. Paul, MN: West Pub. Co., 1979).

19. Thus *Dulieu v. White & Sons* must reconstruct the case's details from its references in other opinions.

20. The former government payment is mandatory and long-term, the latter voluntary and short-term.

21. Letter to John Hodge, M.P., Ministry of Pensions, 26th December 1917. PIN 15/1399, Public Record Office.

22. PIN 15/1399, Public Record Office. The memo, initialed "JH," was most likely written by John Hodge in the Ministry of Pensions.

23. Lily Beatrice MacDonald was eventually awarded a grant of ten pounds from the European War Fund Voluntary Contribution—not the military pension for which she had petitioned, but presumably more generous than the compassionate allowance. A strange twist in the story arose, however, when the woman administering the grant sent a letter to Ministry of Pensions reporting that following the publicity generated by the MacDonald case, Mrs. MacDonald had received a marriage proposal from a man she hardly knew. The suitor had moved into her home and was financing her family. The letter continued, "I consider that if the man had wished to make her his wife the proper course to pursue would have been to take lodgings in the town and not to be living in her house. My previous record of the woman is not satisfactory as regards morals." The writer recommended giving no further funds to Mrs. MacDonald, but it is unclear from the Ministry of Pensions files whether this in fact came to pass. Public Record Office, PIN 15/1399.

24. Indeed, it is the challenge inherent in this relationship that explains Freud's striking turn in his final articulation of trauma theory, namely the famous shift in *Moses and Monotheism* from the legendary story of Moses (in which the Egyptian Moses is murdered by the Jews and replaced by another Moses) to a more ordinary account of an anonymous individual. The trauma he describes is, significantly, not spiritual or mythical but modern and industrial: "It may happen that someone gets away, apparently unharmed, from the spot where he has suffered a shocking accident, for instance a train collision" (84). Freud makes one last attempt here, near the end of his life, to leap from individual to group psychology, to move from the particularity of case histories and even the theory of traumatic nightmares in *Beyond the Pleasure Principle* to a more global proposition. Society, he contended in *Moses and Monotheism,* contains trauma at its very core, atop and around which it constructs an entire civilization. Although Freud never overcame the problem of converting a theory of individual trauma into one of collective trauma, he nonetheless provides us with a fitting model to grasp the law's difficulties in adjudicating psychological harm. In this model, latency is the operative principle, manifested in the law's belated response to those who are "apparently unharmed"—the deferred process through which their harms become apparent, whether following court martial and execution or in their or their families' prolonged suffering. Sigmund Freud, *Moses and Monotheism,* trans. Katherine Jones (1939; New York: Vintage Books, 1967).

25. The tendency for courts to uphold the common-law standard of physical impact persists, even as it continues to be debated, to this day. Even this narrowly construed

liability of psychological injuries as by-products of physical contact did not dispel worries over fraudulent claims—and so ironically, it was the very ephemeral nature of such injuries which had anchored to the impact rule that caused courts to turn away from it: "The mere fact of a physical injury, however minor, does not make mental distress any less speculative, subject to exaggeration, or likely to lead to fictitious claims." *Cullison v. Medley*, 570 N.E. 2d 27 at 30 (Indiana 1991). For other recent examples, see *OB-GYN Assocs. v. Littleton*, 386 S.E. 2d 146 (Georgia 1989), *Hammond v. Central Lane Communications Ctr.*, 816 P.2d 593 (Oregon 1991), *Shuamber v. Henderson*, 579 N.E.2d 452 (Indiana 1991) and *Marchica v. Long Island R.R. Co.*, 31 F.3d 1197 (2d Cir. 1994). For a recent and incisive examination of how tort law fundamentally misunderstands injury, see Sarah Lochlann Jain, *Injury: The Politics of Product Design and Safety Law in the United States* (Princeton: Princeton UP, 2006).

26. Some soldiers, albeit only a small percentage, did indeed pretend to be shell-shocked so as to return home. For an account of the military politics of shell shock, see Wendy Holden, *Shell Shock* (London: Macmillan-Channel 4 Books, 1998). Among the many facets of the interpretation and treatment of shell shock was its relation to soldiers court-martialed for cowardice. Holden notes, "In the minds of the top brass, men were either wounded or well; there was no middle ground. Crucially, shell shock was not admissible as a plea in a court-martial for crimes of cowardice or desertion—for which the ultimate penalty was death" (26).

27. Preston Lockwood, "Henry James's First Interview," *New York Times Magazine*, 21 Mar. 1915, p. 4.

28. Indeed, scholars like Paul Fussell and more recently, Jay Winter, have documented the ways in which emotional responses to the war drew upon traditional explanatory models or mourning rituals. See Paul Fussell, *The Great War and Modern Memory* (London: Oxford UP, 1975) and Jay Winter, *Sites of Memory, Sites of Mourning: The Great War in European Cultural History* (Cambridge, UK: Cambridge UP, 1995).

29. Samuel Hynes, *The Soldier's Tale: Bearing Witness to Modern War* (New York: Penguin, 1997) 56. My emphasis.

30. As a powerful illustration of this idea, Fussell draws our attention to the talismans that soldiers took with them to the war, noting how "no front-line soldier or officer was without his amulet, and every tunic pocket became a reliquary. Lucky coins, buttons, dried flowers, hair cuttings, New Testaments, pebbles from home, medals of St. Christopher and St. George, childhood dolls and teddy bears, poems of Scripture verses written out and worn in a small bag around the neck like a phylactery, Sassoon's fire-opal—so urgent was the need that no talisman was too absurd" (124).

31. Geoff Dyer, *The Missing of the Somme* (1994; London: Phoenix Press, 2001) 122. Historian John Keegan extends this unchanged landscape to the whole of Europe:

> It is true that the Great War, by comparison with that of 1939-45, did little material damage. No large European city was destroyed or even seriously devastated during its course, as all large German cities were by aerial bombardments during the Second

World War. . . The war inflicted no harm to Europe's cultural heritage that was not easily repaired: the medieval Cloth Hall at Ypres stands today as it did before the bombardments of 1914–18, so do the town squares of Arras, so does the cathedral of Rouen, while the treasures of Louvain, burnt in an uncharacteristic act of vandalism in 1914, were replaced piece by piece in the war's aftermath. [John Keegan, *The First World War* (1998; New York: Vintage-Random House, 2000) 7–8.]

32. Dyer 122. Douglas Davies has argued that the rituals and emotions that accompany the death of an individual can reshape an entire social world, galvanizing change in the lives—both collective and individual—of survivors. This process, however, would change radically with World War I, since these rituals were no longer possible; the changes Davies describes would have to take place through other means. See Douglas Davies, *Death, Ritual and Belief: The Rhetoric of Funerary Rites* (London: Cassell, 1997).

33. This lack of return has meant, too, that World War I continues to haunt us today, when not only shell fragments but also bodies of fallen soldiers continue to be discovered on the former battlefields of Europe. One recent harrowing incident of this sort was the discovery of the bodies of twenty British soldiers from the 10th Battalion Lincolnshire Regiment, affectionately known as the "Grimsby Chums." The skeletons were discovered arm in arm in northern France in June 2001. In a turn at once ironic and entirely fitting of recent trends of globalization, the remains of the British soldiers were discovered by French archaeologists, who were preparing the ground for a German BMW car factory. See Owen Bowcott, "Arm in Arm, Soldiers Lie in their Grave," *Guardian* [London] 20 June 2001: 3; John Lichfield, "Arm in Arm they Lie, 'Grimsby Chums' in Death as in Life, Twenty Soldiers Killed by Friendly Fire," *Independent* [London] 20 June 2001: 13; Adam Sage and Michael Evans, "The Grimsby Chums, Brothers in Arms even after Death," *Times* [London] June 20, 2001: 5.

34. Dyer 122.

35. Virginia Woolf, *Jacob's Room: The Holograph Draft* (New York: Pace UP, 1998) xxiii; Edward L. Bishop, Introduction.

36. Virginia Woolf, *The Essays of Virginia Woolf, Vol. II*, ed. Andrew MacNeillie (London: Hogarth Press, 1986) 60.

37. Woolf, *The Essays of Virginia Woolf, Vol. II*, 214–17. This conviction did not translate immediately into the development of a new form. In 1919, Woolf published *Night and Day*, which was met with severe criticism by her contemporary Katherine Mansfield, who called it "a lie in the soul." Privately, Mansfield commented that Woolf's novel proceeds as though history did not matter.

The war has never been: that is what its message is . . . the novel can't just leave the war out. There *must* have been a change of heart . . . I feel in the *profoundest* sense that nothing can ever be the same that as artists we are traitors if we feel otherwise—we have to take it into account and find new expressions new moulds for our thoughts & feelings . . . What *has* been—stands. But Jane Austen could not write *Northanger*

Abbey now—or if she did I'll have none of her. [Cherry A. Hankin, ed., *Letters between Katherine Mansfield and John Middeton Murry* (London: Virago, 1988) 204–205].

Publicly, Mansfield was no less vociferous, writing in her review of *Night and Day:* "We had thought that this world was vanished for ever, that it was impossible to find on the great ocean of literature a ship that was unaware of what has been happening; yet there is *Night and Day,* new, exquisite—a novel in the tradition of the English novel. In the midst of our admiration it makes us feel old and chill. We had not thought to look upon its like again" (Robin Majumdar and Allen McLaurin, eds., *Virginia Woolf: The Critical Heritage* [London: Routledge, 1975] 381). David Bradshaw claims that *Jacob's Room* reads as though Woolf wrote it in direct response to Mansfield's criticism. See David Bradshaw, "The socio-political vision of the novels," *The Cambridge Companion to Virginia Woolf,* eds. Sue Roe and Susan Sellers (Cambridge, UK: Cambridge UP, 2000) 196–197.

38. Winifred Holtby, in her 1932 biography of Woolf, was the first to see *Jacob's Room* as Woolf's "war book": "It is as much a war book as *The Death of a Hero* or *Farewell to Arms;* yet it never mentions the trenches, camps, recruiting officers, nor latrines. It does not describe the hero's feelings on the eve of battle; not an inch of barbed wire decorates its foreground. These things, of course, are relevant to modern war, but Mrs. Woolf does not describe them. She knew, perhaps, that her talent is unsuited to the description of violence in action, though she can measure with extraordinary range and accuracy its effect when action has ceased" (Winifred Holtby, *Virginia Woolf: A Critical Memoir* [Chicago: Academy Press-Cassandra, 1978] 116). As I will argue here, however, I understand Woolf's turn away from realism not as testament to the fact that her talent does not lie in vivid war-front description; rather, I see it as her commitment to the trauma of those on the home front, for whom the war remained largely invisible. For a detailed account of the significance of 1922 to modernism, see Michael North's *Reading 1922: A Return to the Scene of the Modern* (New York and Oxford: Oxford UP: 1999).

39. Benjamin 94.

40. John Mepham, "Mourning and Modernism," *Virginia Woolf: New Critical Essays,* eds. Patricia Clements and Isobel Grundy (London: Vision-Barnes and Noble, 1983) 143.

41. One of the most publicized poems of the Great War, John McCrae's "In Flanders Fields" was published in December 1915 in *Punch* magazine. With its call to arms—its speaker is a dead soldier exhorting the living to "Take up our quarrel with the foe"—the sonnet quickly became a recruiting tool, encouraging young men throughout England to enlist in the military. Its instant popularity meant that the name Flanders came to be associated with the war even before it was halfway over. McCrae himself, like the speaker in his poem, would not survive the war, dying of pneumonia in France in 1918. See Jon Silkin, ed., *The Penguin Book of First World War Poetry,* 2nd ed. (London: Penguin, 1996) 85.

42. Virginia Woolf, *Jacob's Room* (1922; New York: Harcourt Brace, 1950) 39. All subsequent references will be cited parenthetically in the text.

43. Christine Froula, *Virginia Woolf and the Bloomsbury Avant-Garde: War, Civilization, Modernity* (New York: Columbia UP, 2005) 70, 69.

44. Virginia Woolf, "Jane Austen," *The Common Reader*, ed. Andrew McNeillie (New York: Harcourt Brace, 1925) 139.

45. Holtby 83. Katherine Mansfield sounded a similar note in her review of *Night and Day*: "It is impossible to refrain from comparing *Night and Day* with the novels of Miss Austen." *Virginia Woolf: The Critical Heritage*, eds. Robin Majumdar and Allen McLaurin (London and Boston: Routledge and Kegan Paul, 1975) 80.

46. Virginia Woolf, *A Writer's Diary*, ed. Leonard Woolf (New York: Harcourt Brace, 1953) 56. As Michael Levenson has argued, "One of the great concealed dramas of the modern novel is the struggle between certain enduring traits in literary character and certain innovations in narrative structure, the contest between a notion of fictional self inherited from nineteenth-century precedents and the new literary forms designed to contain it." Michael Levenson, *Modernism and the Fate of Individuality: Character and Novelistic Form from Conrad to Woolf* (Cambridge: Cambridge UP, 1991) xii.

47. Like Conrad and many others, Woolf was critical of the press' inability to communicate the war's brutality. She concluded her 1917 story "The Mark on the Wall" with an anonymous figure announcing, "I'm going out to buy a newspaper . . . Though it's no good buying newspapers . . . Nothing ever happens. Curse this war; God damn this war!" Virginia Woolf, "The Mark on the Wall," *The Complete Shorter Fiction of Virginia Woolf*, ed. Susan Dick (San Diego: Harcourt Brace-Harvest, 1989) 89. Paul Fussell notes how "A lifelong suspicion of the press was one lasting result of the ordinary man's experience of the war" (316). Woolf's privileging of feeling over understanding can be gleaned from her reading of the French philosopher Julien Benda. She records in her reading notebook: "They think that to feel a thing means that you understand it but a mere prolongation of feeling does not produce understanding—there is an hiatus— you must perhaps just(?) have lived it: but the understanding is a separate process" (Virginia Woolf, reading notebook, Monks House Papers, [MHP/B.2.d], University of Sussex).

48. Benjamin 208. "Seine Begabung ist; sein Leben, seine Würde; sein *ganzes* Leben erzählen zu können." Benjamin, *Illuminationen* (Frankfurt: Suhrkamp, 1972) 410.

49. Virginia Woolf, "How Should One Read a Book?" *The Second Common Reader*, ed. Andrew MacNeillie (1932; San Diego: Harcourt Brace-Harvest, 1986) 258.

50. Compare, in this regard, the fact that Jacob does not return and so will not be buried at home, with the reflections on this father's death that begin the novel. "'Merchant of this city,' the tombstone said; though why Betty Flanders had chosen so to call him when, as many still remembered, he had only sat behind an office window for three months . . . Had he, then, been nothing?" (16).

51. Wilfred Owen, "Anthem for Doomed Youth," *The Poems of Wilfred Owen*, ed. John Stallworthy (New York and London: W.W. Norton and Co., 1986) 76.

52. Virginia Woolf, *Jacob's Room: The Holograph Draft* 275. For Bishop's further elaborations on Woolf's rewriting of this ending, see Edward L. Bishop, "The Shaping of *Jacob's Room*: Woolf's Manuscript Revisions," *Twentieth Century Literature* 32 (1986): 115–35; Charles G. Hoffman, "From Lunch to Dinner: Virginia Woolf's Apprenticeship," *Texas Studies in Literature and Language: A Journal of the Humanities* 10 (1969): 609–27; Christine Froula, "The Death of Jacob Flanders," *Virginia Woolf and the Bloomsbury Avant-Garde* 63–84. In taking the chapter as a confirmation of Jacob's death, my reading parts ways with Karen Levenback's suggestion that the conclusion does not necessarily verify Jacob's death but rather makes it "as uncertain as the war." See Karen Levenback, *Virginia Woolf and the Great War* (Syracuse: Syracuse UP, 1999) 42.

53. Edward Bishop, Introduction, Woolf, *Jacob's Room: The Holograph Draft* xx.

54. Woolf, *Common Reader* 139.

Chapter Two

1. "The Faces Emerge," editorial, *New York Times,* 16 September 2001, 4:10.

2. Barbara Johnson, *A World of Difference* (Baltimore and London: Johns Hopkins UP, 1987) 16.

3. John T. Noonan Jr., *Persons and Masks of the Law: Cardozo, Holmes, Jefferson, and Wythe as Makers of the Masks* (1976; Berkeley: University of California Press, 2002) xv.

4. G. Edward White, *Tort Law in America: An Intellectual History* (New York and Oxford: Oxford Univ. Press, 1985) 16. For a perceptive account of these stranger cases in nineteenth-century American literature, see Nan Goodman, *Shifting the Blame: Literature, Law and Accidents in Nineteenth-Century America* (Princeton: Princeton UP, 1998).

5. Oliver Wendell Holmes Jr., "The Theory of Torts," *7 Am. L. Rev.* 660 (1873).

6. *Palsgraf v. Long Island Railroad Company,* 248 NY 339 at 340–41 (1928). All subsequent references will be cited in the text as P, followed by page number.

7. Noonan uncovers these details in his research on *Palsgraf* in *Persons and Masks of the Law.*

8. See Pierre Bourdieu, "The Force of Law," 38 *Hastings Law Journal* 819 (1987).

9. Along these lines, see Leon Green, "The Palsgraf Case," 30 *Col. L. Rev.* 789 (1930); William Lloyd Prosser, "Palsgraf Revisited," *Selected Topics on the Law of Torts* (Ann Arbor: U of Michigan Press, 1953) 191–242; Ernest J. Weinrib, "The Passing of Palsgraf?" 54 *Vanderbilt L. Rev.* 803 (2001).

10. Noonan 127.

11. Noonan 127.

12. Oliver Wendell Holmes Jr., "The Path of the Law," 10 *Harv. L. Rev.* 457 (1897), 457.

13. Virginia Woolf, diary entry, April 8, 1925, *A Writer's Diary,* ed. Leonard Woolf (New York: Harcourt Brace, 1953) 70.

14. Paul Fussell, *The Great War and Modern Memory* (London: Oxford UP, 1975) 87.

15. This does not suggest, however, that no official efforts were made to assist return-ing soldiers and to compensate them for war injuries. For a rich account of the treatment of World War I veterans in England and Germany, see Deborah Cohen's *The War Come Home: Disabled Veterans in Britain and Germany, 1914–1939* (Berkeley: U Calif. P, 2001).

16. Editorial, *Shrewsbury Chronicle*, 4 April 1919, National Inventory of War Memo-rials, Imperial War Museum, London.

17. Letter to the editor, *Shrewsbury Chronicle*, 23 April 1920, National Inventory of War Memorials, Imperial War Museum, London.

18. Maria DiBattista, for instance, saw in the novel a "philosophy of anonymity" (63), which she attributes to the narrative technique of placing the artistic mind at a distance from its creations. See *Virginia Woolf's Novels: The Fables of Anon* (New Haven: Yale UP, 1980). Compare Pamela L. Caughie, who also notes this dialectic of involvement and de-tachment: "Just as the narrator merges with characters yet remains, for the most part, de-tached, so Clarissa participates in scenes even as she stands apart from them. She shares Woolf's artist figure's dual perspective of being both within a scene (creating) and with-out (observing)." This sense of balance, however, elides the novel's commitment to so-cial chaos, to the chance encounters that throw even the most carefully planned event— Clarissa's party—off balance. (Pamela L. Caughie, *Virginia Woolf and Postmodernism: Literature in Quest and Question of Itself* [Chicago: U of Illinois Press, 1991] 74). For a related but subtler account of the novel's narrative technique, compare J. Hillis Miller's dictum of the text's necessary precondition of disunity: "The cogito of the narrator of *Mrs. Dalloway* is, 'They thought, therefore I am.'" (J. Hillis Miller, *Fiction and Repetition: Seven English Novels* [Cambridge, MA: Harvard UP, 1982] 180–81).

19. Virginia Woolf, *Mrs. Dalloway* (New York: Harcourt Brace Jovanovich, 1925) 5. All subsequent references will be cited parenthetically in the text.

20. Holmes, "The Path of the Law" 457.

21. John Mepham, for instance, understands the move from *Jacob's Room* to *Mrs. Dal-loway* as one in which "[t]he emphasis was no longer on Jacob's silence but on Clarissa's interior sounds and images." *Virginia Woolf: A Literary Life* (New York: St. Martin's Press, 1991) 89.

22. Paul K. Saint-Amour, "Air War Prophecy and Interwar Modernism," *Compara-tive Literature Studies* 42:2 (2005): 131. See also Vincent Sherry's reading of this scene as "a restaged memory of the Great War" in *The Great War and the Language of Modernism* (Oxford: Oxford UP, 2003) 265.

23. Wilfred Owen, *The Poems of Wilfred Owen*, ed. John Stallworthy (New York: Norton, 1986) 76.

24. And yet the man Woolf had in mind as she developed Septimus Smith's charac-ter was precisely an individual who pursued justice in the unlikeliest of circumstances. Siegfried Sassoon, who expected to be court-martialed for his antiwar poems and *non-serviam*, "A Soldier's Declaration" (1917), was instead advised by a medical board to seek

rest at a mental sanitarium in Scotland. He eventually returned to the front, and in 1918 published another antiwar volume, *Counter-Attack and Other Poems,* which Woolf reviewed in the *Times Literary Supplement.*

25. W. H. R Rivers, "Repression of War Experience," *Instinct and the Unconscious* (1920; Cambridge: Cambridge UP, 1922) 187.

26. Freud explained this gatekeeper as standing guard between the "large entrance hall" of the unconscious and the "drawing room" of consciousness: "But on the threshold between the two rooms a watchman performs his function: he examines the different mental impulses, acts as a censor, and will not admit them into the drawing-room if they displease him." See Freud, "Nineteenth Lecture: Resistance and Repression," *Introductory Lectures on Psycho-Analysis,* trans. and ed. James Strachey (1920; New York: W. W. Norton and Co, 1966) 366.

27. Aristotle, *The Nichomachean Ethics,* Book 5, trans. J. E. C. Welldon (Amherst, NY: Prometheus Books, 1987) 151–53.

28. Proportion's companion piece—her "sister"—is never far behind: "Conversion is her name, and she feasts on the wills of the weakly, loving to impress, to impose, adoring her own features stamped on the face of the populace" (100). Here, then, is Woolf's figure for judgment, which accompanies and reinforces the limiting principles of proportion. Like its sibling, Conversion too deals in blindness, seeing only the interest of a larger, but not necessarily clearer, principle.

29. On the representation of death in Woolf's novels, see Mark Spilka, *Virginia Woolf's Quarrel with Grieving* (Lincoln, NE, and London: U Nebraska P, 1980).

30. On the gendered differences between the clocks' acts of keeping and disrupting time, see Rachel Bowlby, *Feminist Destinations and Further Essays on Virginia Woolf* (Edinburgh: Edinburgh UP, 1997) 78–79.

31. This connection between the woman and Septimus contrasts with that offered by Elizabeth Abel, who takes this moment as illustrative of the changes in female intimacy over time: "Clarissa's willingness to contemplate an emblem of age instead of savoring a memory of youth suggests a positive commitment to development." This reading, which approaches the novel as inward-turning and meditative, overlooks its force as a normative, outward-turning text. See Elizabeth Abel, *Virginia Woolf and the Fictions of Psychoanalysis* (Chicago: U Chicago Press, 1989) 40.

32. Levinas, "The *I* and the Totality," *Entre Nous: Thinking-of-the-Other,* trans. Michael B. Smith and Barbara Harshav (New York: Columbia UP, 1998) 32.

33. Levinas "The *I* and the Totality," 35.

34. Virginia Woolf, notebook entry, Monks House Papers(MHP/A 20), University of Sussex. In a letter to Woolf on March 23, 1941, E. M. Forster would echo these very thoughts in connection to *Jacob's Room:* " I opened Jacobs Room to find a quotation yesterday and was so much moved, also so sad that 'all that' has stopped working for the moment; all that hope of learning and loveliness steadying and spreading. But these are great

times and occasionally one stretches oneself toward being in [scale?] with them, and is helped by work like yours." (Monks House Papers [Letters III], University of Sussex.)

35. Virginia Woolf, diary entry, September 13, 1940, *A Writer's Diary* 335.

Chapter Three

1. Margaret Atwood, *Morning in the Burned House* (Boston: Houghton Mifflin, 1995) 126–27.

2. Vera Brittain, *Testament of Youth: An Autobiographical Study of the Years 1900–1925* (1933; New York: Penguin Books, 1989) 251. Brittain served as a war nurse in London, on Malta, and on the Western Front.

3. Brittain 252. Emphasis added.

4. These questions acquired renewed urgency and contemporary relevance in the United States in the aftermath of September 11, which saw an overwhelming rise in the number of people rushing to make wills. *The New York Times* reported that "[a] number of lawyers suggested that the very nature of the attack meant that the rush in estate planning was not about to fade. Since so many of the victims were so young, it is just a matter of time until their estates wind up in court, the subject of litigation and confusion over the intentions of men and women who never expected to die without a will" (Adam Nagourney, "Jolted by Sept. 11, Many Rush to Make Wills," *The New York Times* 13 Dec. 2001: A.1.)

5. Jeremy Bentham, *The Theory of Legislation,* ed. C. K. Ogden (1802; Littleton, Colorado: Fred B. Rothman and Co., 1987) 112. Originally published in French as *Traités de legislation civile et pénale,* 3 vols., trans. Etienne Dumont (Paris, 1802).

6. Bentham 112.

7. Bentham 112. Emphasis added.

8. Indeed, the surge in estate planning immediately following September 11 has been attributed to people imagining their deaths not as remote possibilities but as vivid realities. One attorney interviewed by *The New York Times* noted, "Sept. 11 took away the ability to do what people do when they come in to talk about wills, which is to say, 'Here's what I'd like to do if I die.'—as if they have a choice . . . Now it's not if but when." Nagourney A.1.

9. Bentham 111.

10. Cathy Caruth, *Unclaimed Experience: Trauma, Narrative, and History* (Baltimore: Johns Hopkins University Press, 1996) 7.

11. Virginia Woolf, *Jacob's Room* (1922; New York: Harcourt Brace-Harvest, 1950) 176.

12. A notable exception to this critical gap is Douglas Mao's *Solid Objects: Modernism and the Test of Production* (Princeton: Princeton UP, 1998) and its sustained treatment of Woolf's materiality. Deborah Esch approaches the subject through Woolf's connection to Hume's philosophy in "'Think of a kitchen table': Hume, Woolf, and the Translation of Example," *Literature as Philosophy, Philosophy as Literature,* ed. Donald G. Marshall (Iowa City: Univ. of Iowa Press, 1987) 262–276.

13. Arnold Bennett, rev. of *To the Lighthouse, Evening Standard,* 23 June 1927: 5, in *Virginia Woolf: The Critical Heritage,* eds. Robin Majumdar and Allen McLaurin (London and Boston: Routledge and Kegan Paul, 1975) 200. In her next novel, *Orlando,* Woolf would reply to Bennett by embedding his criticism in her own prose, simultaneously acknowledging and disparaging it. The span of years, her narrator notes in that novel, does indeed bring little change, "a conclusion which, one cannot help feeling, might have been reached more quickly by the simple statement that 'Time passed' (here the exact amount could be indicated in brackets) and nothing whatever happened." *Orlando* (1928; New York: Harcourt Brace & Co., 1956) 98.

14. Virginia Woolf, *To the Lighthouse* (1927; New York: Harcourt Brace & Co., 1951) 128–129. All subsequent references will be cited parenthetically in the text.

15. Gaston Bachelard, *The Poetics of Space,* trans. Maria Jolas (1958; Boston: Beacon Press, 1969) 14.

16. Bachelard 106.

17. Penelope Lively, *A House Unlocked* (New York: Grove Press, 2001) xi.

18. On the relationship between the philosopher (Mr. Ramsay), the artist (Lily), and the text (Mrs. Ramsay) in *To the Lighthouse,* see Gayatri Chakravorty Spivak, "Unmaking and Making in *To the Lighthouse,*" *In Other Worlds: Essays in Cultural Politics* (New York and London: Routledge, 1988) 30–45.

19. *The Collections* (London: Imperial War Museum, n.d.) 30.

20. Christopher Hussey, *The Life of Sir Edwin Lutyens* (London: Country Life Ltd., 1950) 392.

21. Hussey 393. Emphasis added.

22. G. S. Cooper, *The Outdoor Monuments of London* (1928), quoted in Penelope Curtis, "The Whitehall Cenotaph: An Accidental Monument," *The Cenotaph Project* (Derry: Orchard Gallery, 1991) 12.

23. Quoted in David Cannadine, "War and Death, Grief and Mourning in Modern Britain," *Mirrors of Mortality: Studies in the Social History of Death,* ed. Joachim Whaley (New York: St. Martin's Press, 1981) 225. Emphasis added. Geoff Dyer echoes this sentiment in a similar but decidedly less enthusiastic vein: "Over the years, passing by in a bus or on a bike, I have seen the Cenotaph so often that I scarcely notice it. It has become part of the unheeded architecture of the everyday. The empty tomb has become the invisible tomb" (Geoff Dyer, *The Missing of the Somme* [1994; London: Phoenix Press, 2001] 19).

24. "Cenotaph Blunder Reconsidered by the Cabinet," *Daily Chronicle* [London] 22 Oct. 1923. Public Record Office HO 45/11557/392664. In the end, the ceremony was abandoned altogether that year because November 11th fell on a Sunday.

25. "At the Cenotaph," *Daily Chronicle* [London] 19 Oct. 1923, Public Record Office HO 45/11557/392664.

26. Cannadine 197.

27. Quoted in Hussey 394.

28. Curtis 2.

29. Concerns over the Cenotaph, in fact, often related to containing the public's emotional response to it, particularly on Armistice Day. A Home Office document from 1922 notes the worry over crowd control following the events of the previous years' celebrations: "Last year when the troops marched off, the crowds broke through the Police and surged in a seething mass round the Cenotaph. This might be borne in mind and some force of Police concentrated immediately North and South of the Cenotaph before the troops march off." Public Record Office HO 45/11557/392664/30.

30. Brittain 252.

31. Brittain 251.

32. Erich Auerbach, "The Brown Stocking," *Mimesis: The Representation of Reality in Western Literature,* trans. Willard R. Trask (1946; Princeton: Princeton UP, 1968) 540.

33. Auerbach 529.

34. Virginia Woolf, "To Roger Fry," 27 May 1927, *Congenial Spirits: The Selected Letters of Virginia Woolf,* ed. Joanne Trautmann Banks (San Diego: Harcourt Brace Jovanovich, 1989) 228.

35. Bill Brown, "Thing Theory," *Critical Inquiry* 28 (2001) 4.

36. John Locke, *Second Treatise on Civil Government* (1690) (Amherst, NY: Prometheus Books, 1986) 87.

37. This moment might be taken, too, as Woolf's jab at realism, as her literal depiction of art not measuring up to life. For in spite of her efforts, Mrs. Ramsay finding that the stocking is "too short . . . ever much too short" is a failing that would keep her at her knitting for the remainder of the novel.

38. Auerbach 552.

39. Rebecca West would express a similar notion of selectivity and things in 1928, in the title essay to her volume *The Strange Necessity.* "The problem of art," West writes, "is to communicate to the beholder an emotion caused in the artist by a certain object; and though it is possible that every attribute of that object, all its relations in time and space, are relevant to that emotion, it is not very probable. It is far more likely that the object will have a number of attributes which are merely cords that secure it a place in the world of physical fact, in the world of naïve realism, which is the world in which it must be for the artist to catch sight of it, but from which he must remove it in order to treat it; and that it has yet other attributes of a sort which might interest another artist but not this particular one." *The Strange Necessity: Essays by Rebecca West* (Garden City, NY: Doubleday, Doran & Co., 1928) 22.

40. Woolf made a more explicit case against such still life in an essay on Joseph Conrad, "Mr. Conrad's Crisis": "But in a novel we demand something more than still life, and where the still life is thus superbly designed we want humanity as largely modeled and inspired by a vitality deep and passionate in proportion to the magnificence of the conception." (*The Essays of Virginia Woolf,* ed. Andrew MacNeillie, vol. 2 [London:

Hogarth Press, 1986] 227.) She had, moreover, a powerful public model for this stillness in her own time, for the Cenotaph, which she witnessed in its full public grandeur while attending the Armistice Day celebration, soon became an official model of stillness—a stillness, literally, on a monumental scale. In 1919, the British government instituted a two-minute silence, an interval that became known as the Great Silence, at eleven o'clock on the morning of Armistice Day, November eleventh ("the eleventh hour of the eleventh day of the eleventh month"). During the Great Silence's observance, which continues to the present day, the nation grinds to a halt for two minutes: traffic is instructed to stop in the street and pedestrians are expected to stand at attention. For a discussion of the connection between the Great Silence and Woolf's previous novel, *Mrs. Dalloway,* see Vincent Sherry, *The Great War and the Language of Modernism* 265–66.

41. Roland Barthes, *Camera Lucida: Reflections on Photography,* trans. Richard Howard (1980; New York: Farrar, Straus and Giroux, 1981) 26–27.

42. This partial acquisition, I would suggest, is something that Bentham did not imagine outside the law. Law, for him, was the only way to induce individuals to work for gains in the future, since it was the only thing that would guarantee a lasting claim to the fruits of their labor: "Law alone has done that which all the natural sentiments united have not the power to do. Law alone is able to create a fixed and durable possession which merits the name of property . . . Nothing but law can encourage men to labours superfluous for the present, and which can be enjoyed only in the future" (Bentham 110). Yet the brown stocking, in its perpetual near-completeness, prompts the very labors that will never be realized in the present.

43. Hermione Lee, *The Novels of Virginia Woolf* (New York: Holmes and Meier Publishers, 1977) 123.

44. M. R. Cohen, "Property and Sovereignty," 13 *Cornell LQ* 8 (1927) 12.

45. The abortive efforts to convene an international criminal trial following World War I suggest as much. For an analysis of how these attempts foregrounded the international trials after World War II, see James F. Willis, *Prologue to Nuremberg: The Politics and Diplomacy of Punishing War Criminals of the First World War* (Westport and London: Greenwood Press, 1982).

Chapter Four

1. Rebecca West, *The Meaning of Treason* (London: MacMillan & Co., 1949) 70.

2. Patricia Meyer Spacks, *Boredom: The Literary History of a State of Mind* (Chicago: U of Chicago P, 1995) 24.

3. See in this regard Marc Osiel, *Mass Atrocity, Collective Memory, and the Law* (New Brunswick, NJ: Transaction Publishers, 2000).

4. Although there were twelve trials conducted under the American occupation authorities in Nuremberg between 1946 and 1949, I refer in this chapter only to the first

Nuremberg trial of the major war criminals, which is commonly referred to as the Nuremberg Trial.

5. Indeed, the decade following these trials saw the field of jurisprudence grappling with questions of law's constitution and basis. The 1958 debate between legal scholars H. L. A. Hart and Lon Fuller, which grappled with the question of whether unjust law nonetheless constituted law, illustrated the force with which the issues raised by Nuremberg—and in the case of the Hart-Fuller debate, the tension between positive and natural law—resonated in the wake of the trials. See H. L. A. Hart, "Positivism and the Separation of Law and Morals," 71 *Harv. L. Rev.* 593 (1958), and Lon L. Fuller, "Positivism and Fidelity to Law—A Reply to Professor Hart," 71 *Harv. L. Rev.* 630 (1958).

6. Laurel Leff, "Jewish Victims in a Wartime Frame: A Press Portrait of the Nuremberg Trial," in *From the Protocols of the Elders of Zion to Holocaust Denial Trials: Challenging the Media, the Law, and the Academy,* Debra Kaufman, Gerald Herman, James Ross, and David Phillips, eds. (London: Valentine Mitchell, 2007) 82. For a broader account of journalism in the United States during the Holocaust, see Leff's *Buried by The Times: The Holocaust and America's Most Important Newspaper* (Cambridge: Cambridge UP, 2005).

7. Gloria Fromm has proposed that trials held particular appeal for West because of their limited framework, one that "provided a ready-made structure" into which she was able to integrate psychological reflections about the individuals on trial. As I will argue with respect to West's essays on Nuremberg, however, her focus shifted away from the experience of those on trial, settling instead on the experience of those who sat and watched the proceedings—thereby pushing the conventional format of trial reporting to its limits. See Gloria G. Fromm, "Rebecca West: The Fictions of Fact and the Facts of Fiction," *New Criterion* 9.5 (1991) 44.

8. See, for example, Zofia P. Lesinska, *Perspectives of Four Women Writers on the Second World War: Gertrude Stein, Janet Flanner, Kay Boyle, and Rebecca West,* Studies in Literary Criticism and Theory Ser. 17 (New York: Peter Lang, 2002) and Brian Hall, "Rebecca West's War," *New Yorker* 15 April 1996: 74–83.

9. For an important and much-needed corrective reading of the continuity between *The Return of the Soldier* and West's postwar writing on the state, see Patricia E. Chu, "Soldiers and Traitors: Rebecca West, the World Wars and the State Subject," in *Race, Nationalism and the State in British and American Modernism* (Cambridge: Cambridge UP, 2006) 79–114.

10. Rebecca West, *A Train of Powder* (London: MacMillan, 1955) 8.

11. Rebecca West, undated note, Box 38, Folder 1402, Rebecca West Papers. General Collection of Rare Books and Manuscripts. Beinecke Rare Book and Manuscript Library, Yale University.

12. Rebecca West, *A Train of Powder* (London: MacMillan, 1955) 3. All subsequent references will be cited parenthetically in the text.

13. Robert E. Conot, *Justice at Nuremberg* (New York: Harper & Row, 1983) xi.

14. Robert H. Jackson, "Opening Address for the United States, Nuremberg Trials," in *Philosophical Problems in the Law,* ed. David M. Adams (2d edition; Belmont, CA: Wadsworth, 1996) 5.

15. Otto Fenichel, "On the Psychology of Boredom," in *The Collected Papers of Otto Fenichel: First Series* (New York: W.W. Norton and Co, 1953) 301. Emphasis in the original.

16. "During the Nuremberg trial, the *Times* reporters fully accepted the prosecutors' version of the case, so much so that they departed from standard journalistic practices. They abandoned even the pretense of objectivity or journalistic balance, never referring to 'alleged crimes' or bothering to couch the defendants' guilt in terms of the presumption of innocence. Nor did they challenge the authenticity or reliability of the prosecution's evidence, or suggest an alternative interpretation of witnesses' testimony." Leff, "Jewish Victims in a Wartime Frame" 85.

17. Rebecca West, *Ending in Earnest: A Literary Log by Rebecca West* (Garden City, NY: Doubleday, Doran & Co., 1931) 34–35.

18. West, *Ending in Earnest* 38.

19. West, *Ending in Earnest* 38–39.

20. West, *Ending in Earnest* 38.

21. Janet Flanner, "Letters from Nuremberg," in *Janet Flanner's World: Uncollected Writings 1932–1975,* ed. Irving Drutman (New York: Harcourt Brace Jovanovich, 1979) 109.

22. Flanner would repeat this contrast in various ways throughout her reports, as she does in her description of the trial's ceremonial grandeur: "One of the sights outside the courthouse is the glorious daily arrival of Sir Geoffrey in a magnificent black limousine, glistening against the dusty ruins of the bombed walls. Attired in a long, blue broadcloth coat and a bowler, he passes through the courthouse door while the Allied guards of the day—the Russians with medals or the French with berets or the Tommies with battle ribbons or the Americans in snow-white helmets—stiffly present arms. In the courtroom itself, the same physical dignity and sartorial elegance of prosecutor Sir David Maxwell Fyfe, impeccable in his Foreign Office attire, have unquestionably affected the Nazis, hypersensitive to formality and chic in the male." Flanner, "Letters from Nuremberg" 120.

23. The same lack of distinction extends West's understanding of the relationship between public and private in her sweeping work *Black Lamb and Grey Falcon.* As Janet Montefiore has argued with regard to this volume, "The story of Rebecca West's own journey cannot, then, be separated from the wider story of Yugoslavia, which is itself a stage for the European crisis. You cannot distinguish private from public: personal friendships express political hope and divisions, no more and no less than the mine at Trepcha, the buildings in the cities, the marketplaces. Yugoslavia is not only a border country; it is a stage where tensions of Europe are acted out, in intimacies as well as in

battles." Janet Montefiore, *Men and Women Writers of the 1930s: The Dangerous Flood of History* (London: Routledge, 1996) 207.

24. Flanner, "Letters from Nuremberg" 117.

25. As Laurel Leff reminds us, most of the coverage on the trial focused on its beginning; as the months wore on, the headline stories declined dramatically, suggesting that few people had any sense of what was going on beyond those in the courtroom. Leff, "Jewish Victims in a Wartime Frame" 87–88.

26. Less than a decade later, Chief Prosecutor Robert Jackson underscored this point in his Introduction to Whitney Harris's history of Nuremberg: "During the almost year-long trial, it was not practicable for the daily press to present American readers with more than occasional, sketchy, and sometimes inaccurate accounts of the evidence and proceedings, nor was there in this country the wide and sustained reader-interest felt by the peoples of Europe, whose countries had been occupied. As a result, no sound and general foundation of public information about the trial was laid." Robert H. Jackson, "Introduction," Whitney R. Harris, *Tyranny on Trial: The Trial of the Major German War Criminals at the End of World War II at Nuremberg, Germany, 1945-1946* (Dallas: Southern Methodist UP, 1954; revised edition 1999) xxxvi.

27. Robert Jackson, "Report to the President, June 6, 1945," in Michael R. Marrus, *The Nuremberg War Crimes Trial 1945-46: A Documentary History* (Boston: Bedford Books, 1997) 40.

28. Jackson, "Opening Address" 6.

29. Victoria Glendinning, *Rebecca West: A Life* (New York: Fawcett Columbine, 1987) 194.

30. Pierre Nora, *Les lieux de mémoire* (Paris: Gallimard, 1984). As Shoshana Felman has argued with respect to the relation between the legal process and memory, "a legal case truly becomes a locus of embodied history, a 'site of memory' or a material, literal 'lieu de mémoire' in Pierre Nora's sense, only when it is spontaneously endowed with what Freud calls a 'historical duality,' when it reverberates, in other words, with what I have defined as a *cross-legal* resonance, or triggers inadvertently the movement of a repetition or the dynamics of a *legal recall*." Shoshana Felman, *The Juridical Unconscious* 84.

31. Mary Carruthers, *The Book of Memory* (Cambridge: Cambridge UP, 1990) 16.

32. Luria, *The Mind of a Mnemonist* 31–32.

33. Virginia Woolf advances a similar approach to remembering through familiar surroundings in "A Sketch of the Past": "I see it—the past—as an avenue lying behind; a long ribbon of scenes, emotions. There at the end of the avenue still, are the garden and the nursery. Instead of remembering here a scene and there a sound, I shall fit a plug into the wall; and listen in to the past." Virginia Woolf, "A Sketch of the Past," in *Moments of Being* (1976; San Diego: Harcourt Brace, 2nd ed. 1985) 67.

34. Luria, *The Mind of a Mnemonist* 28.

35. Jerome Bruner, Forward to the First Edition, in Luria, *The Mind of a Mnemonist* xxii.

36. Luria, *The Mind of a Mnemonist* 116.

37. Rebecca West, *The Meaning of Treason* (London: MacMillan & Co., 1949) 70.

38. West's statement underscores the force of form, and the inadequacy of this form—both legal and artistic—in shaping the trial, and her words echo those of Jackson's opening address: "Despite the magnitude of the task, the world has demanded immediate action. This demand has had to be met, though perhaps at the cost of finished craftsmanship." Jackson, "Opening Address" 8.

39. West's approach thus draws boredom's relationship to time, as it is noted by Otto Fenichel: "The very word '*Langeweile*' indicates that in this state there are always changes in the person's subjective experience of time. When we experience many varying stimulations from the outside world, the time, as we know, appears to pass quickly; but should the external world bring only monotonous stimuli, or should subjective conditions prevent their being experienced as tension-releasing, then the 'while is long'" (Fenichel, "On the Psychology of Boredom," 301).

40. Walter Benjamin, "The Storyteller," *Illuminations*, ed. Hannah Arendt, trans. Harry Zohn (New York: Schocken Books, 1968) 91. For a discussion of boredom's function in psychoanalysis, see Adam Phillips, *On Kissing, Tickling, and Being Bored: Psychoanalytic Essays on the Unexamined Life* (Cambridge, MA: Harvard UP, 1993).

41. Jon Silkin, ed., *The Penguin Book of First World War Poetry*, 2nd ed (London: Penguin, 1996) 85.

42. Geoff Dyer, *The Missing of the Somme* (1994; London: Phoenix Press, 2001) 130.

43. Avishai Margalit, *The Ethics of Memory* (Cambridge, Mass.: Harvard UP, 2002) 34.

44. Rebecca West, letter to Mary Andrews, 21 Oct. 1939, Box 2, Folder 32, Rebecca West Papers. General Collection of Rare Books and Manuscripts. Beinecke Rare Book and Manuscript Library, Yale University.

45. Carl Rollyson, *Rebecca West: A Life* (New York: Scribner, 1996) 201.

46. Rollyson, *Rebecca West: A Life* 203.

Chapter Five

1. Cited in *Miranda v. State of Arizona*, 86 S. Ct. 1602 (1966) 1654–1655.

2. Haim Gouri, *Facing the Glass Booth: The Jerusalem Trial of Adolf Eichmann*, trans. Michael Swirsky (1962; Detroit: Wayne State UP, 2003) 73.

3. Emmanuel Levinas, "Is Ontology Fundamental?" *Entre Nous: Thinking-of-the-Other*, trans. Michael B. Smith and Barbara Harshav (New York: Columbia UP, 1998) 9.

4. Gideon Hausner, *Justice in Jerusalem* (New York: Harper and Row, 1966) 453.

5. Hannah Arendt to Karl Jaspers, April 13, 1961, *Hannah Arendt-Karl Jaspers: Correspondence 1926–1969*, ed. Lotte Kohler and Hans Saner, trans. Robert and Rita Kimber (New York: Harcourt Brace Jovanovich, 1992) 415.

6. Hannah Arendt, *Eichmann in Jerusalem: A Report on the Banality of Evil* (1963; New York: Penguin, 1994) 253. Hereafter cited parenthetically in the text.

7. Tom Segev, *The Seventh Million: The Israelis and the Holocaust,* trans. Haim Watzman (1991; New York: Hill and Wang/Farrar, Straus and Giroux, 1994) 359

8. The Silence = Death project was formed in 1987, and eventually became the logo of the AIDS activist organization ACT UP. See http://www.actupny.org, accessed April 20, 2006.

9. See Hanna Fenichel Pitkin, *The Return of the Blob: Hannah Arendt's Concept of the Social* (Chicago: U of Chicago P, 1998), for an examination of how the social was a particularly vexed category in Arendt's thought.

10. Wendy Brown, *States of Injury: Power and Freedom in Late Modernity* (Princeton: Princeton UP, 1995) 68.

11. Brown 66.

12. Segev 332.

13. Hannah Arendt to Karl Jaspers, December 23, 1960, *Correspondence* 417.

14. Seyla Benhabib, *The Reluctant Modernism of Hannah Arendt* (Lanham, MD: Rowman and Littlefield, 2000) 185.

15. Hannah Arendt, "German Guilt," *Jewish Frontier Anthology 1934–1944* (New York: Jewish Frontier Association, 1945) 479–80.

16. Segev 339.

17. The writer Yechiel De-Nur [Dinoor in Arendt's spelling], who was already known at the time of the trial under the pen name K-Zetnik, fainted during his testimony of June 7, 1961. K-Zetnik represented KZ, the initials of Konzentration Zenter or concentration camp (inmates were referred to as "Ka-Zetnik number [x]," where [x] indicated the number tattooed onto their flesh). He later wrote about his experiences in *Shivitti: A Vision,* trans. Eliyah Nike De-Nur and Lisa Herman (1987; Nevada City, CA: Gateways Publishers, 1998). For a penetrating treatment of this moment in the trial, see Shoshana Felman's *The Juridical Unconscious* (Cambridge, MA: Harvard UP, 2002).

18. Hausner 327.

19. Deborah Nelson, "Suffering and Thinking: The Scandal of Tone in *Eichmann in Jerusalem,*" in *Compassion: The Culture and Politics of an Emotion,* ed. Lauren Berlant (New York and London: Routledge, 2004), 227–28.

20. Hausner 453–54.

21. Hanna Yablonka, *The State of Israel vs. Adolf Eichmann,* trans. Ora Cummings with David Herman (2001; New York: Schocken, 2004), 3–4.

22. Hannah Arendt to Karl Jaspers, December 23, 1960, *Hannah Arendt-Karl Jaspers: Correspondence 1926–1969,* ed. Lotte Kohler and Hans Saner, trans. Robert and Rita Kimber (New York: Harcourt Brace Jovanovich, 1992), 415.

23. See Hayden White, *The Content of the Form: Narrative Discourse and Historical Representation* (Baltimore: Johns Hopkins UP, 1987).

24. Arendt, September 16, 1963. *Between Friends* 146.

25. Dana Villa, *Politics, Philosophy, Terror: Essays on the Thought of Hannah Arendt* (Princeton: Princeton UP, 1999), 58–59.

26. As Arendt observed, "Foremost among the larger issues at stake in the Eichmann trial was the assumption current in all modern legal systems that intent to do wrong is necessary for the commission of a crime. On nothing, perhaps, has civilized jurisprudence prided itself more than on this taking into account of the subjective factor. Where this intent is absent, where, for whatever reasons, even reasons of moral insanity, the ability to distinguish between right and wrong is impaired, we feel no crime has been committed" (277).

27. Hannah Arendt, "On Hannah Arendt," in *Hannah Arendt: The Recovery of the Public World*, ed. Melvyn A. Hill (New York: St. Martin's Press, 1979), 301.

28. Benjamin, "The Storyteller," *Illuminations* 83–84.

29. Villa, *Politics, Philosophy, Terror* 59.

30. This position, it is worth noting, was also expressed in Arendt's 1958 Lessing Prize speech, in which she tied the phenomenon of inner emigration to the tendency in postwar Germany "to act as though the years from 1933 to 1945 never existed" (19). "On Humanity in Dark Times: Thoughts About Lessing," *Men in Dark Times*.

31. Walter Benjamin, "The Storyteller," *Illuminations,* ed. Hannah Arendt, trans. Harry Zohn (New York: Schocken, 1968) 83.

32. This formal principle of the silhouette guides Arendt's thinking in *Men in Dark Times,* one of her most uncharacteristic works. The essays in this volume bring together individual portraits of figures including Gotthold Lessing, Rosa Luxemburg. Karl Jaspers, Walter Benjamin, and Randall Jarrell, to posit a relationship between personal experience and collective history.

33. Hausner 453.

34. Leviticus 19:18, Luke 10:25.

35. *Donoghue v. Stevenson* (1932), AC 562 at 580.

36. See Joanna Conaghan and Wade Mansell, *The Wrongs of Tort* (London: Pluto Press, 1993), particularly chapter 2, "The Duty of Care in Negligence."

37. Hannah Arendt, *Love and Saint Augustine,* trans. Joanna Vecchiarelli Scott and Judith Chelius Stark (1929; Chicago: U Chicago P, 1996) 93.

38. Arendt, *Love and Saint Augustine* 102.

39. Slavoj Žižek, "Neighbors and Other Monsters: A Plea for Ethical Violence," *The Neighbor: Three Inquiries in Political Theology,* ed. Slavoj Žižek, Eric L. Santner, and Kenneth Reinhard (Chicago: U Chicago P, 2006), 153.

40. Hannah Arendt, "Truth and Politics," *Between Past and Future* (1968; New York: Penguin, 1993) 236.

41. Arendt, "Truth and Politics" 238.

42. It is in this sense that we can understand Jean-François Lyotard's insistence on justice that predates or transcends the state. Lyotard writes in "The Differend": "By forming

the State of Israel, the survivors transformed the wrong into damages and the differend into a litigation. By beginning to speak in the common idiom of public international law and of authorized politics, they put an end to the silence to which they had been condemned. But the reality of the wrong suffered at Auschwitz before the foundation of this state remained and remains to be established, and it cannot be established because it is in the nature of a wrong not to be established by consensus." Jean-François Lyotard, *The Differend: Phrases in Dispute*, trans. Georges Van den Abbeelle (Minneapolis: U Minnesota P, 1988) 56.

43. Susan Sontag, "Reflections on *The Deputy*," in *The Storm Over the Deputy* 118.

44. Hannah Arendt, "The Deputy: Guilt by Silence?" (1964), *Responsibility and Judgment,* ed. Jerome Kohn (New York: Schocken, 2003) 214–15. For Sontag, Hochhuth's play was "a moral event" rather than "playwriting of the highest order." Sontag, "Reflections on *The Deputy*" 121.

45. Robert Brustein, "History as Drama," in *The Storm Over the Deputy* 21.

46. See, for example, Leora Bilsky's work in *Transformative Justice: Israeli Identity on Trial* (Ann Arbor: U Michigan P, 2004).

47. Segev 350.

48. Felman, *The Juridical Unconscious* 124.

49. Shoshana Felman, "Response to Marianne Torgovnick," *Critical Inquiry* 28 (Spring 2002).

Epilogue

1. Virginia Woolf, "How It Strikes a Contemporary," *The Essays of Virginia Woolf,* ed. Andrew MacNeillie, vol. 3 (San Diego: Harcourt Brace Jovanovich, 1988), 357. Emphasis added.

2. See John Rawls, *A Theory of Justice* (1971; Cambridge, Mass.: Harvard UP, revised ed. 1999).

3. James Boyd White, *Justice as Translation: An Essay in Cultural and Legal Criticism* (Chicago: U Chicago P, 1990) 262–63.

4. Sigmund Freud, "Thoughts for the Times on War and Death" (1915), *Collected Papers* 4, trans. Joan Riviere (London: Hogarth Press, 1953) 316.

5. Jean-François Lyotard, *The Differend: Phrases in Dispute,* trans. Georges Van den Abbeelle (Minneapolis: U Minnesota P, 1988) 57.

6. Lyotard 57.

7. Lyotard 8. He continues, "A lot of searching must be done to find new rules for forming and linking phrases that are able to express the differend disclosed by the feeling, unless one wants this differend to be smothered right away in a litigation and for the alarm sounded by the feeling to have been useless. What is at stake in a literature, in a philosophy, in a politics perhaps, is to bear witness to differends by finding idioms for them." (8) Lyotard positions law as anathema to trauma, which requires a delay, a period

of time in which the silence symptomatic of this trauma can be heard and, finally, broken by new ways of speaking. This, then, is behind the necessary lag time between literary and legal modernism.

8. Roberto Mangabeira Unger, *Law in Modern Society: Toward a Criticism of Social Theory* (New York: Macmillan, 1976), 175.

9. Thomas Keenan, *Fables of Responsibility: Aberrations and Predicaments in Ethics and Politics* (Stanford: Stanford UP, 1997), 2.

10. Emmanuel Levinas, "The *I* and Totality," *Entre Nous: Thinking-of-the-Other*, trans. Michael B. Smith and Barbara Harshav (New York: Columbia UP, 1998), 20.

References Cited

Abel, Elizabeth. 1989. *Virginia Woolf and the Fictions of Psychoanalysis*. Chicago: University of Chicago Press.

Arendt, Hannah. 1995. *Between Friends: The Correspondence of Hannah Arendt and Mary McCarthy*. Ed. Carol Brightman. New York: Harcourt Brace.

———. 2003 (1964). The Deputy: Guilt by Silence? In *Responsibility and Judgment*, ed. Jerome Kohn. New York: Schocken.

———. 1994 (1963). *Eichmann in Jerusalem: A Report on the Banality of Evil*. New York: Penguin.

———. 1945. German Guilt. In *Jewish Frontier Anthology 1934–1944*, 479–80. New York: Jewish Frontier Association.

———. 1992. *Hannah Arendt-Karl Jaspers: Correspondence 1926–1969*. Ed. Lotte Kohler and Hans Saner, trans. Robert and Rita Kimber. New York: Harcourt Brace Jovanovich.

———. 1996 (1929). *Love and Saint Augustine*. Trans. Joanna Vecchiarelli Scott and Judith Chelius Stark. Chicago: University of Chicago Press.

———. 1995 (1968). *Men in Dark Times*. New York: Harcourt, Brace & Company.

———. 1979. On Hannah Arendt. In *Hannah Arendt: The Recovery of the Public World*, ed. Melvyn A. Hill. New York: St. Martin's Press.

———. 1993 (1968). Truth and Politics. *Between Past and Future*. New York: Penguin. 227–264.

Aristotle. 1987. *The Nichomachean Ethics*. Trans. J. E. C. Welldon. Amherst, NY: Prometheus Books.

At the Cenotaph. 1923. *Daily Chronicle*, 19 October, London edition.

Atwood, Margaret. 1995. *Morning in the Burned House*. Boston: Houghton Mifflin.

Auerbach, Erich. 1968 (1946). *Mimesis: The Representation of Reality in Western Literature*. Trans. Willard R. Trask. Princeton, NJ: Princeton University Press.

Austen, Jane. 1995 (1818). *Northanger Abbey*. Ed. Marilyn Butler. London: Penguin Books.

Bachelard, Gaston. 1969 (1958). *The Poetics of Space.* Trans. Maria Jolas. Boston: Beacon Press.

Barthes, Roland. 1981 (1980). *Camera Lucida: Reflections on Photography.* Trans. Richard Howard. New York: Farrar, Straus and Giroux.

Bell, Peter, and Jeffrey O'Connell. 1997. *Accidental Justice: The Dilemmas of Tort Law.* New Haven, CT: Yale University Press.

Benhabib, Seyla. 2000. *The Reluctant Modernism of Hannah Arendt.* Lanham, MD: Rowman and Littlefield.

Benjamin, Walter. 1972. *Illuminationen.* Frankfurt: Suhrkamp Verlag.

———. 1968. *Illuminations.* Trans. Harry Zohn. Ed. Hannah Arendt. New York: Schocken Books.

Bentham, Jeremy. 1987 (1802). *The Theory of Legislation.* Ed. C. K. Ogden. Littleton, CO: Fred B. Rothman and Co.

Bilsky, Leora. 2004. *Transformative Justice: Israeli Identity on Trial.* Ann Arbor: University of Michigan Press.

Bishop, Edward L. 1986. The Shaping of *Jacob's Room:* Woolf's Manuscript Revisions. *Twentieth Century Literature* 32: 115–35.

Black's Law Dictionary, 5th Ed. St. Paul, MN: West Pub. Co., 1979.

Bourdieu, Pierre. 1987. The Force of Law. 38 *Hastings Law Journal* 819.

Bowcott, Owen. 2001. Arm in Arm, Soldiers Lie in their Grave. *Guardian,* June 20: 3, London edition.

Bowlby, Rachel. 1997. *Feminist Destinations and Further Essays on Virginia Woolf.* Edinburgh, Scotland: Edinburgh University Press.

Bradshaw, David. 2000. The socio-political vision of the novels. In *The Cambridge Companion to Virginia Woolf,* eds. Sue Roe and Susan Sellers, 191–208. Cambridge, England: Cambridge University Press.

Brittain, Vera. 1989 (1933). *Testament of Youth: An Autobiographical Study of the Years 1900–1925.* New York: Penguin Books.

Brooks, Peter. 2000. *Troubling Confessions: Speaking Guilt in Law and Literature.* Chicago: University of Chicago Press.

Brown, Bill. 2001. Thing Theory. *Critical Inquiry* 28: 1–22.

Brown, Wendy. 1995. *States of Injury: Power and Freedom in Late Modernity.* Princeton, NJ: Princeton University Press.

Bruner, Jerome. 1987. Foreword to *The Mind of a Mnemonist: A Little Book about a Vast Memory,* A. R. Luria, ix–xix. Trans. Lynn Solotaroff. Cambridge, MA: Harvard University Press.

———. 1968. Foreword to *The Mind of a Mnemonist: A Little Book about a Vast Memory,* by A. R. Luria, xxi–xxv. Trans. Lynn Solotaroff. New York: Basic Books.

Brustein, Robert. 1964. History as Drama. In *The Storm Over the Deputy,* ed. Eric Bentley. New York: Grove Press.

Butler, Judith. 1997. *Excitable Speech: A Politics of the Performative*. New York: Routledge.

Calabresi, Guido. 1970. *The Costs of Accidents: A Legal and Economic Analysis*. New Haven, CT: Yale University Press.

Cannadine, David. 1981. War and Death, Grief and Mourning in Modern Britain. In *Mirrors of Mortality: Studies in the Social History of Death*, ed. Joachim Whaley, 187–242. New York: St. Martin's Press.

Carruthers, Mary. 1990. *The Book of Memory*. Cambridge, England: Cambridge University Press.

Caruth, Cathy. 1996. *Unclaimed Experience: Trauma, Narrative, and History*. Baltimore, MD: Johns Hopkins University Press.

Caughie, Pamela L. 1991. *Virginia Woolf and Postmodernism: Literature in Quest and Question of Itself*. Chicago: University of Illinois Press.

Cenotaph Blunder Reconsidered by the Cabinet. 1923. *Daily Chronicle*, 22 October, London edition.

Chu, Patricia E. 2006. *Race, Nationalism and the State in British and American Modernism*. Cambridge, England: Cambridge University Press.

Cohen, Deborah. 2001. *The War Come Home: Disabled Veterans in Britain and Germany, 1914–1939*. Berkeley: University of California Press.

Cohen, M. R. 1927. Property and Sovereignty. 13 *Cornell Law Quarterly* 8.

The Collections. n.d. London: Imperial War Museum [pamphlet].

Conaghan, Joanna, and Wade Mansell. 1993. *The Wrongs of Tort*. London: Pluto Press.

Conot, Robert E. 1983. *Justice at Nuremberg*. New York: Harper.

Cover, Robert. 1993. *Narrative, Violence, and the Law: The Essays of Robert Cover*. Eds. Martha Minow, Michael Ryan, and Austin Sarat. Ann Arbor: University of Michigan Press.

Cuddy-Keene, Melba. 2003. *Virginia Woolf, the Intellectual, and the Public Sphere*. Cambridge, England: Cambridge University Press.

Curtis, Penelope. 1991. The Whitehall Cenotaph: An Accidental Monument. In *The Cenotaph Project*, 34–58. Derry, U.K.: Orchard Gallery.

Davies, Douglas. 1997. *Death, Ritual and Belief: The Rhetoric of Funerary Rites*. London: Cassell.

DiBattista, Maria. 1980. *Virginia Woolf's Novels: The Fables of Anon*. New Haven, CT: Yale University Press.

Dyer, Geoff. 2001 (1994). *The Missing of the Somme*. London: Phoenix Press.

Editorial. 1919. *Shrewsbury Chronicle*, 4 April. National Inventory of War Memorials, Imperial War Museum, London.

Esch, Deborah. 1987. 'Think of a kitchen table': Hume, Woolf, and the Translation of Example. In *Literature as Philosophy, Philosophy as Literature*, ed. Donald G. Marshall, 262–276. Iowa City: University of Iowa Press.

Esty, Jed. 2004. A Shrinking Island: Modernism and National Culture in England. Princeton, NJ: Princeton University Press.

Ewick, Patricia, and Susan Silbey 1998. *The Common Place of Law: Stories from Everyday Life*. Chicago: University of Chicago Press.

The Faces Emerge. 2001. Editorial. *New York Times*. 16 Sept., sec. 4:10.

Felman, Shoshana. 2002. *The Juridical Unconscious: Trials and Traumas in the Twentieth Century*. Cambridge, MA: Harvard University Press.

———. 2002. Response to Marianne Torgovnick. *Critical Inquiry* 28 (Spring).

Fenichel, Otto. 1953. On the Psychology of Boredom. In *The Collected Papers of Otto Fenichel*, 292–302. First Series. New York: Norton.

Flanner, Janet. 1979. *Janet Flanner's World: Uncollected Writings, 1932–1975*. Ed. Irving Drutman. New York: Harcourt Brace Jovanovich.

Fleming, John G. 1967. *An Introduction to the Law of Torts*. Oxford, England: Oxford University Press.

Freud, Sigmund. 1966 (1920). *Introductory Lectures on Psycho-Analysis*. Trans. and ed. James Strachey. New York: W. W. Norton and Co.

———.1967 (1939). *Moses and Monotheism*. Trans. Katherine Jones. New York: Vintage Books.

———. 1953 (1915). Thoughts for the Times on War and Death. In Volume 4 of *Collected Papers*, trans. Joan Riviere, 288–317. London: Hogarth Press.

Fromm, Gloria G. 1991. Rebecca West: The Fictions of Fact and the Facts of Fiction. *New Criterion* 9.5: 44–53.

Froula, Christine. 2005. Virginia Woolf and the Bloomsbury Avant-Garde: War, Civilization, Modernity. New York: Columbia University Press.

Fuller, Lon L. 1958. Positivism and Fidelity to Law—A Reply to Professor Hart. 71 *Harvard Law Review* 630.

Fussell, Paul. 1975. *The Great War and Modern Memory*. London: Oxford University Press.

Gilligan, Carol. 1982. *In a Different Voice*. Cambridge, MA: Harvard University Press.

Glendinning, Victoria. 1987. *Rebecca West: A Life*. New York: Fawcett Columbine.

Goodman, Nan. 1998. *Shifting the Blame: Literature, Law and Accidents in Nineteenth-Century America*. Princeton, NJ: Princeton University Press.

Goodrich, Peter. 1995. *Oedipus Lex: Psychoanalysis, History, Law*. Berkeley: University of California Press.

Gouri, Haim. 2003 (1962). *Facing the Glass Booth: The Jerusalem Trial of Adolf Eichmann*. Trans. Michael Swirsky. Detroit: Wayne State University Press.

Green, Leon. 1930. The Palsgraf Case. 30 *Col. L. Rev.* 789.

Haldar, Piyel. 2007. *Law, Orientalism, and Postcolonialism: The Jurisdiction of the Lotus Eaters*. London: Routledge Cavendish.

Hall, Brian. 1996. Rebecca West's War. *New Yorker,* 15 April: 74–83.

Hankin, Cherry A., ed. 1988. *Letters between Katherine Mansfield and John Middleton Murry.* London: Virago.

Harris, Whitney R. 1999 (1954). *Tyranny on Trial: The Trial of the Major German War Criminals at the End of World War II at Nuremberg, Germany, 1945–1946* (revised edition). Dallas, TX: Southern Methodist University Press.

Hart, H. L. A. 1958. Positivism and the Separation of Law and Morals. 71 *Harvard Law Review* 593.

Hausner, Gideon. 1966. *Justice in Jerusalem.* New York: Harper and Row.

Hilberg, Raul. 2003 (1961). *The Destruction of the European Jews.* 3 vols. New Haven, CT: Yale University Press.

Hoffman, Charles G. 1969. From Lunch to Dinner: Virginia Woolf's Apprenticeship. *Texas Studies in Literature and Language: A Journal of the Humanities* 10: 609–627.

Holden, Wendy. 1998. *Shell Shock.* London: Macmillan-Channel 4 Books.

Holmes, Oliver Wendell Jr. 1991 (1881). *The Common Law.* New York: Dover Publications.

———. The Path of the Law. 1897. 10 *Harvard Law Review* 457.

———. The Theory of Torts. 1873. 7 *Am. L. Rev.* 660.

Holtby, Winifred. 1978 (1932). *Virginia Woolf: A Critical Memoir.* Chicago: Academy Press-Cassandra.

Hussein, Nasser. 2003. *The Jurisprudence of Emergency: Colonialism and the Rule of Law.* Ann Arbor: University of Michigan Press.

Hussey, Christopher. 1950. *The Life of Sir Edwin Lutyens.* London: Country Life Ltd.

Hynes, Samuel. 1997. *The Soldier's Tale: Bearing Witness to Modern War.* New York: Penguin Books.

Jackson, Robert H. 1996. Opening Address for the United States, Nuremberg Trials. In *Philosophical Problems in the Law* (2nd ed.), ed. David M. Adams, 7–13. Belmont, CA: Wadsworth.

———. Report to the President, June 6, 1945. 1997. In *The Nuremberg War Crimes Trial 1945–46: A Documentary History,* ed. Michael R. Marrus, 40–43. Boston: Bedford Books.

Jain, Sarah Lochlann. 2006. *Injury: The Politics of Product Design and Safety Law in the United States.* Princeton, NJ: Princeton University Press.

Johnson, Barbara. 1987. *A World of Difference.* Baltimore, MD: Johns Hopkins University Press.

Katz, Tamar. 2000. *Impressionist Subjects: Gender, Interiority, and Modernism Fiction in England.* Urbana: University of Illinois Press.

Ka-Tzetnik 135633 [Yechiel De-Nur]. 1998 (1987). *Shivitti: A Vision,* trans. Eliyah Nike De-Nur and Lisa Herman. Nevada City, CA: Gateways Publishers.

Keegan, John. 2000 (1998). *The First World War.* New York: Vintage-Random House.

Keenan, Thomas. 1997. *Fables of Responsibility: Aberrations and Predicaments in Ethics and Politics.* Stanford, CA: Stanford University Press, 1997.

Lee, Hermione. 1977. *The Novels of Virginia Woolf.* New York: Holmes and Meier Publishers.

Leff, Laurel. 2005. *Buried by The Times: The Holocaust and America's Most Important Newspaper.* Cambridge, England: Cambridge University Press.

———. 2007. Jewish Victims in a Wartime Frame: A Press Portrait of the Nuremberg Trial. In *From the Protocols of the Elders of Zion to Holocaust Denial Trials: Challenging the Media, the Law, and the Academy,* eds. Debra Kaufman, Gerald Herman, James Ross, and David Phillips. London: Valentine Mitchell.

Lesinska, Zofia P. 2002. *Perspectives of Four Women Writers on the Second World War: Gertrude Stein, Janet Flanner, Kay Boyle, and Rebecca West.* Studies in Literary Criticism and Theory 17. New York: Peter Lang.

Letter to the editor. 1920. *Shrewsbury Chronicle,* 23 April. National Inventory of War Memorials, Imperial War Museum, London.

Levenback, Karen. 1999. *Virginia Woolf and the Great War.* Syracuse, NY: Syracuse University Press.

Levenson, Michael. 1991. *Modernism and the Fate of Individuality: Character and Novelistic Form from Conrad to Woolf.* Cambridge, England: Cambridge University Press.

Levinas, Emmanuel. 1998. *Entre Nous: Thinking-of-the-Other.* Trans. Michael B. Smith and Barbara Harshav. New York: Columbia University Press.

Levmore, Saul. 1994. *Foundations of Tort Law.* New York: Oxford University Press.

Lewis, Pericles. 2000. *Modernism, Nationalism, and the Novel.* Cambridge, England: Cambridge University Press.

Lichfield, John. 2001. Arm in Arm they Lie, 'Grimsby Chums' in Death as in Life, Twenty Soldiers Killed by Friendly Fire. *Independent* 20 June: 13, London edition.

Lively, Penelope. 2001. *A House Unlocked.* New York: Grove Press.

Locke, John. 1986 (1690). *Second Treatise on Civil Government.* Amherst, NY: Prometheus Books.

Lockwood, Preston. 1915. Henry James's First Interview. *New York Times Magazine* 21 March: 4–5.

Luban, David. 1994. *Legal Modernism.* Ann Arbor: University of Michigan Press.

Luria, A. R. 1987 (1968). *The Mind of a Mnemonist: A Little Book about a Vast Memory.* Trans. Lynn Solotaroff. Cambridge, MA: Harvard University Press.

Lyotard, Jean-François. 1988. *The Differend: Phrases in Dispute.* Trans. Georges Van den Abbeelle. Minneapolis: University of Minnesota Press.

MacNeil, William P. 2007. *Lex Populi: The Jurisprudence of Popular Culture.* Stanford, CA: Stanford University Press.

Majumdar, Robin, and Allen McLaurin, eds. 1975. *Virginia Woolf: The Critical Heritage.* London: Routledge; Boston: Kegan Paul.

Manganaro, Marc. 2002. *Culture, 1922: The Emergence of a Concept.* Princeton, NJ: Princeton University Press.

Mao, Douglas. 1998. *Solid Objects: Modernism and the Test of Production.* Princeton, NJ: Princeton University Press.

Margalit, Avishai. 2002. *The Ethics of Memory.* Cambridge, MA: Harvard University Press.

Mepham, John. 1983. Mourning and Modernism. In *Virginia Woolf: New Critical Essays,* eds. Patricia Clements and Isobel Grundy, 137–156. London: Vision-Barnes and Noble.

———.*Virginia Woolf: A Literary Life.* 1991. New York: St. Martin's Press.

Mezey, Naomi. 2001. Out of the Ordinary: Law, Power, Culture, and the Commonplace. *Law and Social Inquiry* 26, 1:145–167.

Miller, J. Hillis. 1982. *Fiction and Repetition: Seven English Novels.* Cambridge, MA: Harvard University Press.

Montefiore, Janet. 1996. *Men and Women Writers of the 1930s: The Dangerous Flood of History.* London: Routledge.

Morrison, Mark S. 2001. *The Public Face of Modernism: Little Magazines, Audiences, and Reception, 1905–1920.* Madison: University of Wisconsin Press.

Nagourney, Adam. 2001. Jolted by Sept. 11, Many Rush to Make Wills. *New York Times,* 13 December: A1.

Nelson, Deborah. 2004. Suffering and Thinking: The Scandal of Tone in *Eichmann in Jerusalem.* In *Compassion: The Culture and Politics of an Emotion,* ed. Lauren Berlant, 219–244. New York and London: Routledge.

Noonan, John T. Jr. 2002 (1976). *Persons and Masks of the Law: Cardozo, Holmes, Jefferson, and Wythe as Makers of the Masks.* Berkeley: University of California Press.

Nora, Pierre. 1984. *Les lieux de mémoire.* Paris: Gallimard.

Norris, Margot. 2000. *Writing War in the Twentieth Century.* Charlottesville: University Press of Virginia.

North, Michael. 1999. *Reading 1922: A Return to the Scene of the Modern.* New York: Oxford University Press.

Nussbaum, Martha. 2001. *Upheavals of Thought: The Intelligence of Emotions.* Cambridge, England: Cambridge University Press.

Osiel, Marc. 2000. *Mass Atrocity, Collective Memory, and the Law.* New Brunswick, NJ: Transaction Publishers.

Owen, Wilfred. 1986. *The Poems of Wilfred Owen.* Ed. John Stallworthy. New York: Norton.

Phillips, Adam. 1993. *On Kissing, Tickling, and Being Bored: Psychoanalytic Essays on the Unexamined Life.* Cambridge, MA: Harvard University Press.

Pitkin, Hanna Fenichel. 1998. *The Return of the Blob: Hannah Arendt's Concept of the Social.* Chicago: University of Chicago Press.

Prosser, William Lloyd. 1953. Palsgraf Revisited. *Selected Topics on the Law of Torts,* 191–242. Ann Arbor: University of Michigan Press.

Rabin, Robert. 1995 (1976). *Perspectives on Tort Law*. Boston: Little, Brown.

Rawls, John. 1999 (1971). *A Theory of Justice*. Cambridge, MA: Harvard University Press.

Rivers, W. H. R. 1922 (1920). *Instinct and the Unconscious*. Cambridge, England: Cambridge University Press.

Rollyson, Carl. 1996. *Rebecca West: A Life*. New York: Scribner.

Sage, Adam, and Michael Evans. 2001. The Grimsby Chums, Brothers in Arms even after Death. *Times*, 20 June: 5, London edition.

Saint-Amour, Paul K. 2005. Air War Prophecy and Interwar Modernism. *Comparative Literature Studies* 42:2: 130–161.

Sarat, Austin. 2001. *When the State Kills: Capital Punishment and the American Condition*. Princeton, NJ: Princeton University Press.

Sassoon, Siegfried. 1918. *Counter-Attack and Other Poems*. New York: E. P. Dutton.

Schnapp, Jeffrey T., and Matthew Tews, eds. 2007. *Crowds*. Stanford, CA: Stanford University Press.

Schor, Naomi. 1987. *Reading in Detail: Aesthetics and the Feminine*. New York: Methuen.

Segev, Tom. 1994 (1991). *The Seventh Million: The Israelis and the Holocaust*. Trans. Haim Watzman. New York: Hill and Wang / Farrar, Straus and Giroux.

Shapo, Marshall. 1977. *The Duty to Act: Tort Law, Power, and Public Policy*. Austin: University of Texas Press.

Sherry, Vincent. 2003. *The Great War and the Language of Modernism*. Oxford, England: Oxford University Press.

Shklar, Judith N. 1990. *The Faces of Injustice*. New Haven, CT: Yale University Press.

Silkin, Jon, ed. 1996. *The Penguin Book of First World War Poetry* (2nd ed.). London: Penguin.

Silver, Brenda R. 1999. *Virginia Woolf Icon*. Chicago: University of Chicago Press.

Sontag, Susan. 1964. Reflections on *The Deputy*. In *The Storm Over the Deputy*, ed. Eric Bentley. New York: Grove Press.

Spacks, Patricia Meyer. 1995. *Boredom: The Literary History of a State of Mind*. Chicago: University of Chicago Press.

Spilka, Mark. 1980. *Virginia Woolf's Quarrel with Grieving*. Lincoln: University of Nebraska Press.

Spivak, Gayatri Chakravorty. 1988 (1987). Unmaking and Making in *To the Lighthouse*. In *In Other Worlds: Essays in Cultural Politics*, 30–45. New York: Routledge.

Tratner, Michael. 1995. *Modernism and Mass Politics: Joyce, Woolf, Eliot, Yeats*. Stanford, CA: Stanford University Press.

Unger, Roberto Mangabeira. 1976. *Law in Modern Society: Toward a Criticism of Social Theory*. New York: Macmillan.

Villa, Dana. 1999. *Politics, Philosophy, Terror: Essays on the Thought of Hannah Arendt*. Princeton, NJ: Princeton University Press.

Walzer, Michael. 1992 (1977). *Just and Unjust Wars*. New York: Harper Collins.

Weinrib, Ernest J. 2001. The Passing of Palsgraf? 54 *Vanderbilt Law Review* 803.

West, Rebecca. 1994 (1941). *Black Lamb and Grey Falcon: A Journey Through Yugoslavia*. New York: Penguin Books.

———. 1931. *Ending in Earnest: A Literary Log*. Garden City, NY: Doubleday, Doran and Co.

———. 1949. *The Meaning of Treason*. London: MacMillan.

———. 1998 (1918). *The Return of the Soldier*. New York: Penguin Books.

———. 1928. *The Strange Necessity: Essays by Rebecca West*. Garden City, NY: Doubleday, Doran and Co.

———. 1955. *A Train of Powder*. London: MacMillan,

West, Robin. 1997. *Caring for Justice*. New York: New York University Press.

White, G. Edward. 1985. *Tort Law in America: An Intellectual History*. New York: Oxford University Press.

White, Hayden. 1987. *The Content of the Form: Narrative Discourse and Historical Representation*. Baltimore, MD: Johns Hopkins University Press.

White, James Boyd. 1985. *Heracles' Bow: Essays on the Rhetoric and Poetics of the Law*. Madison: University of Wisconsin Press.

———. 1990. *Justice as Translation: An Essay in Culture and Legal Criticism*. Chicago: University of Chicago Press.

Willis, James F. 1982. *Prologue to Nuremberg: The Politics and Diplomacy of Punishing War Criminals of the First World War*. Westport and London: Greenwood Press.

Winter, Jay. 1995. *Sites of Memory, Sites of Mourning: The Great War in European Cultural History*. Cambridge, England: Cambridge University Press.

Witt, John Fabian. 2004. *The Accidental Republic: Crippled Workingmen, Destitute Widows, and the Remaking of American Law*. Cambridge, MA: Harvard University Press.

Wollaeger, Mark. 2006. *Modernism, Media, and Propaganda: British Narrative from 1900–1945*. Princeton, NJ: Princeton University Press.

Woolf, Virginia. 1925. *The Common Reader*. Ed. Andrew McNeillie. New York: Harcourt Brace.

———. 1989. *The Complete Shorter Fiction of Virginia Woolf*. Ed. Susan Dick. San Diego: Harcourt Brace-Harvest.

———. 1989. *Congenial Spirits: The Selected Letters of Virginia Woolf*. Ed. Joanne Trautmann Banks. San Diego: Harcourt Brace Jovanovich.

———. 1986. *The Essays of Virginia Woolf*. Ed. Andrew MacNeillie. Vol. 2. London: Hogarth Press.

———. 1988. *The Essays of Virginia Woolf*. Ed. Andrew MacNeillie. Vol. 3. San Diego: Harcourt Brace Jovanovich.

———. 1922. *Jacob's Room*. New York: Harcourt Brace & Co.

———. 1998. *Jacob's Room: The Holograph Draft*. Trans. and ed. Edward L. Bishop. New York: Pace University Press.

———. 1985 (1976). *Moments of Being* (2nd ed.). Ed. Jeanne Schulkind. San Diego: Harcourt Brace-Harvest.

———. 1925. *Mrs. Dalloway.* New York: Harcourt Brace Jovanovich.

———. 1956 (1928). *Orlando.* New York: Harcourt Brace & Co.

———. 1986 (1932). *The Second Common Reader.* Ed. Andrew MacNeillie. San Diego: Harcourt Brace-Harvest.

———. 1927. *To the Lighthouse.* New York: Harcourt Brace & Co.

———. 1953. *A Writer's Diary.* Ed. Leonard Woolf. New York: Harcourt Brace.

Yablonka, Hanna. 2004 (2001). *The State of Israel vs. Adolf Eichmann.* Trans. Ora Cummings with David Herman. New York: Schocken.

Žižek, Slavoj. 2006. Neighbors and Other Monsters: A Plea for Ethical Violence. In *The Neighbor: Three Inquiries in Political Theology,* ed. Slavoj Žižek, Eric L. Santner, and Kenneth Reinhard. Chicago: University of Chicago Press.

Zwerdling, Alex. 1986. *Virginia Woolf and the Real World.* Berkeley: University of California Press.

List of Cases

Attorney General v. Adolf Eichmann, Criminal Case No 40/61 (1962)

Cullison v. Medley, 570 N.E. 2d 27 at 30 (1991)

Donoghue v. Stevenson, A.C. 562 at 580 (1932)

Dulieu v. White & Sons, 2 K.B. 669 (1901)

Hammond v. Central Lane Communications Ctr., 816 P.2d 593 (1991)

Holmes v. Mather, L.R. 10 Exch. 261 (1875)

Indiana Springs Co. v. Brown, 74 Northeastern Reporter 615 (1905)

Lynch v. Knight, 9 H.L.C. 577 (1862)

Marchica v. Long Island R.R. Co., 31 F.3d 1197 (2d Cir. 1994)

Miranda v. State of Arizona, 86 S. Ct. 1602 (1966)

Monteleone v. Co-Operative Transit Co., 36 S.E. 2d. 475 (1945)

OB-GYN Assocs. v. Littleton, 386 S.E. 2d. 146 (1989)

Palsgraf v. Long Island Railroad Company, 248 N.Y. 339 (1928).

Shuamber v. Henderson, 579 N.E. 2d 452 (1991)

Smith v. Johnson. Unreported.

Spade v. Lynn & Boston R.R. Co., 47 N.E. 88 at 89 (1897)

Index

Abel, Elizabeth: on Woolf's *Mrs. Dalloway*, 180n31
accidents: deaths in war as, 26–27, 28; inevitability of, 19–21; and tort law, 8, 16, 18–21, 40, 41, 42–49, 172n8; Woolf on, 8, 49–50, 52, 53, 54–55, 63–64
AIDS crisis, 137
Andrews, William, 45–46, 47, 62
Arendt, Hannah: on banality of evil, 10–11, 116, 133, 136, 147; on the bourgeois individual, 140; on care for the world, 11; and ethical judgment, 147; "German Guilt," 140; and Grynszpan's testimony, 142–46, 149, 153, 159–60; vs. Hochhuth, 156–57, 158; the individual vs. collective in, 139, 142–43, 144–45, 146–47, 148–49, 150, 156, 157, 190n32; on Israeli public, 135; and justice, 10, 137, 146, 150, 151, 155, 163, 164; and legal modernism, 99; Lessing Prize speech, 190n30; and literary modernism, 145–46; "Love and Saint Augustine," 153–54; on love of neighbor, 153–54; *Men in Dark Times*, 149, 190n32; on motives, 147, 148–49, 190n26; on prosecution witnesses, 140–41, 142–46, 149, 150, 155, 159–60; on responsibility, 11, 136, 137, 146, 148, 153–54, 164; and tort law, 11, 136, 137, 138, 149–60; "Truth and Politics," 154–55; vs. West, 2, 10, 99, 163, 164; vs. Woolf, 2, 11, 133, 163, 164

Arendt, Hannah, *Eichmann in Jerusalem*, 10–11, 99, 116, 133, 164; the court as theater, 141, 157; Epilogue, 139; Grynszpan, 142–45; ideal of law in, 135–36, 146; and Jewish councils (*Judenräte*), 139, 154–55; and prosecution witnesses, 140–41, 142–46, 149, 150, 155, 159–60; reply to critics in "Truth and Politics," 154–55; as report of facts, 136, 138, 145–49, 154–55, 157; vs. *The Deputy*, 156–57, 158
Aristotle: on justice as equilibrium, 57; *The Nicomachean Ethics*, 57
Atkin, Lord, 151–52
Atwood, Margaret: "Morning in the Burned House," 66
Auerbach, Erich: *Mimesis*, 82, 90–91; on stocking in *To the Lighthouse*, 82, 90–91, 94
Augustine, St., 153–54
Austen, Jane: on injury and responsibility, 15–16, 18, 27–28; *Northanger Abbey*, 15–16, 18, 27–28, 175n37; on novels, 15–16, 18, 27–28; vs. Woolf, 28, 31–32, 33, 39, 175n37, 177n45
Austin, John, 162

Bachelard, Gaston: *The Poetics of Space*, 72, 73; on shells, 73; on Valéry, 73
Barrie, J. M.: on the Cenotaph, 78
Barthes, Roland: *punctum* in *Camera Lucida*, 93–94

THE CULTURAL LIVES OF LAW

Austin Sarat, Editor

The Cultural Lives of Law series brings insights and approaches from cultural studies to law and tries to secure for law a place in cultural analysis. Books in the series focus on the production, interpretation, consumption, and circulation of legal meanings. They take up the challenges posed as boundaries collapse between as well as within cultures, and as the circulation of legal meanings becomes more fluid. They also attend to the ways law's power in cultural production is renewed and resisted.

Fault Lines: Tort Law as Cultural Practice
Edited by David M. Engel and Michael McCann
2009

Lex Populi: The Jurisprudence of Popular Culture
William P. MacNeil
2007

The Cultural Lives of Capital Punishment: Comparative Perspectives
Edited by Austin Sarat and Christian Boulanger
2005